D1634180

STEPHEN POTTER AT THE BBC

STEPHEN POTTER
AT THE BBC

'Features' in War and Peace

By Julian Potter
with extracts from the Stephen Potter Diaries

ORFORD BOOKS

First published in Great Britain in 2004 by Orford Books

A CIP catalogue record for this title is available from the British Library.

ISBN 0 954 66530 9

Typeset in Minion by Miranda Potter, 132 Blinco Grove, Cambridge, UK.

Printed and bound at the University Press, Cambridge.

Published by Orford Books, Orford, Suffolk, UK.

Contents

Acknowledgements

Thanks are due to Cathy Henderson, the Research Librarian of The Harry Ransom Humanities Research Center at the University of Texas at Austin. Over the past few years she and her staff have sent me photostats of at least 5000 pages from my father's diaries. To guide me in my selection, they have re-catalogued all the papers in the Stephen Potter boxes. Since acquiring the archive in 1970 they have cared for it well, making it available without fuss to anyone wanting to use it.

The BBC's archive centre at Caversham has also been most helpful. There, over a series of visits, Neil Somerville took on the task of telling me what was available and finding what I wanted. The Mary Hope Allen archive is also kept at Caversham and I am grateful to her niece Julia for allowing me to see it.

The British Library has not only made available many of the books listed in the bibliography, but also provided facilities for me to listen to some of the few Stephen Potter programmes still extant. Much use has been made of the Library's back numbers of *The Listener* and the *Radio Times* and thanks are due to the BBC for allowing me to quote from them.

Extracts from books have been quoted and I thank those heirs, agents or executors who have given me permission to do so. For anything longer than a one-liner, efforts have been made to get such permission. An acknowledgement is due to The Society of Authors as the Literary Representative of the Estate of Compton Mackenzie. Where I have failed to trace the appropriate authority, I apologise.

Finally, thanks to my daughters and son for cutting out old fogey excesses in the text and helping with the production process; and to my wife Valerie for her careful read-through of the manuscript, for her many useful criticisms and suggestions and above all, for her prolonged encouragement.

Illustrations

Note 'Potter family prints' have been in possession of the family since they were taken, but were probably arranged through the BBC.

Preface

by Libby Purves

When I first joined the BBC in the early seventies, it was still just about recognizable as the house that Reith built. There was a sense that we were a kind of cross between a major university, a prelapsarian *Times* newspaper, the Royal Shakespeare Company and a particularly dignified department of state. There was a lot of talk about not 'Bringing the Corporation Into Disrepute', which in the case of my lowly technical post mainly meant not putting tapes out with bad edits or doing uneven fades on the old bakelite training desks. Someone said to me at that time – when I was enjoying the eccentricities of a particular boss – that the man was 'Old BBC. The definition of an Old BBC man is that he is basically a civil servant, with a secret spangled tutu underneath his suit....'

So the world of Stephen Potter and the ground-breaking 'Features' department, as sketched in his diaries within this book, are not wholly unfamiliar, even to those of us who joined nearly four decades later than he did. Potter always had the spangled tutu well in evidence; from his dry, literate, hilarious books to his subtle radio Features, he was a man who always knew just how far to go, and when to push a bit further. The picture painted here – lunch with Vivien Leigh, brushes with Larry Olivier and the rest – is not just a thing of period charm. It is a hymn of praise to the craftsmen and women who created, in Britain, an art form which remains to this day almost uniquely ours: the well-constructed radio Feature.

In 1946, when a confident postwar BBC first opened the Third Programme (now Radio 3), its first programme was a piece of mild, literate self-mockery. Stephen Potter and Joyce Grenfell were already well-loved for their 'How to...' series; Potter a stalwart, trusted maverick within the Corporation's famous Features Department. For the new network they did 'How to Listen'. I love this scrap of tape from the beginning of that programme, because it manages simultaneously to mock the dinner-jacketed Oxbridge pretensions of the corporation, and to convey the authentic thrill of live radio, of connecting directly and intensely with an invisible audience, an electric mind-to-mind communication unhampered by appearances and prejudices. A low, studious voice says reverently that the green light is coming on, and the performers ready:

'One minute to go … we can hear the music of the programme before … the producer hands over to the actors and the engineers … less than a minute now … the work in the writing and the rehearsing of the programme is all now coming to a head, all boiling down to this one supreme moment … half a minute to go … and the producer, suspended in space as it were, seems to see the whole as it ought to be … and for a second his vision extends beyond, to the audience, to a million wireless sets at the other end … a million separate audiences … are they ready? are they listening?'

And then, of course, it cuts to wireless licence number 865432, Mrs Moss, who is chattering away to her friend and tells her to turn up the set a bit. Gently, he mocks the faith of those who throw out their best efforts to an audience which may not be there, or not paying attention. Gently, he laughs at the earnestness and tensions of the trade. But you can tell all the time how much he loves it.

And so do we, today. The BBC itself may infuriate at times (just read the Heppenstall threnody on the accountants and time-and-motion men, in the final chapter on the death of Potter's old department). But the craft of radio is greater than the institution which brought it into being, and from time to time even the accountants and the time-and-motion men stand back and admit this with grace. Long may it continue; and long may we remember the brilliance of pioneers and craftsmen like Stephen Potter. His son, in this book, does him proud.

Introduction

Features in the forties

The heyday of radio was in the 1940s. Before the war, attitudes to the new invention were very similar to early reactions to the telephone, television and the Internet. All were wondrously clever, but not things that would seriously affect our lives. During the war, radio became a lifeline. While a dismissive attitude was still to be found amongst the intelligentsia, most of the population listened. And with the new Third Programme in 1946, and an influx of new script writers, this blossoming of radio continued for a few more years, until its partial eclipse by television.

It was in 'Feature' programmes that the novelty of the new medium was most apparent. Talks were not very different from going to a lecture or reading an article. Drama (with exceptions) consisted of adaptations, either of plays intended for the stage, or of novels. Music heard on the air was the same as that heard in the concert hall, except for the addition of atmospherics. News bulletins were admittedly a day more up to date than newspapers, but not otherwise different in content. Only Features were new and not a reflection of anything else.

Surprisingly, no book focuses on Features at this time. Lord Briggs, in his *History of Broadcasting in the UK*, of course covers Features along with every other department; but inevitably he gives a top management, bird's eye view. Remote Director Generals and their departmental Controllers are quoted, rather than those who made the programmes. Rayner Heppenstall, a writer/producer in Features, wrote revealingly in *Portrait of the Artist as a Professional Man* about his experiences in the BBC – but he did not join it full time until after the war. His colleague D. G. Bridson spent a lifetime on the same job and was writing Features for the Northern Regions even before the word had acquired its later BBC usage. His book, *Prospero and Ariel*, gives a vivid account of the pre-war innovative techniques he used in those regions and has been drawn on in this book. Like Heppenstall, he writes of what it was like to be in the front line, writing and producing programmmes. But again, partly because he was seconded for eighteen months to America, he says little about what was happening to Features during the war in London, a time and place crucial to their development. Val Gielgud, Head of the Features and Drama Department, would have been the one to do that. His two autobiographical works both include chapters on his time at the BBC, with many wonderful anecdotes and a few more solid paragraphs on Features. But his main interest was in Drama – as was that of his brother John. Laurence Gilliam, who ran the Features half of Gielgud's domain, produced an anthology of the best Feature programmes but never wrote a book.

The diaries of Stephen Potter, who worked full time in the department from 1939 to 1948, provide new perspectives on this golden age of Features. Of course he writes mainly about his own programmes; but in doing so he provides a day-to-day record of how Features were made and what they were like. He also discusses the work of his colleagues and describes how the output of all of them was affected by their Home Guard duties, the blitz and the twists in the course of the war.

This book will use Stephen's diaries to illustrate and bring to life the development of Features and the people in it during his ten BBC years. It is not a definitive history: too much of it is taken up with Stephen's writings about his own programmes for that. However, an attempt has been made to round out the diary extracts with enough background information to put them in their context. Some account is given of the major trends and developments within the department and of landmark contributions by other writers. Policy, propaganda and censorship decisions filtering down from top management are also covered and for this files at the BBC research centre at Caversham have been consulted. Some of the wartime documents there have only recently been released.

Stephen Potter

Born in 1900, my father worked in his twenties and thirties as a lecturer on English Literature, mainly at Birkbeck College, London. He also wrote books. His was the first biography of D. H. Lawrence (1930). A second biography, *Coleridge and STC*, was published in 1935, following on from his editorship of the Nonesuch Coleridge in 1933. Then, in 1937, came *The Muse in Chains*, an attack on the way literature was taught in universities. All three were highly praised in literary and academic circles and in the press; but few copies were sold. The last had a slightly more extended circulation in the universities and there are still English scholars around who remember reading it as students. The element of satire in the book resurfaces in most of Stephen's radio programmes. It mellowed through his radio collaboration with Joyce Grenfell and peaked in the tongue-in-cheek instruction manual that was *Gamesmanship*.

When Stephen accepted a full-time job at the BBC in 1939, it was in one way a defeat. He had always wanted to be an author and even now still saw it as his vocation to produce books worthy of note in the academic world. He was reluctant to give up the freedom of being self-employed, which he thought he needed to write such books; yet he had never been good at managing his time. Freelance work had in practice meant continually giving in to the distraction of one or other of his wide range of interests, the most insidious of which were the golf course and the snooker table. Now that he had a job, he quickly became too absorbed in his work to worry about the course of his career. He found himself faced with a series of deadlines which had to be met; and his writing flowed. In the next ten years he wrote and/or produced about 230 programmes, which included some of his best and most original work. Now, only eighteen sound recordings survive, together with half a dozen typescripts. All writer/producers worried about their work disappearing into the ether, and Stephen was no exception. But in his case, the flavour of many of his programmes is caught in his diaries.

If Stephen Potter is remembered at all today, it is by the 70+ generation, some of whom still joke about gamesmanship. The 'art of winning games without actually cheating' and the cult of being 'one-up' in all situations were the inescapable in-jokes of the fifties and early sixties. The initial success of *Gamesmanship*, written in 1947, must have been to some extent due to the fact that millions already knew of Stephen Potter, thanks to his radio programmes. Ironically, the success of his book gave him the confidence to leave the BBC – and trapped him into a series of sequels, of which the first and the best known were *Lifemanship*, *One-Upmanship* and *Supermanship*. For twenty years here and in America he was famous for these. His BBC work was, and is, forgotten. Who would have thought that the author of *Gamesmanship* was the writer/producer chosen for the BBC's main appreciation of Winston Churchill on the day after VE day?

STEPHEN POTTER AT THE BBC

The diaries were acquired by the University of Texas after Stephen died in 1969 and over the last few years I have been deciphering photostats. Stephen had dickered with a diary from 1930 onwards but it was not until 1940 that he set himself the task of daily entries, which often run to several pages. These cover everything: his work; his golf, snooker and other games; his enthusiasms such as the theatre, music and botany; his family, friends and lovers; his money worries; his health; his Home Guard duties, the bombing and his thoughts on the war. If he had had the time and the temperament to edit them and cut them down to a manageable size, he would still have had enough to publish a volume of diary for each year – as did his contemporary James Agate.

Stephen worked on his diaries obsessively, often writing up yesterday before getting down to scripts that should have been ready the previous week. A confessional, a way of exorcising the frustrations of the day, a historical record of notable people and of momentous times, a way of keeping his hand in at writing, a way of sorting out his thoughts – the diaries were all these things, but perhaps their most important purpose was to provide the material for an autobiography. They contain periodic invocations to his friends and descendants to write the book for him, in the event of his not getting around to it. He never did. *Steps to Immaturity*, published in 1959, took him up to the age of nineteen. His second volume of autobiography, incomplete and unpublished, covered his life from then until his marriage in 1927.

On 8 December 1942, after lunch with a publisher, Stephen was asked to consider putting his diaries into book form; but he was immediately daunted by the difficulties:

> For the first time there is a serious possibility that this diary might be published. But how? The whole thing as it is? Expanded from these notes? The personal thing – the picture of myself and therefore also of my age? *A book on the BBC in wartime*? Family connections? Thoughts on books? etc. etc. Or not publish at all and make it the material for a book or plays which will be my prime-of-life, best-I-can-do work.

Stephen did none of these things and the diaries are untapped. One day someone may take on the task of writing a biography based on them.

Meanwhile, this book will use only those bits of them that are relevant to Features. Of the options listed above, it will attempt to fulfil the one italicized by me, extended to cover all Stephen's ten years at the BBC.

Editorial note

Chapter one contains no diary extracts, as it deals with Features before Stephen joined the BBC. Chapters two and three, which cover Stephen's early freelance work for the BBC and take the story up to the beginning of 1940, are both short on diary, as until then his entries were sporadic. Sources consulted to fill in the gaps are indicated in the Acknowledgments and in the Bibliography.

The diary extracts have been selected so as to follow through each strand from start to finish. Thus the visit to Cowley on 13 November 1942 is quoted in the passages about Lord Nuffield; the meeting with Lord David Cecil on the same day is in the section on *New Judgments*; and the interview with the Poet Laureate John Masefield, also on the same day, is discussed under *Contemporary Portraits*. That way I hope the narrative will gain in coherence more than it loses in day-to-day drama.

Where relevant entries are too notey to be reproduced, I have built them into my own text. The quoted extracts have been edited only to eradicate obvious awkwardnesses, avoid repetitions and complete unfinished sentences – Stephen never went through and amended his diaries himself. Where I cannot read a word I have guessed it. I have sympathy with his Oxford examiners who told him at the viva: 'Had we been able to read your papers, Mr Potter, we would no doubt have awarded you a first.'

My mother Mary Potter (the artist) is sometimes referred to as P. (Stephen called her Poppy) and sometimes as Att (her long-term nickname originated at the Slade and was short for Attenborough, her maiden name). The Controller of Programmes (Basil Nicholls until 1944) is throughout referred to as C(P).

Chapter 1
Features pre-Potter

Stephen Potter describes in his diary how at the Café Royal in August 1941, well after midnight, Laurence Gilliam tried to get Cyril Connolly to do a Feature on Tennyson. 'What is a Feature?' asked Connolly crossly.

The question was even more difficult to answer then than now. Features were still evolving, with Stephen and his boss at the centre of the process. Features were whatever they decided to produce. A step back to look at their pre-Potter origins might be helpful.

In the beginning

The origin of Features has been well described by Gilliam, in a short introduction to his 1950 compendium of BBC Features. He had been in charge of the Features Section since 1936. Recognising that to begin with programmes had mostly been straight adaptations from other media, he wrote:

> But slowly, obstinately and with growing success, a group of writers and producers insisted on exploring the possibilities of the radio medium itself. Because what they produced fitted no known formula, and for that reason stood out from the run of programmes stemming from existing forms, they were grouped under the generic title of 'feature programmes'.

Four of the writers and producers referred to above were formed into a think tank by Sir John Reith in 1935, with no brief other than to come up with ideas. The Programme Research Section, as they were called, had no office hours and no specific programme assignments. Hard-working colleagues were jealous and sometimes a little scornful. One difficulty, as pointed out by Val Gielgud in *Years of the Locust*, was that they were a laboratory with no facilities for experiments except on air. Their search for 'pure' radio took time and such programmes as they produced had a mixed reception. By 1937, Reith lost patience and told Gielgud, who was Head of the Drama Department, that either he must absorb the Research Section or it would be disbanded. Gielgud absorbed it and, in recognition of its oddball output, added 'and Features' to the name of his department. He remained head of a combined Drama and Features Department from then until the end of the war. In his book he acknowledges that without the work of the four pioneers, the subsequent triumphs of Features would not have been possible.

Reith was the BBC's first Director General. To him, the number of listeners was unimportant, as long as the programmes were of the highest standard, rewarding and elevating. This philosophy is so different from that prevailing in the media today that it is hard to grasp. Even after the war, when the Third Programme was to be inaugurated, many spoke against it on the grounds that the 'good' programmes would no longer be listened to by the masses. For many years after Reith had left the Corporation, right up to the coming of commercial television in the fifties, his missionary attitude prevailed. John Drummond joined the BBC in 1958. 'No one,' he wrote, '... thought that the main role of the Corporation was just to give the public what it wanted. How could the public know what it wanted?' This was the atmosphere in which Features was born and grew up.

Early protagonists

The four thinkers in the Research Section were Lancelot De Giberne Sieveking (Lance), Mary Hope Allen, E. J. King-Bull and E. A. (Archie) Harding. King-Bull was an ex-naval officer and colonial administrator. Probably because he left the BBC relatively early, his contributions, however excellent, have not made as lasting an impact as those of the other three.

Mary Allen, who at the Slade School of Art had dared to laugh at the domineering Professor Tonks, was now equally unabashed by Reith. She joined the BBC in 1927 and her first job was to read through every play in the repertoire to see which were suitable for broadcasting. This took a year, after which she persuaded Reith to let her write programmes. She put together a series of 'mosaics', which blended verse and music. Notoriously, she wrote a programme about the Great Plague of London which spared the audience nothing of the horrors of the disease. Drawing rooms were invaded with realistic groans and screams. The programme was greeted with outraged reviews and many indignant letters. It caused a ban on any such realistic sound effects and dialogue that was not lifted until June 1940.

When Gielgud took over the Research Section, he insisted that his writers should produce their own programmes. Mary Allen was at first horrified, but before long recognized the advantages of the new system. It made for writing that was more sensitive to the potentialities and peculiarities of broadcasting, and for production skills that were more sensitive to the aims of the writer. 'How right,' she wrote, 'I gradually got confident and had the pleasure of seeing scripts through from start to finish.' The system became the norm and 'writer/producer' is still the only adequate way to describe the job.

Lance Sieveking's early programmes had also been daringly experimental. He saw that 'the art of painting with pure sound is a new thing, peculiar to radio' and this made him attach the greatest importance to sound effects. He listed six categories of them and considered them to be *The Stuff of Radio*, the title of his 1934 book. His 1928 *Kaleidoscope* was a 'panorama of man's life from cradle to grave'. The music included Negro spirituals, Beethoven and jazz. 'It is not merely used as an accompaniment,' noted *The Morning Post*, 'but is part of the very essence of the play, being as necessary as the voices.'

Sieveking's productions were extravagant, requiring five or six rehearsals and more than one studio: for *Kaleidoscope* he had used no less than seven. This was to accommodate the multiplicity of sound effects; to make use of the different acoustics of different rooms, and to enable him to have more cross-fades from one scene to another. He manipulated the control panel, by his own account, 'as if it was a musical instrument'. Sieveking's wayward definition of a 'Feature-Programme' was 'an arrangement of sounds that has a theme but no plot'. He may have been the butt of a later criticism by Laurence Gilliam that such programmes 'exalted the "How" at the expense of the "What".' But at least he boldly experimented with new techniques, some of which were of lasting value.

Archie Harding was the first to achieve, in 1932, a Christmas Day hook-up with Commonwealth countries, which thereafter traditionally preceded the King's broadcast. He worked with Gielgud on adapting plays for radio. He was on the left of the left wing and considered everything put out by the BBC to be propaganda because programmes tacitly accepted the existing political system and social conventions. This is not as extreme as it sounds. The tone of the newscasters and lecturers was *de haut en bas*. Censorship of anything that might possibly lead to social unrest appears to have been more obtrusive at this time than any censorship during the war. The writers were left wing or communist, the bosses Tory. Even after the war had begun, as will be seen in the cases of Priestley and Beatrice Webb, there were still signs of this conflict.

Experimental programmes akin to Features were also being made in the Regions. Their authors were more productive than those inside the Research Section, presumably because they were paid to produce programmes rather than theorise. Not all of them can be named here, but Cecil McGivern in Newcastle and Francis (Jack) Dillon in Bristol were already making a name for themselves and will appear in later chapters.

The most productive of them all was **D. G. Bridson**. Based in Manchester, Bridson was recruited by Harding in 1935. Also left wing, he had one verse play on Social Credit banned as being seditious and in his long verse epic *The March of the 45*, references to unemployment (at the time of Bonnie Prince Charlie!) were censored. It was the BBC's first verse Feature and in its truncated form it was to be repeated nine times.

Accents, live transmissions and scripted broadcasts

Bridson hated the stuffy BBC convention that only one sort of voice – upper middle class – was acceptable on the air. Exceptions were allowed in plays, where three regional accents were recognized: northern, cockney and 'Mummerset', a blend of all the rest. Actors – whose own accents would be public school – were expected to be able to 'do' all three. While Dillon in Bristol was trying to get them to differentiate between, say, Somerset and Suffolk accents, Bridson, whose home town was Manchester and who worked for the Northern Region, went further. He took recording equipment into homes all round the Dales and got the voices of 'real people' onto records. He had created a character called Harry Hopeful, a Lancastrian clockmaker looking for a job. He would come into homes and discuss his prospects with the local inhabitants. Although these conversations had to be rehearsed and later brought back to the studio, fitted together, scripted and then re-spoken for transmission, the dialects heard in the first Harry Hopeful programmes in 1935 were ground breaking in their use of 'actuality'. Another Bridson production with the same idea was his journey by train from London to Glasgow, when he brought his heavy Shellac discs with him and recorded local people at every station, revealing the multiplicity of regional dialects. Most shocking of all, he persuaded a Glaswegian busker to recite on air his (Bridson's) poem *Song for three million*.

With programmes such as these, Bridson claimed to have abolished the boiled shirt, us-and-them image of the BBC and opened broadcasting to all. But progress in the use of actuality and non-toff accents was slow. Recording equipment was cumbersome and it was easier to get an actor to mimic dialects in the studio than it was to record them in the field. Listeners, moreover, had come to believe that the standard BBC accent *was* standard English. When Reith himself announced the results of a general election with a clear Scottish accent, people rang in to complain. As late as 1942, Stephen Potter was writing in his diary of having to tell a schoolmaster who came in for an audition that he had no hope, because of his cockney accent.

The conventions of the time did not help non-actors. All broadcasts had to go out live; and all of them had to be scripted. When confronted with Bridson's recording paraphernalia in the home, off-the-cuff remarks were hard enough. But when the victim had to come into the studio and read out from a script his 'spontaneous' lines, this time live on air, it was difficult not to fluff them. So while it was comparatively easy for the makers of cinema documentaries to film real dockyard workers and coal miners silently at work with a voice-over commentary, radio was mainly dependent on actors.

The insistence on scripting all transmissions seems strange, but is explained by the idea that broadcasts should go out live. A live transmission without an authorised script was thought of as being too risky. Who knows what official secrets, seditious ideas or obscene remarks might slip out, inadvertently or otherwise? Better by far, it was thought, to treat such a potent weapon with respect and fix in advance exactly what was going to be said. The paradox is that while the rule about live transmissions was an attempt to retain the immediacy and audience *rapport* of the theatre and the lecture hall, the rule about scripting eliminated spontaneity.

Role of the writer/producer

Gilliam wrote in 1950: 'The essential quality of the feature programme is that it should be the expression of one mind.' The mind in question was that of the producer, not the writer. Whether the producer had written his own programme or not, it was he who was king-pin and responsible for everything – for coming up with the idea in the first place, researching it, getting it written, casting and producing it.

Research was often a matter of acquiring first-hand knowledge: going down the coal mine, boarding the battleship, going round the factory and talking to the workers as well as to the people in charge. If an outside writer had been commissioned, the producer was expected to accept the script, to reject it or to suggest improvements – sometimes a delicate matter for a young producer dealing with a well-known author. But suggestions for making a script better suited to the medium were usually both necessary and thankfully accepted.

Sometimes at this point the producer was allowed to use one of the BBC's new, specially fitted vans to record sounds, snippets of conversation and the occasional interview, which by the end of the thirties could be slotted in without being re-spoken live in the studio. Then there were the auditions and the casting. Then the choice of suitable music or the commissioning of new music (although here a musical advisor was available for the non-musical producer). Then all these sounds had to be fitted together so that, with the script, they would make a balanced programme matching the time allotted. The climax came with the rehearsals, perhaps one or two on the day before and a final run-through before transmission. This was where the expertise and the personality of the producer could make or break the programme – working with the engineers so that there were smooth transitions between scenes, sound effects, music and so on; and pacing all these elements so as to end the programme exactly on time. If the cast was enthusiastic and working with the producer, his task was eased; but if they were uninterested, or if perhaps they were unhappy with the parts allotted them, then even a skilled producer could be in trouble. Here again, tact and temerity were needed if a young producer was to tell some legend of the stage how to act; but here also the techniques of speaking into a microphone were different from those required in a theatre, and such help as the producer could give was usually welcomed.

During transmission, the role of the producer was less obvious. As broadcasts were live, it was too late to give any further guidance to the cast. Howard Rose, the most senior of the producers in the Drama Department, used to go and listen to his programmes at home, arguing that he had already done all he could during the rehearsals and that during transmission, the engineers could be trusted to work the cross-fades and the cuts. No-one else dared to do this; but probably in Features no-one would have wanted to. A play adapted from the stage was one thing, but a Feature usually contained a variety of special effects and many more changes of scene. The producer had to be present to see that all was well, intervene with any necessary adjustments and deal with crises.

Gielgud emphasised the variety of talents required of a producer of Features:

> At one end of the scale ... he will handle a programme such as that on Christmas Day, 'putting a girdle round the earth in forty minutes'. At the other he will be assigned an anthology of un-published modern poetry and music. To be ideally suited to his job, he should be not only a producer of competence and force, but a writer of parts, with a journalist's instinct for the topical, a scholar's background and an artist's taste. His work has the advantage of being immensely diversified; freed as far as humanly possible from routine activities; with almost complete elasticity of working hours; of never being completed; of desire almost invariably and inevitably outrunnng performance....
> The producer must have a musical ear, a razor-edged sense of timing, and an innate aptitude or an acquired capacity for the smooth handling of mechanical controls.

Definition of Features

The answer to Connolly's question has not yet emerged. Rayner Heppenstall's cynical 'anything put out by a producer in the Features Department' is too easy a way out. The suggestion that 'Features deal with original work while Drama deals with adaptations' is unfair on Drama, as a few plays were written specifically for radio – and Features were certainly not the only department to broadcast original work. Perhaps it is best to look at the definitions by the men in control, Val Gielgud and Laurence Gilliam. Gilliam said succinctly: 'Drama deals with fiction, Features with facts.' This is a useful pointer, but does not always hold water. Gilliam's emphasis on facts was appropriate to all his own programmes: even as a propagandist during the war, he maintained that the best propaganda was the truth. But the work of the Arts side of Features was often more imaginative than factual. Gielgud touches twice on the problem, in a more discursive way:

Definition, heaven knows, is a dangerous and thankless business, but it may not be too far wide of the truth to reply: a Feature Programme is any programme item – other than a radio play – whose author makes use of the specialised technique of radio-dramatic production. Its range is therefore exceedingly wide.

I do not think it is unfair to claim for the work of 'Features' that it is the most essentially 'radio' of all programmes broadcast. If broadcasting ceased upon the morrow's midnight with no pain, music and the theatre would and could go on.

Gielgud implied that Features alone could not exist outside radio; and this is nearer the mark. But even here it has to be said that some of the documentary films made in the thirties by Humphrey Jennings and the GPO Film Unit were not all that dissimilar from the documentary type of radio Feature. Yet Gielgud's and Gilliam's definitions cannot be bettered. As these two weave in and out of the rest of this book, a word about them on their own is appropriate.

Val Gielgud

Gielgud joined the BBC in 1928 (aged twenty-eight) as assistant to the editor of the *Radio Times* (*RT*), Eric Maschwitz. He then moved to the Public Relations side, but after a short spell there, to the surprise of some and wounded pride of older hands, he was appointed in 1929 Productions Director, which meant he had been put in charge of Drama and Variety. He was to retain control of Drama for thirty-four years.

The many family connections with the stage must have helped. Gielgud was the nephew of Ellen Terry and his brother John was already a star. But it was the quality of his dramatic instincts and his dedication to the job that enabled him to overcome any initial eyebrow-raising. Again, when in 1937 he took over the Research Section, relations with its four idiosyncratic members were at first strained, as he admits in his book; but this too he was clever enough to smooth over. He may not have been easy to get along with, but perhaps he deliberately distanced himself from his staff. Mary Allen recorded that he was not very approachable and that at meetings he was subject to fits of temper and would bring down his fist on the table and shout 'God's teeth!' She thought he was something of a poseur, wearing a red-lined black cape on first nights.

Winston Graham knew Gielgud after he had retired, as a fellow member of the Savile Club. His memories only go back fifty years, but accord well with Mary Allen's. He wrote in a letter: 'I always felt he was an actor manqué and he dressed like one: plum-coloured velvet smoking jacket, corduroy trousers, long cigarette-holder.'

It has been said that Gielgud and his staff spent too much time adapting stage plays for radio and not enough on getting plays written especially for the medium. Against this it must be remembered that when Gielgud first took over Drama in 1929, no-one questioned that his main job was to make the West End plays, hitherto only seen by the select few, accessible through radio to the masses; and this he achieved. By 1935 there were seven million radio licences and many listeners were getting their first introduction to drama. Later, during much of the war, most theatres and music halls were closed, so that even regular theatre-goers became dependent on radio. And Gielgud did offer a few plays specifically for radio. They get little attention in this book, which concentrates on the Features half of his Department.

Responsible for Drama under Gielgud was Moray McLaren, previously Programme Director in the Scottish Region. Head of the Features Section, also reporting to Gielgud, was Laurence Gilliam. However, it is clear that, to an ever increasing extent, Gielgud allowed Gilliam to run his own show, perhaps because of Gilliam's competence and Gielgud's absorption with Drama. The reality of Gilliam's independence was not made official until after the war, when Features became a separate department.

Laurence Gilliam

Reith recruited the twenty-six-year-old Gilliam for the BBC in 1933. He was a journalist and, like Gielgud, had been working for the *RT*, where he had praised Bridson's innovative and politically radical programmes. In 1936 he was put in charge of feature-type programmes: this responsibility he retained until his death and the dissolution of the Features Department in the sixties.

Gilliam's achievement was immense. Under his aegis, Features explored new techniques and exploited the possibilities of radio. It developed from nothing to become the most widely admired section of the BBC, both at home and abroad. Many Features were given to American companies, so that they could be re-made for audiences over there. D. G. Bridson, in *Prospero and Ariel*, wrote:

The feature programme as such was purely a BBC invention: no radio service in America or anywhere else had developed it so effectively.

It does not seem to have occurred to Gilliam to write his memoirs, but as he died in office, perhaps he never had time. What is more extraordinary is that no-one has ever written his biography. He attracted loyalty, affection and even veneration from his staff and a number of them gave him generous space in their own autobiographies or other writings. Three extracts are quoted below: the picture of Gilliam that emerges will later be modified by Stephen's diary entries – not always adulatory.

From *Portrait of the Artist as a Professional Man*, by Rayner Heppenstall:

His was a creative personality, that is certain. I am inclined to think that it was the only creative personality ever to emerge in broadcasting in this country.... Louis MacNeice will be remembered as a poet, his career in broadcasting being thought ancillary to this. Stephen Potter will be remembered as a wit, who also happened to work in broadcasting (for which, as it happens, I think he did his best work). Laurence created nothing which has survived.... Anything which is interesting in the Third Programme owes its inception to Laurence, to whom no monument exists or can exist, unless it is what I am writing.

[When the above was written, Features had been disbanded, but the Third Programme still survived.]

From *Feelings have changed*, by P. H. Newby (Third Programme Controller):

He was against those figures in the system who frustrated good ideas; administrators in general but network planners in particular. Inverted Micawbers, he called them, waiting for something to turn down.... He laughed a lot. He liked good food and good wine. He was a good mimic. He could do real Digger talk, Cape Dutch and various north-country accents to perfection.

From *Prospero and Ariel*, by D. G. Bridson:

There was a flamboyance about Gilliam which impressed every-one who came into contact with him and quickly earned him the nickname Lorenzo the Magnificent. He was lively, generous and witty – a man with a gift for making friends and among the most amusing company I ever kept. To the physique of one of Michel-angelo's Sistine athletes, he joined the grin and features of a genial white Negro. That, in fact, was how he described himself; and his broad nose and crinkly hair well fitted the description.

Gilliam was a voracious eater and a dedicated drinker – provided the food and drink were all that he demanded they should be. I once had the pleasure of taking him on a gastronomic tour of Blackpool. In a crowded fishmonger's shop at lunchtime, he noticed some crayfish on the slab, and shouldering his way to the front, selected ten of the largest and most succulent. As the shopman reached for *The Lancashire Daily Post*, preparatory to wrapping them up, Gilliam waved it firmly aside. 'Put them on a plate,' he ordered, 'we'll eat them here at the counter.' Encouraging me to join in, this he proceeded to do – to the stunned surprise of the management. Watching him with no less awe, the customers edged away to a respectful distance. After we had demolished half the pile, Gilliam handed the plate back to the shopman again, explaining that he needed some Black Velvet. 'Keep them on one side,' he said, 'we'll be back to finish them later.' This again the fishmonger accepted: the plate was carefully placed on a shelf behind him. I led the way round the corner to a nearby Yates's Wine Lodge, where Black Velvet was still to be had for a mere one and sixpence a half-pint tankard. Only at closing time did Gilliam deign to return to the shop, where the rest of the crayfish were again made available to us on the counter.

Chapter 2
Sliding into the BBC

John Pudney

In the sixties, Stephen Potter was due to make a speech about gamesmanship in America. His host wanted help with his introductory remarks. Stephen produced a cod CV, in which he wrote that in 1936–1938 he was 'sliding into the BBC via Schools and Empire'.

The man responsible for bringing Stephen into the BBC was John Pudney, a poet, a producer at the BBC and a friend and neighbour of the Potters in Chiswick. Both Stephen and Pudney had met their wives at boatrace parties given by the independent MP Alan Herbert. In a quiet way, Pudney was responsible for commissioning and producing a number of feature-type programmes before the Features section came into being. One such was *Hadrian's Wall*, which in 1937 he commissioned Auden to write, with music by Britten. He was always on the look-out for new writers and commissioned from Rayner Heppenstall his first radio script – on Frozen Meat, for transmission to the colonies.

Similarly, Pudney was the first to suggest to Stephen that he might write something for the BBC. Throughout the early thirties Stephen had been mainly preoccupied with his literary books; but these did not bring in enough to live on. He was therefore constantly, and for the most part ineffectually, looking for odd jobs such as book reviews. Considering this, his diary reference on 8 December 1935 to Pudney's offer is casual: 'Pudney not good at squash. He broaches wireless idea. One of those things I must obviously get in with.' Getting specimen 'playlets' two days later, he wrote 'they seem unbelievably trashy, even beyond expectation.' On 30th December: 'Squash Pudney. He is no match for me. Afterwards we discuss my play. He seems to like my effort.'

At some point in later life, Stephen re-wrote his diary entries for the early months of 1936. Although the daily entries are made to look as if they were written at that time, this later edition is less scrappy than the contemporary version and puts far more emphasis on his first BBC job:

2 January, 1936. A curious new thing happened. John Pudney has asked me to do a 'Feature' for his BBC Overseas Department. The theme is The Night Watchman – '12 o'clock and All's Well'. It shouldn't be difficult. A half-hour anthology on the hours of the night – a wonderful theme, really. He shows me some scripts. Surely I can do better than the other authors in this series, who write feebly. Also I come fresh to it. These facts cheer me, but do not help me to start. I begin to write, but it is nonsense. Then, as I was driving over Hammersmith Bridge, the right start seemed suddenly to come to me: a sort of fantastic discourse on time, clocks, etc. [He went on to comment, from the perspective of the 1960s, on the disingenuousness of this line of thought: on how it would have been better to measure himself against the good writers rather than the bad; and how mistaken it was to think that lack of experience was an advantage.]

4 January. Have finished BBC script and handed it to Pudney, who plays squash with Poppy [Stephen's wife]. I have had glimpses of famous producers producing – Sieveking with a wand (I discovered later it was a way of measuring exact distances from the microphone) or Peter Cresswell in white gloves, which I thought was genius mannerism, not knowing about his hand eczema. Have no hopes whatever about this job. [His retrospective reason was that 'in 1936 nothing could be less in fashion than Overseas BBC, or the BBC in general. It was simply a place where the young man of a dozen years ago was doing the same thing less youngly. It was all right for Gielgud and Sieveking ten years ago, when these mad young men were doing marvels with a new art form.']

23 January. I watched Pudney at the control panel, Broadcasting House – one of those mixed dialogue and music programmes which stuff the in-between times of 'Empire' broadcasting. Very thin and tepid at the listener's end no doubt but there is a conspiracy to ignore that fact. The gadgety glistening control panel is so like a Wellsian description of the future that one may soon get the hang of it. Calm hands at the control are important. Pudney if possible calmer than ever, chin more comfortably settled into his neck. This is a last-minute programme written by him last night –

change owing to King's death – and every atom of anything like a joke has to be ironed out. 'No need to tell you what I'm thinking about now.' Should that line be altered? John sits professional and stolid, hands on knobs, to twist in music and slowly twist out words with his left hand, so that it is all a matter of crescendos and diminuendos.

Among the actors and engineers not actually doing anything, there is a mixture of disassociation and bored chatting. When in action they are concentrated and precise.

30 January. Attend final rehearsals of my first BBC script – *Twelve o'clock and All's Well*. It's to be broadcast at midnight – to Tasmania, one imagines. But it seems wonderfully effective and good to me.

1 February. Pudney asks me to do another programme. Good.

Irregular commissions for similar anthologies followed, all for Empire broadcasts. Stephen would select the poems from the Chiswick library and would also write the linking script. 'My linking dialogue seems a little thin between bits of Shakespeare and Milton.' He was under-employed. 'Only having half enough to do,' he wrote, 'I take hours to do this very simple thing.' One bonus was that he was able to include the poems of his friends: one by Robert Nichols, who was always hoping for much more of his work to be broadcast, and one by Francis Meynell, in an anthology of animal poems.

In June 1937 Pudney offered Stephen a Heppenstall-type programme on Water. Researching his subject, Stephen found that cucumbers were 97% water – and called his programme *Three per cent Cucumber. Coal* followed in September, sententiously billed as *Meaning of Life – IV*. 'I am struggling with BBC programmes not to become indifferent,' he wrote. With *Tobacco* in November he achieved some progress, as it was broadcast on the Home Service as well as overseas: he enjoyed the limited kudos that followed.

There were many more commissions from Pudney over the next two years while Stephen was still freelancing – seventeen in the twelve months following Water. With fees ranging from 10 to 20 guineas, they must have helped to pay the bills. Yet Stephen never thought of these oddball programmes as a way in to a possible profession. It was a commission from another department – Schools – that first sparked any real interest in the medium.

Schools

The BBC's Charter had given it three tasks: to Entertain, to Inform – and to Educate. Education was for adults as much as for children, but the greatest importance was attached to the Schools Department, directed from 1929 to 1947 by Mary Sommerville. For at least an hour every weekday, the Home Service was given over to educational programmes for Schools, many of which planned their timetables so as to enable their classes to tune in: by 1943 it was found that over 10,000 schools were registered listeners. In 1936 Stephen wrote a programme for Schools about Chaucer. The first diary reference was on 22nd September: 'Just as I was trying to fit in all my astounding crisis of work for Pudney, a call from Schools. Can I suddenly and urgently do Chaucer programme? Collect Pudney's squash things and go to BBC for meeting with Mary Sommerville.'

The programme was broadcast seven days later. The assignment suited Stephen well. While other programmes had to be researched from scratch, English Literature was his subject: he had read it at Oxford, lectured and written books about it. Moreover he had a didactic streak, as evidenced in his Birkbeck lectures. He wrote the programme in the form of a question and answer lesson with his son Andrew (then aged eight). It began 'Hello Schools – Hello Andrew.' The angle was Chaucer in relation to the Renaissance. He reported Andrew's questions and how he had answered them. It was the first time that Stephen had himself spoken on the air and the diary entry for the day concentrates on that. He was particularly satisfied with having pulled it off because back in 1932 he had taken a voice test at the BBC for reading poetry and had failed – perhaps because his competitors had included Robert Donat. Now he had discovered that he was capable of speaking on the air:

29 September. A good day. The point about this broadcasting is
1. Voice tests, poetry reading a few years ago no good.
2. My voice broadcast back at me a few weeks ago sounded terrible.
3. But by concentrating on distinct leisureliness, I seem to have overcome this.
4. While actually broadcasting, I thoroughly enjoyed it, was able to think what I was talking about.

Stephen was never allowed to read verse – Mary Allen told him it was hopeless and that he sounded like Donald Duck – but he undoubtedly came across well in this programme. *Chaucer* is one of the few Potter programmes that still exists on tape. For all programmes that have been so saved, the BBC writes a synopsis. It is not the compiler's job to comment, but at the end of his synopsis of *Chaucer* he has written: 'Pause for thought. At this cataloguing date 60 years later, Potter still sounds entertaining, informative and amusing.'

Chaucer only brought in 10 guineas, but soon led to another commission in the *Great Writers of English* series, this time on Dr Johnson. Stephen records his nervousness in the studio:

20 October. Memories – drinking a swig of sherry in the lav. Getting confidence by smiling and mating up with the announcer (in the studio with me to begin with). Being on the whole rather rigid (though this didn't apparently show). Miracle of no mistake, no place-losing.
Much congratulation afterwards.

Mary Sommerville approved and three further programmes in the series were arranged for 1937, on Defoe, Coleridge and William Morris. All 'written and presented by Stephen Potter', they were produced by John Pudney, who made helpful criticisms while at the same time feeding Stephen with more work for overseas channels. Now for the first time there is an acknowledgement that the BBC was an employer to be seriously considered. At the top of the page for 5 December 1936 Stephen had earlier written: 'I pray this blank page won't look as frightening to me on Dec 5th as it does on March 2nd.' When 5 December came round, he wrote: 'No it does not, thank goodness. True the selection of Sutherland [as head of his department at Birkbeck College, where he lectured] sent me deeper down, but I have these extra lectures, my books are fairly promising and sought after, and above all, broadcasting possibilities.'

Victorian Negative

Stephen's next breakthrough came at the beginning of 1938. Whatever the success of the literary programmes, no career at the BBC could be based on Schools and Empire alone. Ever since the end of 1936 Stephen had been promoting the idea of a full-length feature on Samuel Butler, for adult listeners. He saw Butler's free-thinking, polymath life as a model for his own. His own breakaway from Victorian conventions and ideas had been influenced by Butler's semi-autobiographical *The Way of all Flesh*. He had been able to track down Butler's ageing manservant, Alfred Enery Cathie, who had also been the companion and walking partner of Butler in his old age. Alfred was eager to talk about his friend and master and Stephen's idea was to build his programme round recorded extracts from his reminiscenses. Such extended use of actuality was new, as was Stephen's impressionistic script, with short scenes merging into each other. It took time to get the proposal approved. In December 1936 he wrote that his 'embryonically excellent – that I know – programme' had been read by Mary Allen and that he was hoping to get the go-ahead from Gielgud and Gilliam. But it was not until 13 January 1938 that the hour-long *Victorian Negative* was at last broadcast, starting at the prime time of 7.30 pm. Apart from its value as a historical record, it must have been a success, as it led to a part-time contract for Stephen later in the year and was re-made twice during the war. However, his only diary reference to it was on the day after the broadcast (his first entry of the year), when he wrote: 'Well – this year was a delightful one up to the 13th – my Butler broadcast. Then, the feeling that I had rather shot my bolt in the Radio world (not a single newspaper notice) made me feel gloomy.' Later versions did better. In November 1940 *The Times* critic wrote: '… a refreshingly honest and curiously vivid impression of the man and the writer. Stephen Potter used acted extracts from *Erewhon* and *The Way of all Flesh* with due emphasis on their relationship to the writer's personal history. An unconventional attempt to catch the characteristic note of Samuel Butler.'

Part time

22 February, 1938. Have been chosen for the small Feature prog-rammes job. Three months at £400 p.a., schools contracts intact and can still do lectures. I find myself saying what I would come on full time for (£800, I say, rapidly rising to £1000). I walk up and down the corridors of the BBC with quite a new feeling.

The contract, which was later extended until the end of the year, committed Stephen to only twelve hours' work a week. His output was nonetheless extensive and varied. Although work for Schools and Empire continued, from then on most of his programmes were for adult audiences in the UK. Thus on 25 March he presented a collection of poems of his own choice called *Gathering Samphire, or Lines that have stuck in my Head*. Living by the river in Chiswick Mall, he wanted to write about it and its tributaries. In the same month he produced *The Tyburn still flows*, tracing it from its source on Hampstead Heath, winding down below the (still bendy) Marylebone Lane and crossing under the aptly named Brook Street. This was perhaps a trial run for the much more ambitious *Guide to the Thames* in July. The title was deliberately misleading. As one critic described it: 'Mr Potter followed the Thames from its source to its mouth in anything but a guide-book style, with little scratches of conversation, phrases and tunes which made an exact picture of each place he was describing. The criss-crossing of gramophones on the river awoke one's memory of days in punts. There is about Mr Potter's writing a hint of mockery which is delightful, but which does not obtrude when the picture should be serious.'

In September Stephen was working on *Gateway to the World*, a Feature on the Southampton docks, and for the first time he was given the use of one of the BBC's recording vans. A later *RT* article on 'How a Feature is made' used this programme to demonstrate how much care the producer took to find the right sounds to illustrate his theme. Thus Stephen recorded the sound of the meat hurling down the shoot, the sound of the grain being unloaded, the overheard goodbyes as *The Queen Mary* departed – and many more. He was less successful in his interviews. He could not find the dockers who had been detailed for work on that day, and when he did, he could not find the recording van. When that turned up, the men were taciturn. Of the casual labour system, Stephen wrote:

> During this Southampton trip I have often thought if only the men, and especially the Cunard men, were let into it more. Everything possible seems to be done to disassociate them from the job and to make them feel they are hired labour.

Meetings with the white collar staff were worse. '80% of them live in fear of putting a foot wrong and are in a state of nerves, fearing a tick off from above. More like slaves than the dockers who care too little to be in fear of that.'

Although Stephen wrote at this time of his inner content over his BBC job going well, there was an air of unreality about what he was doing. At the top of everyone's mind was the Munich crisis. Arguments raged at his club (the Savile) about whether a war should be fought over the Sudetenland. At the BBC Maurice Brown, whose normal job was musical advisor to Features and Drama, became involved in emergency schedules and in one of his round robins to the Regions, took it on himself to add: 'It is hoped that the BBC will not be able to be accused of fostering patriotism or hate....' The day before leaving for Southampton, Stephen wrote: 'P., A. and J. [his wife and sons] all listen to the zoo roars and Sieg Heils of Hitler's speech, Edith Popper [the refugee nanny] translating as he goes.' Stephen concluded that war was likely, packed the boys off to Scotland, and wondered whether his new-found career was not about to disintegrate.

Stephen's last programme as a part-timer was about the Spanish Armada. It might be thought that it was the first of his propaganda programmes, on the lines of a brave little country resisting the foreign invader – but this would be wrong. Based entirely on contemporary documents, it was written largely from the point of view of Spain. It was called *The Last Crusade* because King Philip saw the Armada as a Catholic offensive against heretical England. According to *The Times* review, the chanting of monks in Philip's private chapel was heard in the background as he conducted affairs of State. 'Contemporary accounts were freely drawn on to give us the atmosphere of the time ... no scenes were so telling as those in which simple Cornishmen, guarding the beacons along the coast, saw the hilltops flare into flame [Stephen had used "real" Cornishmen, auditioning them and rehearsing those chosen in London] ... at the court of Queen Elizabeth, the Polish ambassadors spoke Latin, giving a sense of contemporary authenticity ... the broadcast ended with the Queen's speech at Tilbury ... it was always alive, and gave a splendid picture in sound of one of the turning points in English history.'

Even before *The Last Crusade*, which was to be re-presented many times, the decision had been taken to offer Stephen a full-time job. Gilliam had sent a memo to Gielgud in September saying that 12 hours a week was too limiting and an internal meeting report on 7 October confirms that Potter should be taken onto the permanent staff at a salary of £800 from the beginning of the following year.

Joyce Grenfell, with whom Stephen was later to collaborate in the 'How' series, was at this time unknown to him. She was radio critic of *The Observer*, and was well informed. A long article on 18 December began:

I hardly dare even whisper the good news in case it all turns out to be a beautiful dream, but it really does look as if the feature prog- ramme has swung out of its rut into a wide new spaciousness that leaves one breathless. The man behind this revolution is Stephen Potter. There were hints of what might come as far back as July, when his 'Guide to the Thames' made us sit up and start noticing. 'The Last Crusade', heard on Sunday … told the story of the Spanish Armada from both sides…. [A eulogistic account of the prog- ramme follows, together with a résumé of Stephen's career with the BBC to date]…. And now comes the glad news that, in January, he is to join the Department as a full-time writer and producer. Our entertainment, of the more intelligent sort at any rate, should be well taken care of in 1939.

© *The Observer*

Chapter 3
1939

Full time and flat out

During 1939 the Drama and Features Department moved twice: with the outbreak of war to Evesham; and in November, to Manchester. Stephen's diary in this eventful year is still patchy, and there are few substantial entries for the first four months. Probably he could not spare the time. His secretary's appointments diary (a copy of which was also sent to me by Texas University) helpfully notes the planned transmission days of all his programmes. In this early part of the year he had a busy schedule:

20 Jan	Tom Moore (Schools)	20 March	*The Discovery of France*
30 Jan	*Silence for Take*	23 March	*The Voice of Paris*
11 Feb	*The Tyburn still flows*	13 April	Turner (for Empire)
23 Feb	*Romeo Coates*	22 April	*The Thin Red Line*
5 March	*The Last Crusade*	25 April	*Anzac Day* (for Empire)
7 March	Poetry (Schools)	6 May	*The Great Jowett*
14 March	Oliver Goldsmith (Schools)		

At the end of his first week, Stephen writes: 'My last week's good start has petered away in the wearisomeness of hanging about on the outskirts of this film job.' This referred to *Silence for Take*, a Feature about the making of a film of Edgar Wallace's *The Four Just Men*. It had involved several visits to the Ealing Studios, where Stephen had watched famous directors doing screen tests and 'seen' Michael Balcon at lunch; but he himself had felt too much on the periphery.

Romeo Coates, on the other hand, was more demanding and involved collaboration with Edith Sitwell. He had to adapt and produce a play of hers about a West Indian millionaire's son, who in the eighteenth century had paid to be an actor on the London stage. He was so laughably unconvincing that he attracted huge crowds.

The Tyburn still flows and *The Last Crusade* had both been broadcast in 1938; but in neither case was it just a question of playing a recording. As discussed in the first chapter, all programmes had to go out live; so for 'repeats' actors had to be re-assembled and re-rehearsed – and sometimes there were alterations to the cast. The text itself was usually fine tuned, perhaps to take into account BBC post mortems, usually held the morning after each new broadcast. Revivals could take up almost as much time as the original. Although the quality of recordings then did not match that of tapes, it would technically have been possible to broadcast a straight recording of the original version – and already this was sometimes done with Empire broadcasts, to avoid live transmissions in the middle of the night. It was not concern about the quality of recordings that ruled out canned transmissions at home: rather it was a feeling that it would somehow be cheating not to deliver to listeners a live performance.

The two French programmes are particularly intriguing, as the secretary's desk diary shows a planned absence in Paris of only two days. This would hardly have been long enough: Stephen was a polymath in the range of his interests, but did not speak French and never claimed any expertise in French affairs. Back copies of the *RT* show that both prog-rammes marked the State visit of President Lebrun. *The Discovery of France* was an anthology of essays and poems on France by English writers ranging from Spenser to Dickens. *The Voice of Paris* did involve a trip there, with one of the BBC recording vans capturing sounds of the city. But it was Gilliam and another writer/producer, Bert Lloyd, who went – Stephen must have withdrawn or been eased out at the last minute. The Englishness of his interests and character was not to change. Even after the war, when Gilliam was sending his producers all over Europe, he did not send Stephen.

The Thin Red Line was a series on regiments of the army. The first had been about the Grenadier Guards and was written by Sir Arthur Bryant and produced by Gielgud. Stephen was now asked both to write and to produce one on his own – about the King's Royal Rifle Corps, known as the 60th. It had been the first Regiment to break away from the traditional battle formation of a square; and had been the first to be fully motor-mechanised. Stephen, who had been commissioned in the Guards in the First World War (just too late to go to the front) and whose grandfather Captain 'Josh' Reynolds had been a professional soldier, enjoyed his days with the regimental HQ at Tidworth. He recorded everyday sounds as well as exotica such as what it sounded like to be fired at by 'one of the new Bren guns.' Later, during the war, Stephen was asked to cover various units of the armed forces and these programmes came to be seen as part of the war-related role of the department. The occasion for this first one on the 60th, however, was the centenary year of the regiment.

The secretary's diary notes two appointments for 28 April: '3.00 Benjamin Britten; 4.00 Graham Greene'. The meeting with Britten must have been to discuss the music for *Lines on the Map*, a series on Communications – by land, sea, wireless and air. Stephen had written two of them. Britten noted in *his* diary: 'Wrote some brass music for BBC programme *Lines across May* [sic]. Awful muck.'

Graham Greene had written an hour-long programme on Benjamin Jowett, the famous Master of Balliol fifty years earlier, who had been deprived of his emoluments as Regius Professor of Greek at Oxford on suspicion of heresy (broad-minded religious views). Stephen produced it, advising on the suitability of the script for radio and casting himself as narrator.

The above brief notes, gleaned mainly from sources other than scraps of diary, give an idea of the heavy workload imposed by the BBC. During these months, Stephen and Att had moved house. The new-found regular income, together with an offer to Att of a one-man show at Arthur Tooth & Son, had enabled them to leave their cramped and rented accommodation for a much larger house of their own just down the road in Chiswick Mall. Stephen took the day off on Monday, 8 May and took stock:

Possible re-start of diary because this morning I have a breathing space at last from overwork of last 7 months – but it will be a great effort to organise it again. Well, what is happening? At the moment, it would be one of my record happiest times. We are so enjoying the now nearly completed décor and comfort of Thamesbank. But the shadow – same for us as for everybody – of war again. The house, and familiar London houses of friends, so likely to be spoilt by war and bombing. Also (if war) I separate from P., A. and J. (BBC to Evesham)….

Enjoying my BBC work as I never thought it would be possible to enjoy one's money-earning profession. Why? I feel myself good at it and appreciated and I like the people I work with. I like the little status-plus-publicity and I like to feel that my work, which is all non-writing-down stuff, is being heard.

We can see from this that as early as May the BBC had already laid plans for the evacuation of Drama and Features to Evesham. It was intended that this should be kept secret, and apart from this early lapse, there are no further references to the name of the town in Stephen's diaries.

The next day Stephen for the first time used his diary to make notes for another programme. This again related to the Thames:

> A radio job prospecting Thames dredgers. Brought down to Tilbury by a cheerful, ugly, Daily Maily, human-side journalist Buckley Hargreaves. The lunch in the Port of London Authority hotel, ¾ empty. The journey after lunch in his launch (I fall fast asleep) to the Big Dredger No. 7. The wonderful sight of the buckets, the close-up of that unoiled-metal grind, which grinds and jangles itself away in ten months' continuous dredging. The mud down the shoot. The chains for altering position snapping about on their wheels. The working man's modern oiliness, and its effect on his life.

From such notes were Stephen's Feature programmes built up. Recording equipment was a rare luxury and the noises described would usually be reproduced by the BBC's sound effects department, relying on Stephen's descriptions; while the comments of the stoker would be delivered by one of the actors able to 'do' cockney.

The Oxford Programme

At the end of May, Stephen had an appointment with his old tutors and professors at Merton College, Oxford, for exploratory talks about a programme on the University. He looked forward to this return visit and was to fill eight pages of diary with his impressions, among which:

> Friday, 12 May. Dash down to Merton. I am a shade late and the dons await me. Harrison, Wyld (hearty, sincere greeting from him), Lambert (cold?), padré (unknown, pallid, independent), Garrod, evil old oyster with unexpected charm, pettishly going on to another subject and itching to get on to the handsome don he favours. When I come in, Garrod says: 'You're still looking remarkably young … I

should have guessed that from your books.' Mure talks about himself, his book and about Aristotle *not* being different from Plato. A general air of sad decay about the common room people: of similar talk grown older and gone to seed; of lifelessness. I bless my job.

Saturday, 13 May. In the morning, a nicer Oxford. Wallflowers behind Merton, meadows at back, college garden. I rout out the tall and possessed President of the Union Hugh Fraser, who agrees to a recording of the debate and asks me to dinner. I call on Wyld again and manage, to my surprise, to fix up him and perhaps notable others in a recording of lectures. A glimpse of the 8 before I go [Stephen had rowed for the College].

Stephen's second visit to Oxford was with a recording van and his female assistant, Jo Plummer (later known to many as 'Aunty Jo' of *Children's Hour*). His nervousness about his reception on both visits may well have been due to the publication in 1937 of *The Muse in Chains*, with its anti-academic slant:

18–19 May. Down at 11, and make my first call. How will the wind blow? A bad start. I call (I had sent a note) on the Rt. Hon. H. A. L. Fisher, O.M., Warden of New College. Will he be amenable? A fidgety, big, important man. He (being patient): 'Well, Mr Potter?' I explain. 'How can I help? What do you want me...' I see at once that he is not going to 'play', so I make as quick and neat a get-away as I can, overdoing my grateful enthusiasm over some suggestion about the New College choir. As I go out, I copy down the astounding diversity of notices on the entrance notice board.

Then down to Oxford police and see the chief superintendant. They like seeing BBC, want to make a thing of it. Draw plan of the Union. He wants to be shown round BBC. All well. Then interview with President of OUDS; lunch with Merton lecturer Deane Jones; down to barge for a moment (2nd VIII bumped, but an overbump).

Then to the OUDS rehearsal: Leslie French conducting a cubbish OUDS group in *The Tempest*. Arrange for the take. Then to Union to fix position of van. President Fraser has a rather head prefect manner, but asks Plummer to join us for dinner. I am fixed at Mitre, Plummer at the Eastgate.

Feel good in my good black tie. A sherry with La P., and then with the Union – and with the booted Evelyn Waugh and the nerve-whipped Ronnie Knox [Roman Catholic Chaplain for the University].

After large breakfast with Plum., I call on Isis editor in Oriel. Then record: Merton chimes; Balliol scout; Merton dons; Buttery. After a sandwich, down to the barge to record Joad, who had come to meet me. In the evening, record cocktail party at Christ Church and the OUDS rehearsal. The admirable impromptu talk of the boys – especially O'Donovan, about to be sent down for debts – talks of the bad interview ahead with his father – 'a bit difficult.'

Unforgettable and really self-forgetting day. Tiredness of an efficiently working brain – very pleasant, and rare, for me.

Undergraduate Summer is also one of the few Stephen Potter programmes still preserved in the BBC's archives. Although actors do participate, it is largely a tapestry of 'takes', which for its effect depends on the skill of the producer and his technicians at the control panel: a manuscript would give little idea of the nature of the programme. It includes excerpts from the Union speech by Evelyn Waugh (making fun of the notion that German troops might march into Poland); bits of lectures by Mure on Aristotle; Wyld on English philology; Garrod on Housman; Nichol Smith on Pope; and Deane Jones on the struggle for Constantinople. These are interspersed with shorter takes, such as the Merton chimes, the drinks being ordered in the Buttery, the Isis office on Press Day and snatches from his talk with his old friend Cyril Joad on the towpath. Particularly remarkable were the many quick fades and cuts, building up an impression of University life, as heard by a hidden listener. Also, the liberal use of actuality. Few of the spoken contributions were scripted and re-enacted: they were used as recorded at the time.

Undergraduate Summer was not broadcast until August. Apart from a first-class review in *The Times*, reaction was cool. On 11th August Stephen wrote: 'A day of sadness and self-kicking. I sense lukewarmness in the very very few comments.' But August was not the right time for anything so nostalgic and limited in its appeal. Listeners were pre-occupied with the coming war and such a programme must have seemed irrelevant.

Air Raid

Between fieldwork for *Undergraduate Summer* and transmission in August, Stephen was asked at the end of May to devise a programme that would give listeners some idea of what it would be like to be in an air raid. This was a big assignment, as the government was increasingly worried about the indifference of the public to any kind of Air Raid Precautions (ARP). It was his first war-related programme and was devised with the help of The Air Ministry, The Home Office, Scotland Yard, The Ministry of Health and the War Office. Diary references are scant. 31 May: 'It seems Air Raid prog. definitely on.' 6 June: 'Evelyn to dinner, to talk about ARP and whom I ought to see.' (Evelyn Sharp was later to become the Civil Service's first female Permanent Secretary.)

8 June. To Home Office, Lord Privy Seal's Department, to see Colonel Crutchy, about this Air Raid prog. Then over the bridge to the Air Ministry. Being pushed both ways by the departments, who whisper intimately that the others are no good.

Transmission was on 23 June. Lest any listeners should mistake the programme for a real air raid, it had been preceded by a press campaign warning people of what was coming. (Orson Wells's *The War of the Worlds*, about invasion by another planet, had caused national panic in America.) Alan Jenkins, Stephen's biographer, described it in his book:

Air Raid presented two families, one sceptical – 'It's just a noise' – the other alert, fully prepared. Mr Leversuch, head of the sceptical family, fiddling with his radio, finds a ministerial speech on 'being prepared' and crossly switches off.... Mr and Mrs Leversuch's reasons for not lending a hand *yet* are totally middle-class and suburban: 'But there's the bridge committee, the charity dance, and who would walk the dog?'

In the end, of course, the heel-dragging family is persuaded to be less negative in future. It was a peak-time programme and must have hit the right note, as after the war had started Stephen was to re-introduce Leversuch in a number of Home Front programmes.

Air Raid, probably in a government-inspired attempt to ensure that more people got the message, was featured as a top-of-page news item in

The Times next morning:

A BROADCAST OF AIR RAID
Value of Being Prepared

If anything could bring home to the public the need for A.R.P. and the wisdom of the slogan 'be prepared', it was the excellent broadcast written and presented by Mr Stephen Potter last night.... It was a masterpiece of presentation, bringing home to listeners in forty minutes something that months of canvassing could hardly have achieved.

The column, still posing as a news item, reinforced the message by describing the lack of co-operation of the Leversuch family and went on: 'The imagination of the listener was set on fire not so much by the thrilling air raid which followed as by the brilliant sound picture built up by the co-ordinated measures taken to meet and deal with such an emergency [fighters going up, searchlights, anti-aircraft guns, etc]. It ended: '... the suburban pair who could see no further than their noses found themselves helpless and useless when the end came, because they had not thought it worthwhile to "Be Prepared".'

On the day that *Air Raid* was broadcast the Potters gave a house-warming party for 150 guests – and from my mother's list of drinks to be bought (stuck in the diary), it looks as if 20 bottles of spirit, as well as a great deal of wine and beer, were consumed. The next day Stephen records severe heart palpitations, which must have been the first attack of the tachycardia that was to trouble him later. He took some time off work; then went on holiday with friends to the Lac d'Annecy. He also took the usual August holiday in Swanage, where his recently widowed mother normally rented a house for the whole family. Here he wrote: 'Surely I ought to keep a record of my BBC work – as material for a book on it? But I hope the sight of my scripts will recall the crises and pleasures and failures to mind.' He never did, and the scripts have disappeared.

At Swanage, he had the time to worry about the poor reception of the Oxford programme at the beginning of the month:

17 August. This week there has been, for me, a quite new experience in BBC work. Since my start doing scripts for Pudney 3 years ago it has been in a way a fairy story rise. Now from 2 or 3 centres a

distinct fading. I suddenly feel that I shall have to struggle twice as hard for half or a quarter of the praise. I must not become one of the stranded wrecks of whom Laurence says 'difficult to know what to do with him.' I am no longer alone in my Features glory. Bert Lloyd for one has done a fine Feature on whalers. Archie [Harding] seems a bit off me. Moray won't play golf. Barbara Burnham [she and Mary Allen were the only two female producers in the department] is suddenly frightfully cagey about my long-shot suggestions for doing *The Cherry Orchard* in rehearsal.

Of his autumn programmes, Stephen wrote on 25 August: 'I am doing no preparation for my autumn programmes: shall be rather caught if there is no war after all.' The next day he wrote that he had news of much excitement at the BBC, probably referring to the secret move to Evesham. He tried to arrange for his diaries and photograph albums at Thamesbank to be buried. He then moved his family to a rented cottage just inland from Swanage, judging it to be too dangerous for them to go back to London.

Hogsnorton

Stephen had bought a new wireless in Swanage. As the family was listening in the cottage to Chamberlain's speech on Sunday, 3 September, the sound faded at the crucial moment and Stephen dashed to the nearest pub, only in time to hear the announcer say '… names must be pinned on children.' He had to depart at once for Evesham. He collected his golf clubs (one indefatigable member was still playing) and leaving an anxious family in Dorset, arrived on Monday, the day after war was declared.

The Head of the Drama and Features Department, Val Gielgud, had already arrived, on Saturday. He tells in his autobiography *Years of the Locust* how on the Friday he was in the middle of producing his first full-length play for television when he received a telephone call telling him that Alexandra Palace, the TV centre, was closing down (there was to be no more TV until after the war). The BBC 'emergency period' had begun. The National and Regional radio transmissions were merged into a single 'Home Service', leaving no choice of channel. The number of hours per week allocated to Drama and Features was cut from eighteen to four.

The pre-arranged headquarters of the department (as well as of the Schools department) were in Wood Norton, a mansion previously owned by the Duc d'Orléans, pretender to the French throne. According to

Gielgud, it was 'sprouting *fleurs-de-lys* on everything, from the weather-vane to the bath plug'; and had a bear pit in the garden. It had been quickly dubbed 'Hogsnorton', an imaginary village round which comedian Gillie Potter (no relation) built his radio monologues. Despite the strictest precautions, the attempt to keep the location secret had not worked. Gielgud tells the story of how one of his engineers earlier in the summer had visited a German Radio Exhibition in Berlin. His request to see a new gadget was refused on grounds of secrecy. ' "And by the way," added the Reich official blandly, "how is your little secret hide-out in the Vale of Evesham getting along?" '

Stephen was in contention for one of the better billets and won it by tossing a coin. Gielgud: 'Stephen Potter finds himself, rather typically, billeted at a fantastic farm with the biggest collection of caged birds in the country.' It also contained a mini-zoo and on 12 September Stephen wrote: 'in the evening I help to catch a wallaby galloping round with its baby in its pouch and growling.' His first preoccupation was to find a house for the family, but this proved impossible. 'The house agents laugh at me.' Not only the Drama and Features and Schools departments, but also members of the newly formed BBC Repertory Company had all moved to Evesham. The sudden influx was not at first welcomed by the stunned locals and accommodation was scarce. Stephen wrote to his mother (13 September): 'About 300 people here, all doing usual things in unusual ways – committee meetings on lawns, in pubs. We're all *trying* to get interesting topical programmes done, but we have come up against a wall of Whitehall carefulness so far.'

Within a day of the start of the war the BBC had issued an emergency edition of the *RT*, in which the schedule for 4–10 September had been mostly reduced to News Bulletins and recorded music. The editorial boasted 'Broadcasting carries on!' It said that it was hoped to resume live entertainment soon – possibly by Thursday.

Stephen's first programme from Evesham was – for the third time – *The Last Crusade*, on Friday 8 September. Stephen was up until 3.20 am the previous evening, correcting the script; and a different actor had to be found for the part of Mendoza, the Spanish ambassador. The Chaucer programme for schools was also 'repeated'; as was *Guide to the Thames*. But there was increasing dissatisfaction at the lack of any more imaginative response by the BBC to the war situation: it was expected to do something more than just 'carry on'. News bulletins, official announcements, ministerial pep talks and recorded music predominated; but this pattern had been planned on the assumption that as soon as war started, bombs would be falling on all major cities. The unexpected phoney war, in which life seemed to go on unchanged, brought no change to the emergency schedule. 'I cannot begin to justify our security hide-out and size of staff unless we do really active work,' wrote Gielgud (in a memorandum released in Caversham). He was also worried about the 'reserved occupation' status (i.e. immunity from call-up) of many of his staff. How could this be justified, when no contribution was being made to the war effort? He suspected the motivation of BBC management, hinting that they may have been sitting on the fence, thinking that the war was already lost. He was not encouraged by a memo from Head Office saying that plays of greater length than half an hour should not for the present be envisaged and suggesting that they should be 'of the Children's Hour type'. He made many trips to London to persuade the authorities that it was the duty of the BBC to maintain high quality programmes, especially at a time when civilized standards were at risk. He re-established a reasonable allocation of air-time for his Department. He advocated Shakespeare, Ibsen, Greek drama and other programmes that had previously been banned as unsuitable for a mass market medium.*

Leversuch and Literature

Meanwhile Laurence Gilliam and Moray McLaren, respective heads of the Features and Drama sections, were each working on a major series, each showing that the BBC too had gone to war. First, on 8 October, began MacLaren's *The Spirit of Poland*, which told the story, in a number of episodes, of that country in its most recent configuration, from 1919 to 1939. That Gielgud himself, whose father had been Polish and who had spent years in the country, did not participate is perhaps not strange: he could hardly bear to think about what was happening there. (Towards the end of the war, Stephen wrote: 'Curse the anti-Russianites. Only

---

* An article by Stephen Johnson in the BBC Music Magazine of July 2001 suggests that at the same time Vaughan Williams was fighting a similar battle on behalf of music. In October he wrote to the Director General (now F. W. Ogilvie): 'It has, I think, been a great pain to many people to find that in the early days of the war it was apparently the opinion of your programme-makers that the English people, when their hearts and minds were strung up to great endeavour, only wanted to listen to the loathsome noises of the so-called Cinema "organ".... The result of this policy has been that the discriminating listeners are tuning in to *Germany* for their spiritual sustenance....

forgiveable in Val, a romantic Pole.') Later in the same month, Gilliam launched *The Empire Strikes Back*, an account of the support of the Dominions and Colonies for the war and the first of his many semi-propaganda programmes. *The Listener* hailed both these as 'the first major effort of radio drama since the war began.'

Plans were being drawn up for a series of 'Home Front' programmes, designed to acknowledge the fact that it was not only the Forces that were (or would be) affected by the war. The *RT* 'hyped' the proposed series and promised (rather vaguely) that they would 'reflect all sorts of activities arising out of the war.' As early as 7 September Stephen was typing out a Home Front suggestion. This was probably the origin of *Children in Billets*, in which he recorded on discs the comments of evacuees on their unfamiliar country surroundings. This programme was broadcast on 30 September – twice.

> 26 September. Doing script for Home Front. Laurence to town to see Eden and others.
> 29 September. After golf with Val against Bruce and Moray, Val, feeling strong, suddenly says, in The Star: 'What! Home Front tomorrow at 3.30?' Pause. 'Cut out H. G. Wells's *Purple Pileus* with the BBC theatre orchestra at 8.30 tomorrow evening and run it then as well.' [Fortunately the *RT* had warned that during the emergency, scheduled programmes were liable to alteration.]
> Saturday, 30 September. Fit together records in morning. Lunch hour – learn my part. 3.30–4: my Billets prog. goes out.

Earlier, on 25 September, Stephen had already learnt that he would have a key role in later Home Front programmes: 'All the Feature boys down for a meeting this afternoon…. I am to do second and third H.F. programmes. I don't feel nervous.' In the event, subsequent Home Fronts were of two kinds: non-Potter programmes with titles such as *Farming* and *Harvest of the Sea*; and ones written, researched and produced by Stephen, in which he used again the fictional Leversuch family that had emerged in *Air Raid* in June. The first was called *The Leversuch Family at War*. This was flagged in the *RT*: '… Now the war has started, the Leversuch family is settling down and grappling with such major problems as How to fill up a Form, and whether or not Mr Leversuch could claim extra petrol for that journey to fix up that business point which surely might be considered of national importance….'

When this issue of the *RT* appeared, the programme had not been written and inspiration seems to have dried up. Sometimes Stephen seemed incapable of working until he was at or just past the deadline – a tendency that was to get worse.

6 October. Terribly behind with Leversuch prog. Feel as if I have overdone the putting of it off. Had dream 5 days ago that no prog. appeared and that Val, nice but pained, faked up another. Every evening in this gassy, relaxed, stuffy little sitter, I go to sleep after dinner till 12, perhaps to work without my a.m. clarity till 3.

Sunday, 8 October. Work through morning, Jo coming up (with a push) to type. Get a slight line on Leversuch at last. But God how late.

10 October. The L. prog. finished, rehearsed and performed today. [As usual, an analysis of the performance of each actor follows. It was always important to him that the cast should appreciate the programme; and on this occasion, they did.]

11 October. Apparently L. yesterday was a dazzling success with Val.

12 October. Repeat of Leversuch. Photo in *The Times* of me and Val and Moray.

20 October. Will always remember Moray reading out with great gusto and humour tremendous praise of Leversuch in *Listener*.

This review was headed 'Mr Potter Triumphant'. Parts of it are quoted here as, in the absence of any written or aural record, it gives some description of the programme itself. It also shows that Stephen was beginning to favour simulation in the studio, rather than actuality.

The Leversuch Family at War was, it is true, a minor piece. It was not, for instance, on the scale of *The Last Crusade*. But it had exactly the signs of imagination and of understanding of broadcasting as a medium which made *The Last Crusade* remarkable. And which make *The Tyburn Still Flows* remarkable too. Until lately we had only Mr Bridson to wave as a banner across the seas to foreign broadcasters. Now we can add Mr Potter to our brandishing.

In contrasting the techniques of the two writers, the reviewer went on:

Mr Potter's later programmes show his gift for putting everyday life over the microphone. By this I do *not* mean his recorded 'actuality' programmes. Many people do these as well as Mr Potter. But I do not know anybody who can approach his success in giving us feature programmes which have the unmistakable stamp of actual experience and which are, in fact, imaginative concentrations of reality.

The reviewer describes how voices and themes were superimposed on each other and ends:

Here, in fact, were all the methods of 'expressionism' and 'symbolism' which have sat so uneasily upon the 'advanced' theatre for the past twenty years. And lo! in broadcasting and in Mr Potter's hands they seemed ordinary and proper. This, clearly, is their rightful sphere. This is a line for broadcasting rather than the stage.

Another Leversuch programme was broadcast on 7 November. Each one was partly morale stiffening and partly informative. They may have been inspired by Government officials during visits to London by Gielgud or Gilliam; or they may have originated with the BBC. The idea of Leversuch himself was Stephen's. The way that in the end Leversuch sees reason and co-operates was closely paralleled in Roger Livesey's portrayal of Col. (Gad Sir!) Blimp in the contemporary film *The Life and Death of Colonel Blimp*: at the very end of it, Blimp stops harking back to how things used to be done and goes along with modern methods.

In complete contrast, Stephen was asked once again to produce *Victorian Negative*; and to do another programme about the Irish bard Tom Moore (author of *The Minstrel Boy* and other ballads). It must have been a relief for him to turn from responsibility-laden, semi-official writing; and this alternation between that and literary work set a pattern that lasted throughout the war.

The extent to which the so-called repeat of the Samuel Butler programme was nothing of the kind is shown by the fact that he had to get hold of Butler's manservant again for *Victorian Negative* (although Alfred's contribution to the first production was still available on disc):

17 November. Go furthest East on the District Line to get Alfred at Manor Park. A maze of little streets – it seems quite deserted

and quiet. He is in old clothes – comes down cheerfully. Introduces daughter and granddaughter. I have seldom seen such a sweet family: it seems somehow to have spread from Butler. Alfred says he will come along all right. I get a taxi while he puts on a smart suit and collar and hat. A bit nervous in the taxi of the traffic but otherwise in form. Completely on the spot, he starts talking, as I want, about Butler's last words and the cremation.

Tom Moore built on Stephen's programme for Schools in March. The new version went out at 11 pm and was more experimental. As the *RT* described it, '… the students take notes on how to begin the study of this subject. But as they listen they overhear the voice of Tom Moore himself and seem to be taking part in scenes from his life'.

Bridson land

Work in November and December was disrupted by the department's move from Evesham to Manchester. Evesham had been impractical from the start and the original plan had been to go from there to Cardiff. Gielgud fought another battle over this, mainly on the grounds that in Manchester there was already a core of practised and highly regarded Drama and Feature writer/producers working for the Northern Region. Bridson was the most experienced of these, but among the other producers who were later to achieve fame was Joan Littlewood, who in her poverty had walked all the way from London to Manchester to get a job. Gielgud prevailed and the talents in Evesham and Manchester were fused. Stephen on 13 November recorded his first day in the new offices:

To Manchester. Get up early. Cold northern morning and the car won't start – I twist my thumb on the starting handle. Arriving at the office, I find that Jo has put me in the best desk, bless her. Am shown round. People seem nice, but it is necessary to be humble and modest and like Manchester. Its tall buildings over not-wide-enough streets: no doubt the gloom will descend, but an interesting experience. We like The Haunch of Venison, which is already nabbed as our pub.

Gloom did indeed descend, as is shown in the 29 November entry, when he was returning by train after delivering the second of two lectures on radio to the Royal Society in London:

To the dark – sense of doom – atrophied father feelings, husband, everything. In bad form. Couldn't properly control last Saturday's Butler rehearsal. Losing authority with cast. Stomach bad…. Want the time to rest back, sit and do nothing. Manchester against me in many ways. Bridson land. War going very badly: not much hope.

There are no further diary entries for the year; but Stephen did write and produce at least one programme in December – *The Lying Jade*, which happens to be one of the very few of his programmes for which the full script still exists. While not part of the Home Front series, it may have been inspired by the Ministy of Information, which later commissioned the famous 'Careless Talk Costs Lives' posters by Fougasse. There are two messages. To show the dangers of careless talk, a soldier tries to impress his girl by revealing that he has been 'chosen' to keep watch over a crashed enemy aircraft. As this had a decoding apparatus in the cockpit, the slipping out of the secret that the plane was still intact leads the enemy to change their current code, realizing that we might have cracked it. The other message was a caution against starting rumours. By using the technique of rapid cuts from one scene to another, we hear how idle speculation about an empty farm building can develop, via a suggestion that it is to be used by the military, into a firm belief that it is the site for a secret ray which, when aimed at enemy aircraft, would stop their engines. This particular idea was *not* Stephen Potter's. A 1938 film, *Q Planes*, starring Ralph Richardson and Laurence Olivier, was about just such a malevolent device, on that occasion conceived by 'the enemy'. And the existence of such a ray was in fact a current rumour. While researching Leversuch, Stephen had had a number of meetings with Tom Harrison, master-mind of *Mass Observation*, a series of nationwide surveys employing part-time 2000 researchers to find out what was happening in the minds and daily lives of the population. These meetings had not been of any use for the earlier programmes, but *The Lying Jade* included this credit: 'Use has been made of the dossier of wartime rumours collected by the organisers of *Mass Observation*.'

Chapter 4
Manchester

66 Platt Lane

While Evesham had been a bizarre interlude, Manchester seemed more permanent and again the first priority for Stephen was to find a home for the family. This proved no easier than before: not only had a large section of the BBC converged on the city, but so had many other refugees from London. Att came up to help and eventually the Potters linked up with Laurence Gilliam and his wife-to-be Marianne Helweg – a multi-lingual Dane who did translations for the Department. They rented a large early nineteenth century house in Platt Lane, about a mile from the centre of the city and overlooking Platt Park. Other BBC people came and went, but the Gilliams and the Potters constituted the core of the ménage, and stayed there for just over fifteen months. *Picture Post* ran an article on the BBC in March 1941, from which the picture overleaf is taken. Marianne is serving the food; Maurice Brown is on her right; Att and Stephen are on her left; on their left is Mary Allen and at the head of the table (as befitted the Head of Features and one so large in build and personality) is Gilliam.

An early member of the household was Valentine Dyall, the owner of an extraordinarily deep voice, with which as the 'Man in Black' he introduced the chilling terror series *Appointment with Fear*. (Worries that the the series would terrify children may have been partly defused by my brother and I begging to be allowed to stay up and listen.) *His* wife-to-be got off to a bad start:

> 8 January 1940. Some inter-Platt Lane-necine war on the question of the studio – whether P. or Babette has it. Babette puts L.G. right off by saying 'I must know now.'

Picture Post, March 15, 1941

Att won the battle for the only suitable studio and the Dyalls did not stay long. Ill feeling over this was soon patched up and when they married, Stephen gave them a copy of his Nonesuch Coleridge and Att gave one of her oil paintings, *Golden Privet*. Thanks came in the form of a sonnet, which ended: 'Then let us ever friendly hands entwine; Stephen and Att, Babette and Valentine.'

Stephen sometimes describes home life at No. 66:

Sunday, 11 February 1940. In drawing room at 66 Platt Lane, I am getting on top of one of the endless succession of coughing colds everyone here is suffering from. Dyalls have left, Lance and perhaps Mary [Allen] are about to join. Laurence, who was very funny at lunch time imitating a fag-in-the-mouth Calthrop beginning to a Hitchcock film (his old overcoat is right for it) has gone to a Hallé concert. Marianne getting rid of a cold in bed upstairs. How will she and Mary hit it off, if at all?

Sunday, 25 February. Queer typical day at 66 Platt. L.G. comes home from London at 8 am and goes to bed. A large haddock is brought up to them. I peck at my mountain of work waiting for me in the next fortnight. How has L.G. got on in London? 'No co-ordination from above – just told to "go ahead with Features".' Slip out at 12.30 for brief walk with L.G. and more drinks than I want at pub – we each have 2 light ales and a gin and French. The Moray McLarens have asked themselves to a drink. P. and I are off them as a pair, because we've never had a drop of drink out of them.

The sourness of Stephen's comments merely reflected his mood on the day. Moray McLaren, Head of Drama, is later only referred to in affectionate terms. He introduced Stephen to the Manchester Croquet Club and later in the year, when Manchester was still a refuge from the blitz, Stephen wrote: 'Three passionate games of croquet with Moray – eight hours of it. I have quite got caught up in a passion for this game.' Moray's comments were constantly recorded:

16 January. Moray says that Knutsford Church, where we are going, is ugly inside and nice 18th century out. The sexton told him no, it was the outside that was ugly and it wasn't 18th century anyway, as it was built in 1740. M. says this belongs to the completely silencing type of remark....

Gielgud set himself up in a hotel. A hard worker, he could be critical of the less dedicated; but nonetheless he socialized with his producers on the golf course or in the evenings. The same age as Stephen, he had already been running Features and Drama for over ten years and had the air of having already done everything. After a long talk at the beginning of the year, in which they told each other of their spiritual crises and poetry enthusiasms, Stephen wrote of Gielgud's 'feeling that when he was 17 he was already burnt out, his feeling that, at Oxford, he was too old for the aesthete or any other special set; but of course he was enthusiastic about OUDS. Yet Val still seems in some sense burnt out, wasted and lost.'

On 16 February Stephen wrote: 'At Manchester, Lance Sieveking and Mary Allen are trying out and being tried. They seem to be at the stage of finding it less bad than they expected.' Both these Feature-founders stayed, although before long Lance was moved to Bristol, HQ of the BBC's Western Region. When Stephen wrote *Undergraduate Summer* in 1939, he may have had in mind Lance's 1927 programme about May Week in

Mary Allen

Cambridge. Lance had recorded it 'from a tree in Rectory Meadows' (according to *The Age of Illusion* by Ronald Blythe) and that had been a primitive attempt at Outside Broadcasting and the fly-on-the-wall techniques that Stephen used later at Oxford. As has been seen, Lance had a fastidious approach to his productions. When one of his characters visited a clairvoyant, he insisted that the sound of the curtains being drawn back should be that of *wooden* rings on a *wooden* curtain pole. Stephen describes a conversation with him on a train, returning from London:

L.S. on train (having produced instalment of *The History of Mr Polly* in London). He talks in his usual way – mixed penetration and inconsequence, with a balmy or whimsical remark leading up to a serious point and then when *you* become serious, tripping you up as if you had said something pompous. But he is charming and good-looking, though regarded by DFD [= Director of Features and Drama = Gielgud] as having gone hopelessly to seed, no doubt. L.S. also tells me in one of his sudden thought = word outbreaks that for 18 months he thought I was dislikeable.

Mary Allen had met Att at the Slade, and through her had known Stephen before he had had anything to do with the BBC. Her enthusiasm for *Victorian Negative* and *The Last Crusade* had helped persuade Gielgud to take him on full time. The most wide-awake person imaginable, she kept Stephen on his toes. A *New Yorker* cartoon had shown a gold-digging blonde saying to her elderly and deafish escort: 'I think I could learn to love you.' No response. She: 'Say, what's the matter? Battery gone dead?' Mary would fire this last question at Stephen, whenever his response was not quick enough, or when he went into a dream (as he appears to have done in the photograph three pages back). When retired and in her eighties, Mary wrote this about him: 'Stephen had an immense power of enjoyment … and I know his casts loved working for him…. He remained however totally undisciplined and was incapable of getting his scripts ready for rehearsal. In Manchester, Att told me she dreaded the couple of nights before Stephen had a programme. "He would come to bed in a panic, clutching his type-writer, balance it on his stomach as long as he lay there, and the bed would shake until 2 or 3 in the morning."' Although Mary was without a living in companion, she was constantly visited by J. B. (Jack) Priestley.

Other members of the household were music advisor Maurice Brown (an ex-merchant seaman and author of *We Sailed in Convoy*) and his wife

Thea. Edana Romney, an out of work actress, was later replaced by the actor Robert Eddison. He had joined up as a naval rating. Having already acted in London for nearly ten years, he had just played Oberon at the Queen's Theatre. His departure to the lower deck was for some reason delayed and he continued to act on the stage in Manchester and as a member of the BBC Repertory Company, sometimes cooking spaghetti for the household in the evening. Surprisingly, room was found for my brother and me in the school holidays.

Stephen and his colleagues never got away from each other at home or at work. They listened to each other's programmes and benefited from the professional comments that followed each one. Stephen was particularly worried over what they would say about his New Year's Eve programme *The Face of Courage*, which on transmission had seemed to him sententious and over-patriotic:

1 January 1940. Bad start to year with what I feel to be doubtful programme last night. The 1930s go out to the too vibrant voice of Barbara reciting 'England's green and pleasant land'. Strong desire to bury myself feelings.
But later I get off lightly. 3 or 4 warm pros and about 8 definite antis – including Laurence Gilliam. Bad, because I should know about poetry readings.

As the war news got steadily worse, so the cameraderie at No. 66 Platt Lane built up. There was even a sense of exhilaration as the uncertainty of the future increased and as the bombing began to make their work more difficult. Private thoughts were different. It was not done to express pessimism, but Lionel Millard (a friend from Oxford) sensed 'an unspoken assumption that the war would be lost'. All must have been as dismayed by the ever-worsening news as was Stephen in his diaries:

21 March 1940. With Finland, the news now seems fatally bad. Heard Haw-Haw tonight, skilfully deprecating the results of our Sylt raid. He is clever.
20 April. The bad war news – feeling it is all up. Last Sunday, what seemed great Narvik news, and now we are told nothing.
1 May. News is becoming worse and worse. Some dislocation of work, shown in today's meeting. Some sad faces, e.g. Mary's. People like me think and repeat to themselves over and over again: 'Well,

at least I've had forty good years.' But what about the boys?

12 May. One's often plunged in gloom and heads hang. Only soldiers together look cheerful.

30 May. I am going to London in the train. *The News Chronicle* map of the position of the BEF [British Expeditionary Force] extracts a loud cry from me. During the last week I have been realizing how likely it is, since we are nearly certain to lose the war, that I shall lose my job, if not go to a concentration camp. Also, what chance have I of keeping these diaries, which I am always hoping to base my late writing on. Also invasion and the chances of one of us being killed. Also – the end of about everything in our life which we have liked. It is finished already.

Such comments run throughout the first part of the war, but do not reflect a permanent state of depression. By this time nearly everybody listened to the radio, eager for news and entertainment. The blackout, the closure of theatres, the absence of husbands – all these contributed to the massive increase in listenership. Stephen was producing many of the leading cultural and war-related programmes. He knew that he was doing a worthwhile job and that he was good at it. He did not have time to be permanently gloomy. At the end of the year he wrote: 'I have been reading my 1935 diary and am impressed by my much greater happiness now (full time job) than then (peace time).'

Early 1940 programmes

These included a number of military programmes, two of which were about submarines. Each had a success story to tell and in those days any good news was worth trumpeting. Stephen's preparation of these was eased by the enthusiasm of a submarine expert from the Admiralty, Commander Cross.

A Polish submarine, *The Orzel*, had escaped from Estonia and made it to British waters. Stephen recapitulated the dangers and excitements of that voyage. The programme was researched in Whitehall ('Gloomy, lost-looking Poles fill the corridors'), a harbour somewhere secret in the North of Scotland (where *The Orzel* was) and Portsmouth.

30 January. In London, for one of those blessed holidays from the acid fog and nose and phlegm-blacking dirt of Manchester.

At Admiralty, for another meeting with my grand Commander Cross. He is the man who took the Graf Spee message in to Churchill. 'Most ignominious,' said Winnie. Am staying in London to try to arrange recordings of submarine noises at Portsmouth.

Stephen was nervous during the rehearsal at the beginning of the following week in Manchester: 'I am over-anxious, my name being slightly worn, owing to re-action after early-war successes.' He overran by six minutes and had to make cuts in the text without the opportunity for further rehearsal.

16 February. Lunch at the RAC with Cross and his wife. I am not sure how the Navy liked the sub. prog., but after lunch he and I went to the Savile [Stephen's club] and there he outlined his ideas for what should make a superb programme about the *Salmon*. [In a single fortnight it had sunk a German submarine, sighted the German fleet and torpedoed two cruisers and had been itself depth-charged but managed to return to port.]

18 March. Prepare memo about my overwork. Unnecessary, because Cross rings up, says *Salmon* isn't ready yet. *Orzel* repeat substituted – blessed relief.

3 May. 'Tubby' Cross in great form, giving me the material I need to finish off *Salmon*. He says, by the way, that, in the operations room of the Admiralty, he has just finished the most miserable fortnight of his life, seeing things go wrong which might possibly have come off, if a bunch of young men hadn't been controlled by unconsanguineous old men.

9 May. 10.30 to Chatham, to go over script with Bickford of the Admiralty and then meet the crew of the *Salmon* and take recordings, going out in the harbour and diving. The heat, the salt water drips, the pain in the ears, the mass of gadgets and people sitting gloomily still in cramped conditions. I take a few photographs. In the big officers' mess, the main room, a 'reassuring' voice came over the speaker, to suggest there was no need to worry about this parliamentary crisis – keep smiling, etc. [The next day, Chamberlain fell.]

The programme went out on 16 May. Recordings taken on board and used were of the sounds of, for example, casting off, submerging and rising to the attack. Conversations, however, were still typed up from Stephen's notes and read by members of the BBC rep., using appropriate accents.

The *Salmon*'s patrol had been successfully reconstructed and Stephen planned a celebratory lunch with Cross at the Club. But on 27 May he wrote: 'No lunch with Tubby Cross. I did not know when I arranged it that Cmdr. W. K. R. Cross, the perfect aide to me in my submarine programmes, was at that moment dead, blown up in HMS Hood.' Stephen's last mention of the submarine is on 21 July, with the bleak entry: '... the incredible fact of the *Salmon* reported missing.'

In a third naval programme, about a battleship, Stephen had been struck by the easy relationship between officers and men, which he contrasted favourably with the situation in the Irish Guards, about which he had written and produced a Feature earlier in the year:

9 February. This morning I meet Major Alexander of the Irish Guards at the Savile and he turns out to be nervously admiring of 'our stuff'; a relief. Work should be easier. I haver over a new suit (must get smart for these serious things).
14 February. Most unsatisfactory morning 'taking' sound record of presenting of colours at Wellington Barracks. The recordings were bad and cold-shouldered from Buckingham Palace to start with (they had to sign a declaration not to take the King's voice) – but owing possibly to my non-top-hat clothes [Stephen dressed badly, sometimes using a tie to keep his trousers up] I was somewhat pushed around, not introduced, not given a drink after, which augurs extremely badly for the degree of help likely to be given me next week.

The Irish Guards programme, *A Soldier has a Story to Tell*, followed the life of a recruit from the time he joined up to the time he was 'turned out as a finished Guardsman'. Stephen thought the officers snobby and undemocratic: 'Wodges of loyalty of the subservient kind, from below upwards: scarcely any from above downwards.' He vented his antipathy in his last entry on the programme, written on the evening of the broadcast:

Sunday, 17 March. Well, so ends one of the least pleasant progs. I have ever had to deal with…. The CO appalled me by a hectoring phone call, censoring various human-side records – e.g. a German

lesson with an Irish accent, the sergeants' mess, etc. And then the awful moment when *x* came down with a 'put this thought in the w.p.b. if you don't like it – screw it up and throw it away.' It was a Guards Spirit insertion written with adolescent vulgarity unequalled in my experience. Then, on Thursday, his growing coldness and caginess as he realized I wasn't going to use it.
Three nights this week I am up till 4, after an hour's sleep after dinner. It suits me pretty well, but on Sat. night I ran a temperature of nearly 102 – a spot of flu – which I sweat out during rehearsal on Sunday.

Two days later he got a letter from the CO, expressing the thanks of the Regiment. As so often, Stephen's entries blow hot and cold on his work and it is perhaps unfortunate that the above short extract from his long and bitter account was written with a temperature at the end of a taxing Sunday and a near-sleepless week.

Stephen may have been near breaking-point because while working on this programme he had at the same time been working on two others. One was a re-hash of Daniel Defoe, which was broadcast on 12 March from Evesham, where the Schools Department still was. The other was the *The Rediscovery of Night*. Broadcast on 6 March, it was written jointly with Tom Harrison of Mass Observation. While Stephen welcomes the fact that moonlight and the stars had been rediscovered on account of the blackout (was this the first attack on light pollution?), Tom Harrison analyses the disadvantages to traders and others of darkness. So for four weeks up to the strained Irish Guards entry he had had to draw up a tight schedule of work, every day of which, including weekends, was allocated to scripting, casting, recording for or rehearsing one or another of the three programmes. Travel was mostly by train, at night. Yet he was getting a reputation for late delivery and wrote on 19 March: 'Can I get out of my last-moment-with-programme habit, which has lately been noted and been (on this occasion unfairly, through my overwork) dropped on by Moray?'

Propaganda

Reith's successor as Director General, F. W. Ogilvie, wrote in *Picture Post's* article: 'The BBC works in close co-operation with the Ministry of Informa-tion (MoI), from which it receives guidance on all appropriate matters. The BBC is not itself a Government Department: it speaks authoritatively, but not necessarily with the official voice.' Today, such a statement would be read with scepticism. But, as will be seen later, papers now available at Caversham indicate that interference from the MoI really was minimal. Features certainly played a part in maintaining public morale; yet Stephen's diaries as well as the testimonies of other writer/producers all show that they wrote what they felt, not what they were told by the MoI or even by the BBC hierarchy.

Gilliam, as an ex-journalist, worked mainly on the documentary, war-related side of Features. Following on from *The Empire Strikes Back*, he had begun a second series, *The Shadow of the Swastika*. It had started on 10 November 1939 and traced the rise of the Nazi party up to the start of the war – relying for source material exclusively on contemporary German documents and speeches. Today the carefully selected extracts read as unsubtle propaganda, but they were not fabricated and played a part in opening people's eyes to the nature of the régime.

Gielgud was also involved in the Swastika series and tells in his book of the horrors of casting Hitler: he spent an afternoon listening alternately to Hitler's voice and the voices of candidates for the role, all trying to match his fury and venom. The part went to Marius Goring. The programmes got the full resources of the department, with between twenty and thirty actors in every instalment: they made Stephen feel small. On 11 January he wrote: 'I don't like Swastika programme days – feel dim. L.G. has all the works shooting for him and they are devastatingly good. In evening listen spellbound to the sweep of this programme. Is it Walton's music?'

In May Stephen was given the chance to handle an anti-Nazi programme himself. The editor of *Picture Post*, Stefan Lorant, had some years earlier spent six-and-a-half months in 'protective custody' in Vienna. He had managed to keep a secret diary which was the basis for his book, *I was Hitler's Prisoner*. Stephen's task was to dramatise the book and produce a programme about it. Here he reports on his first meeting with Lorant, on 25 April:

> Lorant said: 'I want to leave the adaptation entirely to you. I know how annoyed I get if someone interferes with my job. The prog-ramme must all be *true*. Every word is true [in the book].' He then said that, contrary to what was written in the book, he *was* beaten up by an SS man, but by asking the self-conscious and embarassed beater a few questions, he managed to [entry ends here.]
> 10 May. Chamberlain to fall after all, it seems. And P. on the phone says they've marched into the Netherlands.

Lunch with Val and Lorant, who wants to make a very big thing of the Hitler programme and tie it up with an article in *Picture Post*. Val infected by this. Hubschmann, the *P.P.* photographer, is around snapping at the Savile. Val calling on me to do the script. He wants Leslie Howard for Lorant, Peggy Ashcroft seemed to be suggested for Mrs Lorant – and I even said the small part of Count S. was a Conrad Veidt part and he said 'have him!' Behold, I go off and see Leslie Howard at his film office in St James's St, find him with his homely girl, Miss Cunningham, and he says 'don't worry about money' but thinks he *would* like to do it – all marvellous – and *then* at 8 I go off and get hold of Peggy Ashcroft at the Globe theatre and after 10 minutes talk she says she will do it. Very, very strange that I should be doing this while the great day of the war is starting. [The day that Churchill became Prime Minister and Germany invaded Belgium and Holland.]

23 May. Prepare for long meeting and lunch at Club with Emlyn Williams, going through the part. [Leslie Howard must have fallen through.] He is quick and very easy to get on with.

29 May. *Picture Post* came out today with pictures of me at the panel. Fitting round off to what I feel to be my last programme. (Only admit this to the diary, needless to say.) [Dunkirk was imminent.]

2 June. My version of Stefan Lorant's book in retrospect. The chief comment has been his tactful collaboration, keeping in the background, etc.... The niceness of all the stars to me except Emlyn Williams, who was a little smug.... I had some agony at his knowledgeableness, in writing and production (see picture opposite). I was very grateful to Val, for the big chance: I liked and admired the timing and face of Peggy Ashcroft: I enjoyed the photography and the jokes about the photos of me in *P.P.* – Lorant certainly did me proud. [The article carried six pictures of Stephen.]

I shall never forget the final production, with Ogilvie [Director General] in the box and Mrs Lorant weeping all through it.

I was Hitler's Prisoner from today's perspective would again be described as propaganda, although at the time it must have seemed to Stephen as if he was simply revealing the truth about the Nazis. If it was propaganda, at least it was more subtle and believable than contemporary films such as *The 49th Parallel*, with its ludicrously fanatical Nazi activists shooting down the Eskimos and trying to convert German settlers in Canada.

Emlyn Williams brilliantly portrayed a prematurely war-weary
Lorant, with only a suggestion of an Austrian accent.

Val Gielgud and S.P. discussing *I was Hitler's Prisoner.*

The lack of Government interference in these propaganda broadcasts is astonishing. The German equivalent of a series such as *The Shadow of the Swastika* would surely have been controlled by the State from the start. Here, a slightly peevish memo in the Caversham files from the MoI, dated January 1940, asks to see copies of the series and says that the Department 'is anxious to get copies of Features dealing with European affairs'. The scripts of the first five Swastika programmes were sent by return. There is nothing to suggest that the Ministry knew anything about them before they were broadcast.

Imminent Invasion

By the summer of 1940 it was assumed that the Germans were about to invade. A taxi-driver, who was smoking Players while Stephen was smoking cheap Woodbines, told him: 'May as well enjoy yourself while you can. In a fortnight, may be all up, everything finished.'

It was a difficult time for those who controlled the department. As the Germans advanced on the Continent, pressure increased from C(P) for programmes to be more 'relevant'. At the same time he again cut the weekly airtime of Features, this time to nine hours, to allow more time for news, talks and Government directives. The question inevitably arose as to whether Features should concentrate exclusively on its war-related progrrammes, with no entertainment. Gilliam asked his producers for suitable ideas and twice drew up seven-week plans, with the emphasis on progrrammes such as a new series on the Dominions; a repeat of *Shadow of the Swastika*; a proposed sequel, to be called *The Nazis at War*; and broadcasts in support of our French allies. However, he left in some of Stephen's non-military suggestions, such as *The Thames in Wartime* (later rejected by C(P)) and the invention of printing (disapproved of by C(P) but nonetheless used).

The trouble was that events were happening so fast that seven-week schedules all too soon had to be revised. After the fall of France, Gilliam sent this telegram: 'DELETE "AU DRAPEAU". INSERT "LOOK TO YOUR MOAT".' A sharp memo from Gielgud read: 'Programmes must be relevant to present conditions and have the enthusiasm of the producer concerned. Otherwise they had better be shifted to some other occupation.'

Stephen wrote in his response to the request for ideas: '... it is appallingly difficult to think of propaganda features when England is on the down rather than on the up.' He wanted firm but cheerful England-gets-back-to-Work programmes and included *Hospitals in Wartime* as one of his suggestions. Also included was *Modern French Painters*, which (surprisingly) Gilliam did not delete from his summarised proposals to Gielgud. He also put forward Stephen's name in relation to programmes about Home Defence in the event of invasion. In a memo dated 17 June he reminded Gielgud how effective Potter's *Air Raid* had been in putting across the Government's policy and suggested that more use should be made of Features in this way. He also pointed out that in order to do this, Features would have to be allocated more time. He got his way on both points.

Stephen wrote on 1 July: 'I am pretty low. No nice programmes in the offing. Nothing to look forward to – till after the invasion.' However, immediately after this, and no doubt as a result of the pressure Gilliam had put on Gielgud, he was asked to write and produce a series of Home Defence programmes under the title of *If the Invader Comes*. These were to amplify the advice and instructions in a leaflet which the government had just put out under the same name. Expectancy of invasion peaked after Churchill's 'We will fight on the beaches' speech and, as never before, people were anxious to know how they could help. The urgency of Stephen's assignment accounts for the extremely short time allowed for preparation. Diary entries show that he had to research, write and produce each programme within the space of a week.

Once again, Stephen decided to tell people what to do – and what not to do – through the medium of Leversuch. The first programme went out on 10 July (produced at too short notice for inclusion in the *RT*). Papers at Caversham show that the subject was 'The defence of a Village'. As usual, the work and responsibility for this not unimportant broadcast cheered him up. His only diary reference to it, on transmission day, was: 'Leversuch programme. Much enjoyed it – cast in very good form.'

Another Leversuch followed on 19 July and was about the defence of factories in relation to the work of The Home Guard (as the Local Defence Volunteers, or LDV, had been renamed at Churchill's request):

> Tuesday, 16 July. 8.45 to Courtaulds, Coventry, beginning to collect first hand material for prog. on Friday! Chief memory of this – the working of the artificial silk machine, which I understand; and annoyance at the presence of an officious ARP officer. [Watchers of *Dad's Army* will recognize the Home Guard–ARP rivalry.] Also, the false feeling I often have on these tours, knowing that I may be mildly satirical at the expense of some of the organisation.

17 July. Writing Home Defence programme and visiting ICI Metals in Manchester – watch the copper and other metals in long sticks being bent straight.

18 July. Writing and Roneo-ing home defence prog. My world record for speed: first hand material on Tuesday and Wednesday, prog. on Friday. Writing it all in one piece doesn't seem to do it any harm.

19 July. Day of my second Leversuch Home Defence series. Again very pleasant – because cast all liked the script – more than I have ever known before. Why? They say it is easy to say, etc. Only just get it in on time.

A third *If the Invader Comes* went out on 31 July. Leversuch, the old soldier, is made to join the Home Guard and get used to this new war. An office note from Gilliam to Gielgud tells us that Stephen was hampered by the reluctance of the War Office to give more than very general directions about the use, equipment and training of the Home Guard, but that it was nevertheless an excellent programme. At least Stephen had been able to draw on his own experience as a Home Guard sergeant.

A later note from Gilliam reads: 'As you know, Stephen Potter has now got some co-operation from the War Office. It appears likely he will have a twenty-minute programme ready in a week from now dealing with –

how to immobilise a car
how to put a garage out of action
the right and the wrong way to pass information
the technique of the road block'

There is nothing in the diaries, the *RT* or the Caversham files to indicate whether this last programme was ever transmitted: so it can be assumed that it was not planned to put it out until after the invasion had started. Equally uncertain is the outcome of the C(P)'s suggestion that there should be a Leversuch programme on what to do if on opening the door you are confronted with armed German paratroopers. It would have been called *Mrs Grant opens the Door*.

Priestley

Thus in the first half of 1940 most of Stephen's programmes had been on military or, through Leversuch, public information subjects. He produced no more such programmes for the rest of that year, probably because he was booked for a major collaboration with J. B. (Jack) Priestley – which never came off.

From early days at 66 Platt Lane, Priestley had become Mary Allen's lover and as such, he was regarded as a half-member of that household. He was touchy, grumbled a lot and never set out to make himself pleasant. An entry near the end of 1940 reads: 'The actors hate Priestley and he despises them. He says they contain no character until the playwright has given it to them: says he has often seen an actor and an actress fall in love through words he has put into their mouths.' So he had enemies; but Stephen, although teased ruthlessly by Priestley, admired him and spoke up for him:

> 21 January 1941. Ever since the ashtray in the guard room broke when I looked at it, which happened to come soon after my shattering of the bathroom basin by dropping a glass on it, Priestley has talked about my 'Pottergeist'.
> 26 February. I am somewhat chippy about my Priestley friendship these days. Dislike of him by e.g. Moray makes my advocacy of him an astounding quirk.
> 18 May. Impact of Jack on me has the effect of making me, to him, inconsequent, long-haired and amateurish, which is my impression of his picture of me. His perception of personality is so strong that I become this while he is present. Mary asks when I am coming back [after an illness] and I say Tuesday. J. says 'Well that's the start of the week, really. And then why not slog straight through to the finish, till Thursday?'

Stephen always retained his admiration for Priestley as a writer and dramatist and wrote later: 'While Ustinov sometimes writes as if he was 100 years old, Priestley has the power (when not acting the glorious universal uncle 50% sincere and 50% with his pipe in his cheek) of writing as if he was 100 years young.'

In 1940 Priestley was broadcasting to America three times a week about life in London and the air raids, speaking at 2.30 in the morning so that he could be heard in the evening over there. Here his most famous wartime broadcasts were his 'Postscripts', which ran on Sunday evenings after the 9 o'clock news from the beginning of June 1940 (just after Dunkirk) until October. Although they offered no easy solutions, nor hid how badly the war was going, because of his own complete self-confidence and ability to make people believe in the values for which the war was being fought, he was listened to by millions – on average each of the nineteen Postscripts was heard by an estimated 30% of the adult population. He spoke, with his Yorkshire accent, not as a leader but as 'one of us'. He was undoubtedly successful in bolstering public morale at a very dangerous time and fan mail came by the sack-load. At the end of the year, Graham Greene wrote in *The Spectator*: 'We shall never know how much the country owed to Mr Priestley last summer. For those dangerous months when the Gestapo arrived in Paris, he was unmistakably a great man....'

Yet there were some who felt not at all indebted. Priestley looked forward to a much more egalitarian society after the war than that sought by many conservative politicians and BBC officials; and this caused growing unease. There were suggestions from high-up sources that such an important slot should not be given indefinitely to a left-wing thinker. The case for keeping him on was put by Harold Nicolson, Parliamentary Secretary

J. B. (Jack) Priestley

to the MoI and soon to be a BBC Governor. 'Let them find their own Priestley,' he said.

In October Priestley began his Postscript by announcing that it was his last, on the pretext that it was time for someone else to take over. He denied having been pushed. Within a month he had submitted the outline of a new series: six fortnightly Feature programmes under the title *The Long Road Home*, with such subtitles as *Freedom and Security*. This was the series that Stephen was to have produced. As first proposed, they were to be primarily entertainment programmes, with a ten-minute chat by Priestley in the middle. He hoped this formula would evade censorship. After much prevarication, the proposal was turned down – much to Stephen's disappointment, as well as Priestley's. He records their frustration at the initial lack of any kind of response from the BBC:

9 December. Priestley fed up he hasn't heard.

11 December. I feel great shame not only with our BBC leaders but also in some degree my friends the leaders of the department – even they reflect the casual coldness of HQ over the 'dangerous' nature of the Priestley programme. And of course I feel disappointed personally. It was to be quite a big thing for me. I would have worked with Jack, at his house, and would have learnt a lot about writing and dramatic techniques in the process.

31 December. Priestley is walking majestically round the ping-pong room. He is usually so stationary. My equivalent would be to pace feverishly up and down. He is smarting to a tortured degree over the fearful BBC coldness and caginess. There is evidence, I think, that they are double-faced to him. His voice on the air is surely a good morale force. Yet on no single occasion has the BBC said 'good'. Or 'that's just what we wanted' – or anything remotely resembling this. I sympathise too: because outside the Department, the Controllers retire behind a curtain of hush-hush and Higher Cares, which nobody believes in though it may involve an occasional toasting from the PM. That was one thing Reith could have taken in his stride: and he was, sometimes, interested.

Papers at Caversham released in 1993 show something of what was going on behind the scenes. Censorship was an important issue. A remark in one of Priestley's broadcasts to the States that life in England was 'wildly and solidly abnormal – almost crazy' delighted the Nazis, who made much of it in their own propaganda. Churchill had already been criticized in the House for the fact that there appeared to be no central control over the BBC. In May he had appointed as Head of the MoI Duff Cooper, who saw it as part of his job to fill that gap. He was not a Priestley fan. He would not sign a conciliatory letter to him that had been drafted by the BBC and said he was 'a second rate novelist made conceited by the success of his broadcasts.' He deleted passages from Priestley's American broadcasts 'on the grounds that German propaganda to the US suggested that Britain was "going Bolshevik" and that this suggestion might be confirmed by the passages in question' (Briggs).

The BBC itself cannot have enjoyed dealing with Priestley. His letter of 12 December proposing *The Long Road Home* was sent direct to the Director General. It begins: 'I shall be much obliged if you will give this proposal serious and immediate attention, especially as many demands are being made on my time….' An earlier letter to the Deputy DG, Stephen Tallents, had even complained about the Prime Minister: 'The first source of dissatisfaction is with the government, especially since the P.M.'s acceptance of the Tory party leadership … it makes sincere advocacy very difficult.'

The series did not survive a letter of 11 December from Ogilvie to Duff Cooper, with which he enclosed synopses of the first two programmes and pointed out how far they had strayed from entertainment into politics, when compared with the original proposal. He asked for Duff Cooper's agreement to turning them down.

The sequel was that within a month Priestley had arrived at some sort of accommodation with Ogilvie and a second series of talks started at the end of January 1941, produced by Mary Allen. Stephen wrote: 'Complete change round of "the authorities". They appeal to him and he is to do a new series of talks. But not *that* programme – working with him would have been a big chance for me. The Priestley interlude has indeed been a fascinating one, with Mary and her real love and pleasure.' These new talks quickly ran into the same sort of political opposition and after the first one Churchill himself complained that Priestley's war aims were not the same as his. The second series was stopped in March. In his book *Margin Released* Priestley wrote: 'I received two letters…. One was from the Ministry of Information, telling me that the BBC was responsible for the decision to take me off the air, and the other was from the BBC, saying that a directive had come from the MoI to end my broadcasts.'

Yet once again pride was swallowed and a third series of talks began in October – *Listen to my Notebook*. On this occasion Stephen was again in the running to work with Priestley on the project, but that was scotched by C(P), who 'said I was too busy to have anything to do with this one'.

That Priestley had ever even considered Stephen for the job requires some explanation. Firstly, Stephen had helped him over a project in the late thirties. It is referred to in the diaries as 'the J.B.P. job', but there is no elucidation. Secondly, both men had similar left-wing sympathies. Although never actively involved in politics, Stephen's views often surface in the diary – as for example when he wrote about the officers of the Irish Guards. His political outlook, shared by many of his colleagues as well as by Priestley, was in sharp contrast (or so he supposed) to that of 'the men in pin stripe suits', the Director General and his staff.

Non-military

Meanwhile, in the second half of the year, Stephen began to pick up again on his literary programmes, which through Schools had been his original route into the BBC and for which his earlier career as an author and lecturer best suited him. Productions included *The Lead Soldiers of Gutenberg*, which celebrated 500 years of printing. It was written jointly with his old friend Francis Meynell, who at one time had conceived, started and developed The Nonesuch Press and who had asked Stephen to edit the Nonesuch Coleridge.

> 24 June. Printing prog. done with F.'s notes and dialogue, but 70% by me.
> 25 June. Up to London, sleeper. See F. at Club. He liked programme. It has been a slight worry, whether he would – difficulty of working with a friend. It turned out a most amiable collaboration.

When Ed Murrow of Columbian Broadcasting Systems (CBS) asked Gilliam to choose six Features for use in America, Gilliam included three of Stephen's in his selection: *I was Hitler's Prisoner*, *Shakespeare Discovery* (see next chapter) and *Lead Soldiers*.

There were also revivals of *Tom Moore* for Schools and of *Victorian Negative*. New programmes on Boswell and on Byron were scheduled for the evening and not, as would have been the case one year earlier, for Schools.

Sunday 27 October. Big Boswell day. On the whole, *not* enjoyable, except for the afternoon croquet. Moray, whom I have often thought of as Boswell, was fresh and amusing as Boswell. Some trying factors. I have only 5 hours for everything. Robert Atkins, who meant everything to me in the twenties, had no mike experience and was imprecise, fluffy and got muddled, forgetting his lines. Moral: don't forget first principles:

1. Has your star mike experience?
2. Don't be too complicated with mikes, if short on rehearsal time.
3. Make sure the audience know who is speaking.
4. Rehearse ensemble scenes quadruply.
5. Don't have actors doing scarcely anything.

The Byron programme dealt with his last journey to Greece. It was criticised by C(P) on the grounds that it 'presupposed a little too much knowledge in the listener and was too specialist for the series'.

Byron had been squeezed into a series called *These Men were Free*, an attempt to give a propaganda edge to a number of disparate biographies. Stephen suggested he should do one about the pre-war leader of the Labour party George Lansbury (whom he knew); but given the political sensitivities displayed over Priestley, it is hardly surprising that he heard no more about it. Gilliam had opened the series with George Washington and this had run into absurd censorship trouble:

18 January, 1941. With the Washington script – a very boring and flat Feature anyhow, I thought – there was the question of some rather heavy propaganda which MoI wants to shove in, to the effect that really we weren't fighting the Americans (when we were). Naturally L.G. objected, and did so in a way which upset them: anyhow, all scripts in 8 days before now.

If this meant that the Ministry was demanding to see all scripts eight days before transmission, it failed utterly to enforce the ruling. Stephen continued to be late with his and would usually change them on the day of transmission, during the course of rehearsals.

Chapter 5
Bombs also in the North

Shakespeare and the Blitz

The London blitz began in the autumn of 1940. Stephen travelled up nearly every week and although his nerves were steady, the work of everyone at that time has to be seen against a background of sleeping in cellars or under tables and dodging in and out of shelters. Att sometimes came up to Chiswick midweek (Thames Bank was still unsold) and on 5th September Stephen wrote: 'We intend to make Thames Bank habitable for ourselves and tonight there we were for dinner with a Watney and a Standard, looking out onto the garden. But immediately after dark, a raid; and then for the whole of the night we are sleeping down below. We carefully sling the bed-cover to avoid the blast and then, as it gets bangy, get the table over us – very friendly. Next morning we see a crater in the E. side of St Peter's Square, a house removed bodily from Black Lion Lane....' [And much other local damage.] Later that month he wrote: 'In tubes, sight of people resting for the night. The realization that some are frightened and that I am not much. P., sometimes alone at Chiswick, is: but far too brave to leave her fellow-frightened friends for the comparative safety of Manchester. Delightful friendliness that goes on owing to these stresses.' Thames Bank remained standing, although its windows were twice blown in. Nearly every day that he is in London, Stephen describes fresh bomb damage. In November Broadcasting House in Langham Place received its first hit: 'I examine B.H. The bomb has been absorbed amazingly well. But that wet, disintegrated plaster smell – a touch of ruin in *that* meticulous place!'

Stephen's output may have been reduced by the bombing, as well as by his Home Guard duties, which included fire-watching at night. Yet the climax of his 1940 literary programmes was still to come. This was a Feature on the discovery by a book dealer, in an old copy of *Hall's*

Chronicles, of notes in the margin that dated from the sixteenth century. There were good reasons for supposing that the handwriting was Shakespeare's.*

> 6 September. Today, a memorable lunch. Alan Keen [book dealer] and Peters [A. D. Peters, literary agent]. Keen calls himself apologetically rather self-made. It is a highly dramatic story and I congratulate myself on getting down to it in this way. One of his eyes is a bit queer – small, round, pop-eyed and shiny. He has the sort of face which could never get brown and is wearing a best suit. He told me the story and showed me the photostats, all carefully prepared and annotated by him. His naïve pride and enjoyment of it all. 'Am I talking too much?' he asks. How his heart beat when he told his wife he had 'discovered Bill'.

The programme was first broadcast on 17 October, from Manchester. Only the previous day, Stephen had been planning to transmit it from Glasgow, but the cast he had been expecting could not be mustered. Consequently the rehearsals in Manchester on transmission day were rushed:

> 17 October. Not very enjoyable to me because it never seemed to me that I really clicked in it. Not *quite* in the writing and certainly not in the production. Back home to find that Gielgud, Priestley, etc. have all been listening – Priestley liked it.

Shakespeare Discovery got good reviews and Ivor Brown, theatre critic of *The Observer*, wrote to Stephen saying how much he preferred this sort of programme to adapted-from-stage radio (what old hands in Features had been saying for years). *The Listener* later commented: '... the intelligentsia are going to discover radio ... Mr Ivor Brown has announced that it is possible to enjoy certain plays without seeing them

---

* Professor Stanley Wells of the Shakespeare Institute at Birmingham University says that while Keen's discovery was useful, it is not thought today that the handwriting was Shakespeare's. Emeritus Professor Andrew Gurr, also an authority on the subject, wrote that he could not confirm the attribution, mainly because research in the last 30 years has shown that Shakespeare's principal source book for the historical plays in question was Holinshead, not Hall.

and that there are entertainments in sound which it is not necessary to see at all.'

A repeat was scheduled for 23 December, with the part of Keen to be played by Wilfred Pickles. By this time Coventry and Liverpool had been blitzed ... while Manchester waited. The storm came on the same night as that scheduled for the repeat. Years later Stephen wrote up his experiences over the three days before Christmas from his diary entries; and sections of this are reproduced below. They give an indication of how he might have treated a book about his life, had he ever got round to it; and they exemplify the way in which BBC work and the blitz were intertwined. Stephen's account includes part of the script of the programme and extracts from this have been included here as so few such scripts still exist. These extracts, together with Stephen's comments, instance some of the characteristics of Feature programmes already discussed, such as the high standard of literary awareness and interest that was then expected of the mass audience and the way in which 'repeats' were improvements on the originals. They also show the awkwardness of finding actors to play the parts of living protagonists (a programme today on the same subject would certainly have included the voice of Keen himself: possibly live, possibly with edited tape). Stephen's method of re-creating conversations based on in-depth interviews is well illustrated. The incidents he contrives and the text he gives to his characters are intended to be true to the spirit of the occasion, but were not meant to detail what actually happened or the words that were spoken at the time. There is no narrator: Keen's retrospective thoughts are simply interspersed with the dialogue during the sorting of the books at the time of the discovery.

The extracts from the programme also show just how inadequate the script is on its own. As Louis MacNeice was to write later, 'radio features, when laid out on the printed page, tend to lose even more than do plays written for the theatre'. Thus even if the text of a programme is retained, its essence may be lost if there is no recording. The bulky Shellac discs used in those days could not all be stored, were easily breakable and in any case deteriorated with time; so very few recordings survive. Stephen would often complain to his diary that after all the sweat and excitement, his works were lost for ever as soon as transmission was over. Yet unlike other writer/producers, such as Sieveking, MacNeice and McGivern, he never published his scripts. The passages from *Shakespeare Discovery* in what follows represent Stephen's only attempt to perpetuate one of his programmes.

**Edited extracts from Stephen's retrospective write-up of his
diaries for the last days of 1940**

In 1940 lecturing on *Hamlet* to half-attentive civil servants is over
for good. The occasional anthology programme for recitation on
short wave to Tasmania has changed to a more full-time BBC job
in hectic early wartime, pumping out programmes on the Services,
closely interleaved with Studies of British Achievement and programmes on Our English Heritage. All these are written and produced
against time, to a war-rattled and still anti-BBC public, in crowded
studios and uprooted from home in the fearsome foreign land of
Manchester. The war is being slowly and steadily lost: but personally
I am ten times happier than I was in '36, when I was able to amble
along on nothing at all, vaguely holding myself in reserve for a
totally unfulfilled mission of being an author. The war was making
me work at last, and though we were pretending most of the time
to be cynical about the quality of the programmes, which had the
depressing unobjectivity of wartime, some of it we believed in, and
some of it was good. An influx of war-job producers, writers and
actors was gradually giving broadcasting a new life which was to
lead to a short Golden Period of Radio. Even at the worst period of
the war, it gave artists extraordinary freedom of self-expression in the
healthy areas of propaganda-free time which were allotted to us;
and no box-office worries whatever.

When this bit of diary starts, the BBC was unpopular. At the
beginning of the war, it had got off on the wrong foot, and was still
paying the penalty. Our Manchester section tended to work within
itself and to itself, dependent on the praise and dispraise of fellow
workers. Comment from BBC HQ in London was practically
non-existent.

My wife ('P.') and the boys – Andrew, aged 12, Julian, aged 9 – have
just been moved by me 15 miles out of Central Manchester into
The Bird in Hand, a little pub on the verge of Cheshire country at
Mobberley. The raids are inclined to be closing in on Manchester.
Droning overhead most nights, now.

21 December, Saturday. In office pleasantly working – patting into
place my tomorrow's programme. This is a repeat of a script I did
first two months ago – *Shakespeare Discovery*. I have been given a
peak hour repeat. Cast, engineers and myself feel that it can't go

wrong, but mustn't relax. On the contrary, enjoy myself making small improvements, getting better gram records for the little bits of effect music, making sure I know the thought approach fitting for each line, and that I'm not too influenced by the possibly different interpretation made by an actor. If only one could always make this leisurely repeat, after an eight weeks' interval! The pleasure of adding these little embellishments. I like my script. But have I marked the excitement of the crisis of the story sufficiently? It only made a story, it seemed to me, if I gave it the long approach. Keen as an apprentice in advertising. Keen in libraries and bookshops for checking copy. A new passion, and Keen turns himself into a book dealer. And then at last The Book turns up, tied in with a bundle as 'Lot 64', The *Hall's Chronicles*, with the strange contemporary handwriting in the margin.

Last month in London I saw the book for the first time, and was shown the mysterious annotator's handwriting. Concentrating on a problem of 1590 – turning oneself into a mole and burrowing underground – what could be pleasanter in December 1940? The handwriting. The letters stood up from the page – a rough crust to the tip of my finger, and some sort of warm spark did seem to flow up my arm from the page. It tingled up my arm like a particularly satisfying or clenching chord played on the piano.

Keen came in at eleven this morning, and we went round to Yarners for some of their doped and sticky sherry. He thinks that *The Times* (which gave good space to the first announcement), the BBC, Gielgud (who agreed to my suggestion it would make a good broadcast) and myself are beneficent angels, all part of the fairy story. Is it really Shakespeare's writing? Is it a fake? How can it be a fake? Keen is pleased today about one thing. The embarrassing difficulty about these dialogue impersonations of living people (exhausting expenditure of diplomacy) is always in the casting. No living person is really satisfied unless they are represented by Robert Donat. I was a bit too realistic with the first production. Philip Wade as Keen was a shade too rough and undercultivated. Keen never criticised his golden benefactors – but he was a little miserable about it. He was so uncomplaining that I determined this time to do him proud. I have got Wilfred Pickles to be him – Pickles, who a) has got exactly the right warmth and b) can talk with the inflection of this latitude of England in various degrees of intensity. I will get him to use his light grade, which is Keen's.

The drama of the actual discovery was not easy to reproduce. Keen was alone in his office when he began *by stages* to realize whose that writing might be. There is no EUREKA moment. We go back to Keen as the successful bookseller who has just bought three thousand volumes as a job lot in a country house sale – a gamble, except that he had spotted some good Brontë firsts. But the actual comprehension of the possibilities of the doodles in the margin of *The Chronicles* was undramatically gradual. So I wrote a scene reconstructing Keen going through books in his warehouse – Keen and his two young assistants, Bobby and George. Well, we got 'spot effects' to bump books together during this dialogue – the semi-technical talk I love writing. What would this Bobby have been saying? I try to get *the atmosphere* of the talk:

BOBBY 'I've never seen so much rubbish. What on earth are you going to do with it all? George, help me to clear a space, will you? I shall want a bath after this, I shouldn't think half the books have been touched for fifty years.'

KEEN (<u>Professionally anxious</u>) 'Careful – careful. It's not rubbish yet, you know.'

BOBBY: It was all lumped together anyhow, Mr Keen, in a railway container.

KEEN I brought the expensive stuff up myself in my suitcase. Those Byron copies were beautiful. First edition of *A Vision of Judgment* – beautiful copy. Have you read it? You haven't. Ought to read the books. I say, you ought to read them.

BOBBY You seem to have got tired of the sixteenth century, Mr Keen.

KEEN No I have not. There's a very nice Peel quarto in this lot. Besides, you haven't seen that lot over there, done up with cords.

[Two more pages of text, as they unpack and comment on the books. Then:]

BOBBY History book. It's an old chronicle. No title page.

KEEN Pass it over. No date – no title page. Look out!

(<u>Drops it</u>)

BOBBY   Was it my fault? Sorry. Which piece will you have?

KEEN   No, it's only a cheap eighteenth century binding, hanging by a thread anyway. Yes, here's the title written on the end page in pencil – *Hall's Chronicles 1550*. That might have been a good book. Right you are.

BOBBY   Got it. (<u>He's caught it</u>)

KEEN   What's the rest of the copy like?

BOBBY   Pretty clean, except for somebody making notes in the margin. Why will people make notes in the margin?

KEEN   Some kind of desire to immortalize themselves, I suppose. Wait a minute – that's sixteenth century handwriting, isn't it? Yes, it is. Don't throw that away – that might be worth a couple of pounds with contemporary handwriting in it. Anyhow, put it on the shelf – I'll take a look at it later. Now then, on we get. Take a note of it, George.

GEORGE   Two pound shelf. *Hall's Chronicles 1550*. No title page, writing in the margin.

BOBBY   *Across the South African Crater* – here we go. *Twixt Tent-peg and Tarpaulin....* (<u>Fade</u>)

KEEN   (<u>He goes on with the story</u>) It is extraordinary how something can be under your nose – right under your nose ... well, it was three weeks *after* that. The beginning of the first heat wave, I was sitting with a book open on my desk. I was very hot, but I wasn't actually asleep. Somewhere across the road the wireless was on.... (<u>Music</u>)

BOBBY   (<u>Leisurely afternoon</u>) Where's the boss?

GEORGE   Upstairs. Do you want him?

BOBBY   I've got this list out for him –

GEORGE   You won't be very popular. He's having his after-lunch think.

(<u>The wireless music</u>)

BOBBY   But I just brought him up the Shakespeare Catalogue –

GEORGE   I should let him be –

KEEN   (<u>Soliloquise on these lines, sleepily</u>) The Tercentenary Shakespeare Catalogue. Items ... imperfect copy ... never comes up now. The office thinks I'm working.

After lunch you feel drowsy … summer…. Now then. I must study the catalogue. Shakespeare items. I haven't seen any for weeks. Golding's Ovid. I should like that. (To the music) *Too good to be true.* Where have I heard that music before? Shakespeare certainly read Ovid. Other source books. Source books. North's translation of Plutarch's Lives. I've got a good North's Plutarch. Good in my opinion. Shakespeare source books. Books which he read for his historical plays. Holinshed's Chronicles. I've got that. In the cellar. Hall's Chronicles. I must get that. Stow. He read Stow, of course. Hall. But I've just found a copy of Hall. (Music) I mustn't let that music send me to sleep. (Suddenly awake) Hall – with handwriting in the margins.

BOBBY	Excuse me, Mr Keen. The list –
KEEN	One moment. I'm just going down –
BOBBY	It's upstairs.
KEEN	Down to the cellar. How was I getting downstairs – my legs? I was up again, with the book. I locked the door. 'In terram Salicam.' Difficult to read, this writing – Latin … George! Get me the big Shakespeare book, the Shakespeare Concordance. I want to look up some references. (Unlocks door) I say, the Shakespeare Concordance.
GEORGE	I haven't had it. Where is it?
KEEN	What? Yes, you do know – the Shakespeare book. (Excited irritation) I want it quickly.
GEORGE	Sorry. Oh yes (stooping). It's underneath this lot.
KEEN	(Excited) It's got a dark brown back. Dark brown back.
GEORGE	OK, OK. Got him.
KEEN	(To himself) In terram Salicam … and it's Henry V. Is there any Latin in *Henry V*? Wait – George, I'm going to take this book home. Give me that bag – no, I mean give me the Concordance.
BOBBY	Mr Keen – I've got the list ready.
KEEN	I'll look at it tomorrow. Ring me at Edgware 3136 if anything turns up. My wife will answer the phone. I shall be busy….

In reality there was no one moment. Later that night, it's true, he came downstairs from his study after checking some of the annotator's comments with the plays and he did say to his wife 'I think I've found him,' or 'I think I've found Bill.' It seemed to me that this true fact would not sound true. So I had to choose another crux – the moment when he first came wide awake, dozing in his office. The music here was a help. I hoped radio music, drifting in through the window, would suggest the entrance of something different from everyday life – and sleepy summer as well. And it must be cheap music – Forces Programme – or it would seem too dramatic.

I was looking forward to tomorrow (final rehearsal and transmission), but tonight was guard night. This means on duty at 6 pm. The siren goes at seven – I've never known it go so early before. Midnight and no sign of the all clear. I am up on the roof – unfortunately very small complement in my section tonight. I have left L.T. (horn player in BBC Northern Orchestra) in the guardroom. The third man should have been recruit Hollis – but when I took him up to the roof, as a new boy, to show him round the beat, going up the little iron staircase to the upper roof, a strange thing. He hung back and began to stiffen up like a waxwork. His face was covered with a glycerine of sweat. Apparently he has a bad height phobia. 'I'm sorry, I simply can't do it.' 'Of course not,' I say, 'get right inside.'
About midnight I heard the sound of planes, and reported it down to L.T. in the guard room. 'Planes overhead in large numbers. High.' (All this duly entered by L.T., in a sarcastically copy book hand, with haloes and flourishes all round it. He didn't see the point of these entries, nor did I. Nobody ever reads them.) The planes were very high. Was this going to be the Manchester Blitz? No sound of distant bombs. Some day there will be a Coventry here, everyone believes. So far, isolated bombs with a group of fire wardens killed last week. Searchlights are wavering ineffectively over the sky, weakly fingering an upper storey of cloud. And high above that, in the clear and freezing air beyond, hundreds of planes are passing, the sound increasing and decreasing within itself, like the sound of a gong lightly rung, sounding both outside and inside the head. I spoke down the phone to L.T. 'I expect those planes are coming back. I'm afraid poor old Liverpool's got it.'

22 December, Sunday. The all-clear didn't sound till 4 am. Didn't feel much like sleep when I finally came down. L.T. wide awake and chatty; and at 4.20 am we go off to the great Studio B and I try the slow movement of the Mozart Horn Concerto on the Steinway, so strong and dependable that it seems almost to put my fingers on the right notes. I can get through it all right. Then I go to sleep in the chair for an hour and wake with a stiff neck. Caught the 7.30 to Altrincham only to find no Mobberley bus till 9.05. A horrible wait in the cold wind and my lust for breakfast is almost unbearable. However, bath and breakfast at Ronnie's [Ronald Simpson, friend and member of the BBC rep.], and croquet till lunch; and then in to rehearse.

Am I ratty after a short night? It seems to me that Sebastian Calm, because he has a small part, is unco-operative. If I say something cutting, then I am *too* cutting, it doesn't work and stops me working. I can only produce, in other words, in a friendly atmosphere.

Actually, this cast is almost perfect. And best of all, Wilfred Pickles is as good in rehearsal as I thought he would be. He has warmth: *and* the sieve of the microphone allows this warm personality to show through.

Why isn't he more used, better known? Answer, he *is* well known, in the North. Everything looks good for this programme. Laddie, the chief programme engineer, is there to manage the knobs, as sure-handed as an expert organist on all those fades and cue lights, always accurately on time and with a rhythm of his own. I enjoy the final run through, and that greatest of all pleasures in my world at this moment – the hearing of a line of my dialogue filled out, improved and *bodied forth* by the actor who is speaking it. Not only Pickles, but in the part of Blakiston the cagey scholar, Cecil Trouncer carves his part out with such clarity and sureness that I want to develop it still further in Trouncer terms, add new phrases as he shows me what the character is, so to speak.

After the final run-through it is seven pm, and I ask Trouncer to join in with me and Ron for the drink-and-food break. Rehearsal and production are not at the BBC, but underground, in the commodious studio beneath the Central Library, St Peter's Square, about 700 yards from Broadcasting House, Piccadilly, and 100 from the scene of Peterloo. As we climb the stairs from below, someone is saying 'There's a raid on.' Something unusual: the mouth of the passage

leading up and out is lined with people. This is a shelter of sorts. A man very breathless rushes past and says 'Where's the fire alarm?' I don't know. I go out. It's daylight – but it should be dark, not excitingly brilliant and gay. In the street are two heaped up piles of burning magnesium; hurtful to the eyes. There is a third cataract half poured into a shop window. SAY IT WITH TWEEDS THIS CHRISTMAS. Averted, polite, modern stylised female dummies in green tweeds stare out on to the bonfire. One has been knocked over. The owner is trying to damp out the bonfire with a carpet. The fact that no one is helping or looking at him seems strange, and gives a slight chill. I must tell the cast. Ronnie and I go back – and already there are twice as many people taking shelter. A family of five with two children are quite badly shocked. The children are not exactly crying but they are shaking – their heads and lips are shaking. Because I had just been staring at burning magnesium all the faces looked green. I happened to know there was a first-aid box down the corridor and said so, and repeated the one fact I know about first-aid to children. 'Glucose is what they want,' I said. Nobody took any notice. Everybody gazed towards the gayness brighter than daylight coming from the doorway. I thought I'd better get in touch with B.H. Both lines were dead. This meant there could be no transmission – no programme. I got through from a call-box outside. They would 'try to send an engineer in about half an hour ... or when it is quiet.' The 'maybe' tone of the voice from B.H. makes me realise. This is Manchester Blitz night. Of course. Up above the whole sky is a sooty crimson and swirling with smoke. Ronnie, Cecil Trouncer and I are in the street, making for the Midland. Across the road from the Midland a corner block is alight from top to toe – and no one there, no one looking. I think: the last fire I saw as big as this was Arding & Hobbs, Clapham Junction, twenty years ago – and one couldn't get nearer than a quarter of a mile because of the of thousands of watchers. Now – no one; because there are buildings alight like this in every street. In the Midland bar is Fay Compton, perfectly neat and perfectly crisp and more contained than ever: every indistinctness planed away, whittled to the shapely essentials. She is down here for panto, and waves to us. 'Here come a lot of gloomy actors,' she says.
Eat plenty of nice thin slices of turkey, then go back to see if production possible. Yes – the line mended. There was a bomb-break

about half way. Dangerous, exposed job, it must have been. Pickles was as good as I had expected – but the raid half spoiled my enjoyment, safe underground as we were. I knew the roof of the building was blazing with a fire bomb, and there were vast, slow, distant reverberations. But the only difference to the cast was an interesting one. Instead of being within ten seconds of their rehearsal time (29' 20") they were 25 seconds less – normally unusual for such experienced people. This was the only way in which the slight tensing showed. Some had families right in Manchester.

After production, most of the cast got ready to sleep in the studio. The raid was getting very heavy. I feel like a drink at the Midland, and was preparing to go when there is a ring for me from Wilkie, Civil Defence Officer tonight at the BBC building. Help wanted. Six of us go. Ronnie, an experienced soldier, calmer than us, suggests waiting a moment: but we want to start at once, before loyal ardour cools, and begin to walk briskly to B.H. The roar in the sky of planes seems continuous, now and then the roar mounts to a breaking wave, a bomb falls in a satisfactory smash. 'You want to trot to a place of relative safety between bombs, ideally,' says Ronnie. Sparks as big as golf balls float quietly down all round. Some big shop or block blazing like an open fire every 200 yards – and deserted. One is tended by a single fireman – one hose and a ludicrously feeble jet. It was as if Gulliver was using his famous fire-fighting method – but on Brobdingnag not Lilliput. We trot and being ahead I half flop down for one screamer, lamely getting up again when the rest appear. 'Is this like the front line?' I said to Ronnie. 'Like a bombardment? Yes, it gives you quite an idea.' Some streets blocked, Chapel Street had completely lost its character of buttoned up respectability, banks and insurance buildings – unrecognisable.

Wilkie was relieved to see us. In almost an excess of helpfulness, Ronnie, Cecil Trouncer and I all go on the roof together. I am inclined to take cover in the shelter hut provided. We gaze down on Manchester, really lively and decorated for the first time in history, gayer than ever in its life, with gold and red. We began to watch small fires starting on roof tops or in passages and left horrifyingly alone. On the top cornice of the huge central Cotton offices of Tommy Barlow (of the Savile) on the other side of Piccadilly we saw one small fragment of fire beginning, and one little figure, like a comic little man on a string, hopping near and banging at it but making no impression. We could only stand and stare. I was glad when my hour was up.

23 December, Monday. After the exhilaration and the fright, and having had only one hour's sleep last night, I fall onto a couch and lie as if felled, to be woken not by the rest of the bombs, which continued to fall for two hours, but by the office cleaners. 'Time you woke up, luv.' Very much business as usual. But out of the window Manchester was burning as if it had been given up for lost.

Later. Tired but mentally very wide awake do a few bits of Christmas shopping in the streets still open. Many fires blazing away as strong as ever but not unattended now – it is said that fire engines have come from as far as London on last night's call, but that the water mains are mostly out of action. No trains, no buses. Cadge somebody's taxi to Altrincham, where the Austin is parked. Two wrong turnings in tired, misty dusk. I remember P., at Mobberley, standing on top of stairs, distrait. Family pleased to see me. Now to enjoy good dinner: but nothing to the meal that I am going to make over my story of last night.

24 December, Tuesday. No transport anywhere, so in that tough little runt of an Austin 7 and a roar of tappetts I first fetch Lila (Ronnie's wife) from Wilmslow – she was Dora in David Copperfield last night. Buzz her round to do a little clear-headed shopping. After lunch there is a crowded journey into Manchester against the stream of Christmas refugees. We pick up a young soldier who talks quietly and nervously with wide open worried eyes. He is longing to talk. 'As a matter of fact,' he says, 'I am taking French leave.' 'No!' 'French leave. Yes. It's just to see my wife, for Christmas. She's just had a baby and I might not see her again. I shall only get a few days C.B. [Confined to Barracks]' Inspecting our Platt Lane house, I am glad to have moved the family out, because although it is still standing, there is a crater in the back garden as big as the house itself, which is loosened in all its sockets though curiously only the windows *in front* are blown clean out (or rather, as is explained to me, were sucked in). Lumps of clay as big as grand pianos were thrown out round the edge of the crater.

The raids had gone on all night, nearly as bad. Moray was in charge on the roof at B.H. We picked him up, then Ronnie, then Moray's wife Aline. We have to make huge detours round conflagrations to get to the simplest places. Then – heaven seems to begin. We are all set for Mobberly, and in the foggy dust, smoke and dirt, we join the road for Altrincham and the East. A solid queue twelve miles long, no doubt: but everybody cheerful and elated because moving *out*. Moving *away* from that horrible bit of dead stinking rubbish behind: and it makes it all the more enjoyable that we were part of it. The queue is walking pace, then stop. Walking pace, stop. During one of the stops, on the edge of the moor, a wild old woman suddenly appears and says 'follow me' and walks into a little bumpy road. 'Keep on through the lane.' I did and it worked – and a good thing for the two or three hundred cars which, in the mist and deep dusk, automatically followed me.

Two more months of Platt

Unlike most Mancunians, Stephen enjoyed a good Christmas Day and Boxing Day with his family. Based in *The Bird in Hand*, most of the time we were the guests of the nearby Simpsons. On 27th, Stephen and Att went back by train to Platt Lane:

> Opposite P. a fidgetty, half depressed half excited young airman who had been to his home in Manchester – and found no house, no family, after searching throughout his Christmas leave.

However loose the sockets of No. 66, the condominium continued, shakily, for two months into 1941.

> 9 January 1941. The food at Platt is getting rather bad. In spite of meals at restaurants, I am at last beginning to feel the pinch of rationing. Mary Allen rattles away to Laurence. Robert Eddison sits quiet and knits, with occasional pedantic little jokes – in a voice that is near pansy but more humorous and dissecting, like a New College don. Yet he has had this vast parochial success at the Players Theatre and often refers to it.
> Raids keep us hanging about, me downstairs in my dressing gown. Mary says that she likes raids less and less – her nerves are wearing out. She isn't at all pleased, for that reason, at the suggestion that we might be going back to London. The pros and cons of this, and the sub-suggestions – Edinburgh? – Evesham? – go round in our heads and give rise to endless discussions. We are set in feeble little whirls

of useless speculation and wish we could be let in officially on the secrets.

Stephen was too old to be called up, but still young enough, by two days, to be in the oldest batch of those who had to register. He got around to this about five weeks after the deadline – but there was 'no tick off – a matey atmosphere.' Valentine Dyall was not so lucky:

10 January. There is an ugly envelope waiting for Val in the green room. He is called up – next Thursday, to the RAMC [Medical

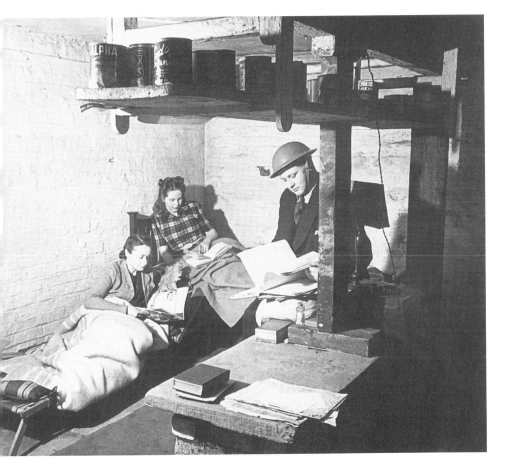

Mary Allen (left), Marianne Helweg and Laurence Gilliam work in the cellar of No. 66 as a night raid begins.

Corps]. Very dull and sordid and no chance of a commission. He has lived for four years with Babette and they are complete 1+1. They have no money.

This drama was resolved a few days later, when Dyall was found to be nearly blind in one eye and failed his medical. 'We of course want to keep him. He has one of the best poetry-reading voices,' wrote Stephen.

Although active service was out, Home Guard duties had, since the blitz, become more demanding. Stephen, as a sergeant, had a truncheon: his corporal had no weapon at all. Later, one rifle was found – for the whole platoon.

2 January. Guard night. We find the pumps frozen and the sand in frozen cement blocks. Take the stirrup pumps down to be melted, but there is no alarm.

8 February. On guard, I load, for door-guard, Robert Eddison's rifle. Laurence, coming in at the end of his spell, volunteers to show him how the safety-catch works. He doesn't know anything about it, nor does he realize this rifle has no cut-out. One goes up the spout – he fires it – it rings through the passage as Tony Holles, the only neurotic in the place, is coming down the passage. 'Had I not flung myself flat at the sound of the rifle...' he says! I feel quite awkward and annoyed – so does Laurence.

Irish Songs, Kew, Mount Everest

Meanwhile Stephen was providing programmes without respite and the first three in 1941 were written up on four consecutive days. One was another co-operation with Tom Harrison of Mass Observation:

3 January. Tom comes in for a drink to talk about a Southampton Gets Back to Work programme. He is full of impetus, working for some unearthly reason for the Admiralty, who have given him a Ford V8 and a commission to Mass Observe all the blitzed areas – Southampton is the worst, he says, and I gather Manchester and Coventry are bracketed next.

The next day Stephen was scheduled to discuss with John McCormack, the tenor, another Tom Moore programme, this time about his Irish songs:

4 January. At 5.30 go to Midland to meet Count John McCormack and his accompanist Gerald Moore. Find McC. noisy and drunkish … he wants to play the part of Moore besides singing it … he sings snippets, playing the piano himself, not very well. Then 'Gerry, where's the drink?' and a good deal of thick brown gin and vermouth is poured out of a jug. Then – 'Stephen, I know when I like a man and when I don't. Stay to dinner.' Though this friendliness and great-man-being-ordinary may be difficult to keep up with, I accept. Very soon the table is laid, with three very large bottles of champagne.

After a very medium dinner – 'See if you can find Leslie Henson' [a famous comedian of the day.] Well, Henson was downstairs, just starting his dinner; but unrebuffed, I felt more and more social and went round the various couples I slightly knew, taking in Fay Compton's table and Lydia Sherwood's. My story became: 'Awkward. My host slightly tight … what would you advise?' In the end Fay Compton came up and tried to make him sing … but by then I realized I was tight myself, and according to my rule in these circumstances, I decided to leave with dignity. Phoning my good-byes from the desk, I swept off with my script. But it wasn't my script, I discovered. It was the call book of the Midland. Of the 200 guests, not one was called at the right time the next morning, nor given the right breakfast.

5 January. Two new members of the BBC Rep. turn up today for my Moore show – Robert Eddison [it was his first job as a member] and Malcolm Keen.

There was little praise for the broadcast, which was under-rehearsed. Another programme into which I put much guts chucked into the void – flung down the crevasse, to be swallowed up for ever.

6 January. Now plunge into next Saturday's programme – a Leversuch réchauffé [a selection from the last three Leversuch programmes]. I like doing these, but it is a little near and C(P)'s secretary has asked for a script.

11 January. The Leversuch rehearsals. On the read-through, a fair amount of the hoped-for laughs. Unless the cast are in exactly the right state, I can't feel in control. I overcame this same feeling with my lectures in 1927 and could do so now too, I always feel, if only I had a stage play reputation and stage production experience.

The reference to stage experience is typical of many entries exhorting himself to work outside the BBC as well as in it. He did not want to be permanently typecast as a writer/producer for radio. Early in 1940 he had written: 'Having shown I can do Radio programmes of entertainment value, now for non-radio stuff … Plays … books. Talked to A. D. Peters the other day and he mentioned the danger of the BBC £1000 a year. Must leave avenue of escape from BBC.'

While Stephen eventually achieved this, in 1941 he was kept far too busy to embark on any extraneous writing. Bits and pieces in the early part of the year included a simulation of the strafing and other noises heard by soldiers as they were escaping from Dunkirk – 'In afternoon, come back to see about a strange but interesting job. Under a psychologist (RAMC) we are to do a 5-minute feature of an air raid, run by me, commentary by Trouncer. Object, to condition Dunkirk shock victims to air raid sounds again, placing them in the calm context of Cecil's voice.' At first Stephen was sceptical about this, but after listening a second time to the 'nerve-racking horror of the sounds' he wrote 'they have certainly conditioned *me*.'

Other work included a new production of *The Last Crusade* (with Lydia Sherwood as a new Queen Elizabeth) and, as usual, a number of abortive projects, including an attempt to get another script from Graham Greene:

4 March. A pleasant interview with G.G. We speak of *The Power and the Glory*, which I thought so good; and I am full of hope for our collaboration.

13 March. A fairly satisfactory G.G. interview in the involved corridors and little eighteenth century rooms of *The Spectator* office, with a snuffy, stuffy ill-tempered-looking editor occasionally appearing.

15 March. This script of Greene's that I have struggled with – and struggled to make him do well – is desperately disappointing. These good authors are batting on such an easy wicket, damn them. If we turn them down they can say 'well, rotten pay anyhow. And surely you don't regard this as inferior to the BBC's average muck?' Which is not the point, not the reason we asked them.

Maybe Stephen was difficult to co-operate with: he certainly preferred producing programmes he had written himself. 'Pulled down by programmes for these *other* people,' he wrote later in the year. When an outside writer was called in – and he was later to produce programmes by Priestley and by Louis MacNeice – he still saw it as very much part of his job to advise them on how to write for radio. This 1940 extract of a discussion with William Gerhardi shows that at times his tact deserted him. Gerhardi's novels were then highly regarded, especially by other novelists. Greene wrote of him: '… to those of my generation he was the most important new novelist to appear in our young life.' But he was about to dry up: until his death 37 years later he added very little to his writings. One of his more recent works was a history of the Romanovs and now a programme was proposed about that:

8 February 1940. Have to see Gerhardi, because his script about the Romanovs is laughably bad. Awkward and touchy point. He suggests I see him during cocktail party of Ann Sheridan's. I go in a rather jumbled suit and find some fairly well, dark-dressed people and some melodramatic floodlit sculpture. I have a 40-minute talk with Gerhardi. I tell him how it is wrong. He starts by being incredulous. I say terrific things about his other books. And as I harden he hardens and things come out such as 'I'm only getting £50 anyway,' and how bad the BBC is anyway.

Stephen's two major programmes at this time were about Mount Everest and Kew Gardens – which had now been open to the public for 100 years. In the early 30s he had been drawn to Kew from Chiswick. A life-long hobby was wild plants and at times he was visiting the long beds in the herbarium at least once a week, occasionally twice in a single day, to draw the plants and to describe them in his botanical notebook. So a Feature on Kew was a double delight, enabling him to visit it again and get away from smog-bound Platt:

19 February. Go down to Kew Gardens with John Green from Talks, an intelligent man and keen BBC-er. We see the Director, a dry and impatient little man, upright and clipped. To him we are obviously non-scientists. His remark to me to 'mind the flowers,' when, in the lovely 18th century room with exquisite green moulded fireplace we sat down to a scone and jam and gingerbread tea and I knocked the winter jasmine so that one of the blooms fell off. It was a special late winter variety. He made a few statements about

himself and his duties 'like a spider in the centre of a web.' He used the same metaphor in a pamphlet about the Gardens. He is obviously a man in a plum job hanging on to it by being careful and unpopular and enjoying the comforts.

Fortunately Stephen got on well with all the other staff he met and describes each of them lengthily, as well as many of the plants and greenhouses. He was dissuaded from making any mention of either the shortage of staff caused by the war or of a disastrous bomb:

25 February. A drama of Kew, which we can't use, is the bombs and the plants. Bomb falls near – little damage. Bomb falls in Kew Road and 3000 panes of glass in the Tropical House are out. There is a great race against time to prevent 500 valuable plants, some unique, some 100 years old, from being ruined.

20 March. This morning I get my interview with the Director over. I can't make out what he wants and I suspect that he wants to feature more himself, so I say to him 'I'm sorry for it, but I understand you want to keep very much in the background, yourself, over this.' A good device, because the answer to that can only be agreement.

25 March. A day at home – perfect conditions – yet I do little to my Kew script although it is desperately urgent. Am I really preparing something in my brain, as I wander aimlessly up and down? Is that why (generally but not in this case) the programme suddenly comes in one piece from the squeezed programme-paste tube, after prolonged pressure with nothing happening?

26 March. I must not do this. It turns me into real fortyhood, in looks and feelings of tiredness. The cast are not put in a good mood either, by receiving the script in two halves.

On this occasion Stephen does seem to have spoilt what should have been an ideal programme for him by leaving it too late. On production day he told the cast that this was the worst programme he had ever written and that they would just have to do their best with it.

Stephen was no expert on mountaineering – indeed he had a phobia about heights. But he was always keen to master a new subject, and given the opportunity to write about F. S. Smythe, who at the time of his last

Everest expedition had got higher up the mountain than anyone else (except Mallory, if it was his bones that were found in 1999), he immersed himself in the technology and jargon, spending three days with Smythe in his Sussex home. His aim was to become familiar with the sort of things the mountaineers said to each other during the ascent, so as to be able to write a realistic dialogue. As with Keen on Shakespeare, nearly the whole story is told in terms of this dialogue, helped with sound effects (also researched in detail) and interspersed with Smythe soliloquising. Stephen believed all this should make the time and place and course of events clear to the listener, without the aid of a narrator.

13 December 1940. A lovely morning. Down to Three Bridges to see Smythe. His house, well in the country, with woods all round it, a real 'door-in-the-wall' after Manchester. He tells me all about Everest, including – thrillingly – unpublished details, such as the dirt of the Tibetans, the child with the black leg, covered with flies, the VD, the man with the hole in his hand, crawling with maggots – he was a shepherd, the hole was right through his hand. 'Go to hospital,' says Smythe. 'My sheep would die.' 'Hold it in a stream.' But he won't. Smythe tells me what it was like at 28,000 feet and demonstrated the eight feverish breaths allowed at each step. The moment when, alone, he thought 'By Jove, I might do it!'

17 January 1941. Today a car was to call at 10.30, with secretary, to take me to Smythe's. Nothing came till 11.20, when behold a blond, sweet-sucking woman appeared, who, apart from complete ignorance of all roads everywhere, was a good driver. Down to Smythes, where F.S. started proceedings by demonstrating the exact sound and method of cutting steps into ice with an axe on his goldfish pond. He was rather difficult for me to deal with as he was inclined to say 'I must go through this thing from A to Z' and 'this is what interests them in my lecture,' whereas all the time I am trying to get out of him material for dialogue.

13 February. Last night I worked in the armchair downstairs all night. Sleep dragged me down but I woke after two hours, cold. The attempt to start work – awful at first but becoming easier. At about 6 I am quite alert and do a good programme.

17 February (transmission day). During the rehearsal we tried to get those quick breathings of high altitude climbing to sound convincing and to get right the sound of climbing the ice. Fred

O'D. *could not* get the hang of the necessity of extreme calmness and non-staginess. Get a big block of ice from the Midland for the ice-axe. A general failure on my part to shape it and a feeling that there should have been something more visual. I count this as one of my shows that 'will do', but considering the magnificence of the subject, a failure.

The only feedback to *Against Everest* was a good review from Wyndham Goldie in *The Listener*, a warm letter from Smythe, a sharp memo from C(P) asking him why he had put 'English' when it should have been 'British' and a stricture from his Uncle Willie at the Club for failing to mention the fact that Smythe had climbed higher than anyone else.

Disintegration of Platt

Despite the mass audience that radio was acquiring, the fashionable view was still that it was a new-fangled gadget and that nothing serious could be put across on it; so the encouragement and intelligent criticism that Platt Lane occupants gave each other had been needed and useful. But now, after fourteen months, this sometimes turned into mockery:

> 22 February. All Platt (bar Laurence) listen to *Three-cornered Moon* – Val's production of Michael Arlen's story – which breaks all records for naïvety of dialogue, heavy treatment of the light, bad effects and Val-ishness (he narrated). Fay Compton's anger at the idiocy of her lines came through very obviously. 'Let me put my dressing-gown on,' she bellows. 'Oh, the pity of it all' was also said. 'I shall go away,' croaks the hero, played by Ronald Squire. Enormous seagull squawk. 'Seagull's got caught in the door,' says Mary. 'My car at once,' says R.S. Bad car effect. 'Sounds as if car's coming up in the lift,' says Mary. 'She's asleep,' says R.S. 'But Paris is not asleep,' says Robert Eddison, in a special voice, and sure enough, out goes R.S. into the night of Paris.

Members of the household were beginning to get on each others' nerves; but there were more practical reasons for the impending break-up. Marianne and Laurence were now married and a baby was due soon. Att was becoming increasingly disillusioned with the amount of cooking and other household work she had to do, although this was supposed to be shared. She insisted that she must find a way of getting back to more painting. Worst of all, continued raids made the strain and danger of living in Platt Lane too great.

The Potters found rooms in Hale, near the home of their Christmas host Ronald Simpson, who now had parts in nearly all Stephen's programmes. (Later he was to play Soames in the BBC's long-running radio version of *The Forsyte Saga*.) In exchange for one of Att's pictures, he had given Stephen the use of his Austin 7, which was often used for the journey between Hale and work. On the last day at Platt, Stephen wrote:

> 27 February. Moray and I have a sad drink, I acting nostalgic for the break-up of Platt and its good jokes and character-revealing scenes. 66 – or sexty sex, as Dillon calls it – is finished at last. In general, a year slightly too social, though often very amusingly social, makes us long to be on our own – also, above all, the country.

Based in Hale

On the plus side, Red Arch, as the house was called, was within walking distance of a 9-hole golf course and bicycling distance of the Simpsons' croquet lawn. But the Potters had never until now lived in lodgings and at first had some difficulty with their landlady, Mrs Redhead, who objected to Stephen's untidiness and excessive use of the telephone and to Att's use of the sitting room as a studio. She had, and used, a wireless, but

> … the fact that Mrs Redhead has it on all day and never turns the knob off, nor even up for the Sibelius 5th, nor down for the news in Gaelic, has the effect of putting me off wireless.

In Hale, the war was more distant but could never be forgotten. A boy from the Channel Islands had been billeted on the household. He had been on a boatload of refugees, but there had been no room on the boat for his sister, his only relative. Stephen describes how every morning he checked the post, but no letter ever came.

The bombing was relatively light:

> 3 May 1941. Tonight more continuous plane drone and more gunfire than last night. At one time I thought that P. ought to come down and went in to her but she wouldn't budge (though she told me

85

later that she had heard shrapnel on the roof). I then went to bed and the bombardment continued, but we went to sleep. P. said my *snores* woke her.

1–2 June. After midnight a sharp raid and I make P. go downstairs and we sit in the bright ugly light of Mrs Redhead's room. There is a whistle and a bomb about half a mile away. I suggest we get under the table for the next; but there is no next. Mrs Redhead comes in and sees our bottoms emerging from the table and suggests we go down to the cellar. 'Oh no!' we say. It gets no worse, though the stars are bursting in big strings over Manchester.

Stephen had to go up to London most weeks. He looked forward to the train journeys, which were always by night. He caught up with his work and with his diary. He caught up with sleep, which on the train was less often interrupted by raids than in either Hale or London. He had discovered that he was entitled to travel first class and booked a sleeper whenever one was available. Others were not so lucky: 'A Blitz blowing up among actors because they are shuttled back and forth on a third class fare and no sleepers. This principle is even being applied to Fay Compton: typical gracelessness of the BBC.'

Arriving in London after the BBC in Langham Place had again been hit, he wrote:

23 April. I look round for signs of last week's raids. A glimpse of my old Broadcasting House office buildings, now in complete ruins. Fresh bomb spots breathing out an exposed smell of wet and rotten dust. The freshly disintegrated rottenness of the bared guts of houses. In Jermyn Street only the middle third remains. In the rest of it, the houses are cascaded over the streets. In the centre of Piccadilly, by St James's, a heaved up swelling is being roughly battered and battened down. Windows of Simpsons and Fortnums out. I go in to Fortnums to buy crab paste and see if any special food is available to the rich. No, except for chocolates at 9/6 a lb.

Nowhere was it possible to miss the war. On 30th April, on the way back from visiting his two boarding school sons in Herefordshire, he wrote:

Journey home punctuated by coffee at Church Stretton and a vision – of a newly blinded soldier. A common young man in civvies, his face looked pitted with blast and his eyes were still in his head but dead and shrivelled. He was sitting in the shop with three cowed friends and a nurse who tried to keep the conversation bright and constantly touched him on the knee, laying her hand on it. He only answered occasionally, with a smile as if he was learning how to smile, and the rest of the time sat with his face averted from them (staring straight at us as if trying to see us) and all the time he was not speaking his mouth trembled and worked. As if he was going to break out, or was still shocked … or couldn't bear it? Do not know.

Although Stephen delayed moving house again until the end of 1941, the centre of action for Features shifted back to London earlier in the year, soon after he first arrived in Hale.

Chapter 6
Features Expand

Gilliam's wider role

Former inhabitants of No. 66 often visited the Potters in Hale, and took the opportunity to get a breath of near-country air. The Gilliams came to Sunday lunch on 23 March 1941:

> They enjoyed it very much, he quite amusing, drinking enormous whiskeys and even going on a little walk, puffing. He tells us the Feature section is to be split – he to make a start going to London with Geoffrey Bridson. I go off to *Last Crusade* rehearsal, they stay till 8.

Since the Northern blitzes, the move to Manchester had been seen as a mistake, as it was clearly no safer than London from air attack – and it was in London that nearly all outside contacts, such as star actors, writers and Government Departments, were to be found. It seems odd that Stephen appears not to have been invited to go with this advance contingent, since he went so often to London in any case. But many programmes were still being produced in Manchester and he may have been reluctant to change house again, so soon after the move to Hale. When he was in London, the Savile was a congenial base.

For the time being Gilliam still spent much of his time in Manchester and sometimes they made the journey to London together. Stephen admired him: 'Laurence is always at his most active when the news is bad, and starts Great Ideas drives.' He appreciated his openness. At Platt he had written: 'Laurence and I usually have about a half hour's talk, last thing, generally about Features and producers. I have learnt much about the BBC this last month, chiefly from him, because of his clear grasp of faces in it, and its committee and bureaucratic, unled nature.' He also appreciated the positive encouragement that Gilliam gave and his instinct to say yes rather than no. Yet Stephen was not uncritical. Perhaps the fact that, unlike colleagues such as Bridson and Heppenstall, he was a few years older than Gilliam made it difficult for him to look up to him in the same way:

> 19 February. Arrive at Euston rather late – trucks off line, had to go round by Northampton. Breakfast with L.G. at station. I don't much like being with him on some occasions – when his 'character' is to the fore, making his weight felt with waiters and taximen. L. and I are drifting – he thinks I am oblique, 'by indirections finding directions out' [*Hamlet*]. I think his directness is false, and built on an ideal of toughness and Americanism which is partly untrue, like his physical toughness and bulk, which collapses into wheezing and perspiration if he walks at over 3 miles an hour. I like his quickness of perception and wit and I hate his muddiness in fundamentals, which once caused him to group a series of prog-rammes under the heading 'values', and makes him talk about Freedom, Realism, Actuality, etc. with paralysing indiscrimination. P. thinks I am sometimes influenced in my judgment of him by the fact that he's boss.

What Gilliam had clearly *not* told Stephen at the lunch at Hale was that he had been given control of all BBC Features, External as well as Home; and that the move back to London had been sparked off by requests for more Features from North American and Empire stations. This required more writer/producers, who were easier to recruit from a London base. The number of hours devoted to overseas broadcasting and the number of stations had been hugely increased, both for propaganda reasons and because of the world demand for news of how the war was going from the only country still at war with Germany.

Caversham papers show that first Gilliam had been offered control of External broadcasts of all sorts, but he had declined this on the grounds that his expertise in Features would not be sufficiently used. He argued that it would be better to combine Home and External Features and put both under his control; and this had been accepted.

The new London headquarters were in Bedford College, next to Queen Mary's Rose Gardens in Regent's Park. On Stephen's first visit, he soon saw that even the Park was not safe from air attack:

21 May. Then to Bedford College to see Laurence. The Saturday blitz fired a big block of it and broke many windows, just as it destroyed Studio 4 at Maida Vale. The day is sunny and the grounds delightful. All seem somewhat vague – L.G. because he has been drinking beer in celebration of Marianne having had a son – or is it bomb vagueness, a bad war vagueness?

This enormous new BBC growing up – this triplicate expansion of Empire – makes me feel rather a stranger and slightly out of it – in contrast to Bridson, for example, who is right in it, and just back from doing a production at Monseigneur [the Marble Arch News Cinema, used by the BBC as a substitute studio for the usual places, St George's Hall and the Drama Studios at Broadcasting House, both of which had been bombed]. General sense that the power of Laurence is upping. Hear him dictate a memo asking for a Grade B

Laurence Gilliam with S.P. at Bedford College.

91

salary for Louis MacNeice, if taken on as a regular, as if he had
refused Grade C.

Gilliam, as well as running the Features section, was developing ways
of presenting the news using the techniques of the Features department.
His *Marching On* (which had started as *War Report*) was in April 1942
allotted an hour-long weekly slot – which after the Allies had landed in
Normandy became daily. In it, 'true stories from the news of the week',
heroic acts and all kinds of incidents were re-created in the studio, without
the use of actuality. Although some of Gilliam's writing may today seem
over-sensational – 'The whole of the British Isles has become one giant
furnace designed to blast the Nazis from the face of the earth' – Gilliam
held to his belief that 'the only propaganda worth telling is the truth'.

The best known series for overseas was *Britain to America*, as it was not
only networked across that country, but also broadcast in the UK. Edited
jointly by Gilliam and Bridson, with Leslie Howard as narrator, it was
designed to inform Americans about the progress of the war and no doubt
to sway opinion in favour of coming in on our side. Stephen was critical,
and beyond attending conferences about the series, was not involved:

> 18 September. After lunch snooker, to a meeting in Laurence's room
> to discuss more *Britain to America* programmes. His great line is to
> make lightning decisions and get things done – the first titles are
> decided in ten minutes: 1. Commandos, 2. Merchant Navy – etc.
> There is much that is good in this. Something bad – insofar that he
> doesn't seem to have a plan in his head to start with. The broad
> blunt pencil – but is that good for radio?
> 19 December. Listen to a baddish Feature, which ought to have been
> good – *Britain to America*. Blush-making self praise about the BBC
> in wartime bringing in John Snagge [leading newscaster] and L.G.,
> neither of whom can act, and both of whom assumed preternaturally
> manly voices, with every aside bellowed. Two good stories well told
> and magniloquent use of large orchestra.

Louis MacNeice's first programmes

Important for Features in 1941 was the signing up of Louis MacNeice.
He was to be instrumental, both by his example and by his advocacy, in
persuading more writers to write for radio. He joined the payroll at Bedford

College late in May, having returned from a prolonged visit to the States the previous November. Not only did he need a job, but he considered that the promising possibilities of radio outweighed his reservations. He wrote to Eleanor, the lady he had fallen in love with in America: '… in spite of the unhealth which goes with a machine that is largely propaganda … it *has* its excitements and (what was less to be expected) its value' [Quoted from Jon Stallworthy's biography].

While MacNeice was later to write landmark scripts such as *The Dark Tower*, his earlier role was to take on propagandist programmes. His first assignment was catastrophic. President Roosevelt, in exchange for a 99-year lease on some British bases, had just leased to us fifty destroyers. This was more than barter: it was a clear indication of which side America was on. It was Gilliam's idea that, as a token of thanks, a programme should be produced for transmission to the States about one of these ships. MacNeice and Jack Dillon were taken on board for a nine-day North Atlantic patrol, but on the last day got so drunk that a letter of complaint came from the Admiralty to C(P) withdrawing all further facilities. Apparently the noise in the wardroom had stopped some of the officers sleeping; MacNeice had tottered up to the bridge at 5.30 am in search of a cigarette and at 7.30 both men were found asleep in the wardroom, which was littered with bottles. The scandal of this abated when it was discovered that the complaints had originated with the captain's wife and not the captain; but because of it, MacNeice's job with the BBC was not confirmed until September.

With the invasion in June 1941 of Russia, making her an ally rather than an enemy, something had to be done to reverse anti-Soviet propaganda. MacNeice was asked to write two programmes with that in mind. The first was a radio profile of Chekhov, with Stephen as the producer. Stallworthy describes it:

> *Dr Chekhov* had been a feature-biography. Beginning on the morning of his last day, it ended with his death. Phases of his early life were presented through flashbacks, but because MacNeice had no experience of studio production, some of the transitions between past and present would have been unproducible but for the skill of the producer, Stephen Potter, who, as the script-writer gratefully acknowledged, 'saved the situation'.

Stephen's diary records, contrariwise, that '… everything went wrong with my MacNeice programme'; but either way, this low-key, experimental production was not what was required when it came to changing Russia's image; and at the end of the year MacNeice wrote *Alexander Nevsky*, based on a Russian film in which the hero defeats an invasion by Teutonic knights. Later he was to write other pro-Russian programmes, even more propagandist: *Salute to the USSR* and *The Spirit of Russia* (8 November 1943). The latter was again produced by Stephen; but from then on MacNeice had acquired enough expertise to produce his own programmes.

In October 1941, to mark the anniversary of Greece's entry into the war, MacNeice wrote *The Glory that was Greece*. The next year, close to the day on which Singapore fell to the Japanese (15 February), he was induced to write a morale-raising programme about that. Stephen (who had by now moved South) commented:

> 12 February 1942. Laurence is trying to convince himself that there *is* a propaganda line which *could* be taken about Singapore. He has got MacNeice onto it. He, with calm resource and acquiescence, seems to have taken on that fearful job willingly.

The *Nevsky* broadcast had coincided with Pearl Harbour; and the entry of America into the war had called forth a similar flurry of pro-American programmes. Many of these were also by MacNeice, culminating in October 1942 with *Christopher Columbus*, a part-verse part-prose Feature celebration of the 450th anniversary of the discovery of America. Olivier was in the title role and Walton wrote the music – Bridson considered it was 'probably the most memorable programme written during the war'. MacNeice was enjoying the producer's role of working with a team of engineers, musicians and actors, and his intensive contribution to the war effort continued into 1943, in which year he wrote no less than nineteen of these semi-propaganda blockbusters. These included one on each of the 'four freedoms', the last of which was *John Milton and the Freedom of the Press*. At the end of that year he was entrusted with the big New Year's Eve Feature, for which he wrote about War Aims. Shortly after that, however, he told Gilliam that he wanted to write no more programmes to do with the war; and Gilliam sympathetically consented.

Blitz Doctor, Tanks and Ballet

For Stephen, the main development in 1941 was his appointment as Literary Editor of Features; but in addition to that and his own literary programmes, he still did his share on the war-related side. An instance of this was his Feature on the Emergency Medical Services (EMS), set up to cope with air-raid casualties. His friend Dr Doyne Bell, although primarily a paediatrician and although he suffered from a painful stomach ulcer, had taken it on himself to get to stricken streets immediately after an air raid to attend the wounded. He had a flat in London where Stephen often stayed – and he was chairman of the Savile Club. Stephen asked Doyne if he could make him the focal point of *Blitz Doctor*, and Doyne agreed.

Already Stephen had recorded a number of journeys with Doyne through the blitzed London streets. For example, in November 1940: 'Come in through the East End with Doyne and pass his two wrecked hospitals and the hit cinema with "down but not out" signs all over it. We see the flaked and pitted St Clement Danes, and he shows me where he put a shot of morphine into a man whose thigh bone was sticking through his trousers.'

On 8 April 1941 Stephen went round children's wards with Doyne in two of his hospitals, recording in his diary the rapport established by Doyne with his child patients and, in grim detail, their symptoms. Back at the Club that evening 'Doyne dictates to a loaned secretary some doctor dialogue for our EMS programme. He is good at it but soon tires, needing glasses of milk.' Later that night they went, again for the programme, to the Vauxhall Hospital to interview a Mobile Aid Post:

My chief impressions were the strength and keenness and happiness of all these people working on a very vital job and also something about people who have seen the worst there is to be seen. They tell me about the Café de Paris job (a to me very differently associated spot), where bombs had killed 70 and badly injured as many more. They rushed to Piccadilly and set up an aid post. There were no pads big enough to go over some of the wounds. One man had lost his testicles and leg, split off at the top of his thigh. He was lying over a woman who said 'please help this man.' They tell her he can't be helped. 'Thank you,' she says, and drops back in a faint, and *then* they notice that her leg is blown clean away.

The full horror of Doyne's work, and perhaps a better idea of what the programme was like, comes through in an entry after it was over, on 21 May:

Doyne at the Club is a terrible sight, much altered and rounded in the stomach – in 'permanent discomfort,' he says – i.e. pain. The Saturday blitz was the worst story conceivable. Doyne and Clarissa [his sister] were in the new flat. Banging starts. Gets worse. C. goes down to the cellar. Doyne stays up, but a near bomb blows the windows in … feels he had better investigate … 20 doors down, a building bursting into flames … officer staggers out, hand over face, blood trickling … 'For God's sake help – not me – others in there' (he faints). Doyne sees some that need moving…. Calls for help – but the street is empty. The Civil Defence is at other incidents: then – eerie – a French lieutenant walks by – Doyne calls him, but he walks straight on, along the middle of the street. Doyne calls again in French. He walks straight on. Then Doyne notices for the first time that the house opposite has collapsed onto its foundations – he knows that there are people there too. Rescue men have turned up to help him get most clear from house A (burning). Now for B. Two hysterics down below, and men too, calling them to be quick. Doyne begins – an arm – but it's difficult – scratches aside to the arm's face. Dead girl. Piles stuff onto her, to clear a way. One out (dies in ambulance). Two out live. Now for the others. But now the flames have suddenly set the debris of the house brightly alight. Doyne and the others, scalded by falling debris and frightened by the flames, have to retire. The flames are put out with water and only one of the buried is burnt alive. The rest are drowned. Doyne is as if himself blasted by this experience, and is not at all recovered from it. 'Blitz Doctor' has more experience than ever.

Blitz Doctor was produced and transmitted on 30 April, not on the Home, but the Empire Service. Stephen was happy with the way in which Ronnie Simpson played Doyne's part and thought the production had gone well. 'I shall be annoyed if it is not on the Home programmes,' he wrote. It was, on 13 June, and received a rave review from Grace Wyndham Goldie in *The Listener*:

> *Blitz Doctor* first. For me, this was the programme of the week. It was a real life affair about medicine and bombs and war. It was by Stephen Potter. And I am prepared to declare, against all comers, first that it was the finest radio feature since *Battle of Britain*; and second, that it made most routine programmes (*War-Time Express*

and *Bren Gun*, for instance) look like the half-baked endeavours of well-intentioned amateurs. The pleasing truth is, in fact, that in Stephen Potter and Cecil McGivern radio has discovered its own bright stars … Mr Potter, more uncertain, sometimes hits and sometimes misses; but everything he handles has a star-like glow, and when he lands upon his target with a *Victorian Negative* or the *Rediscovery of Night* there is no-one in broadcasting who can touch him.

Cecil McGivern, bracketed with Stephen by Wyndham Goldie, had begun to make his name as a Features writer/producer while still based in the BBC's Newcastle offices. He did not join the main Features section until Gilliam's move to Regent's Park, so Stephen hardly knew him. Gielgud wrote that McGivern made his name with programmes such as *Bomb-doors Open* and *Battle of Britain*, but Stephen, while noting the affinity between his own work and McGivern's, was critical. In May 1941 he was using a slow recovery from measles to listen to other people's programmes and comment on them. He marvelled at what radio could do: '… hearing Joad and Gerald Barry and Julian Huxley – friendly voices in this Hale room.' He wrote about the variety and excellence of much of what he listened to, but *Battle of Britain* was the first McGivern prog- ramme he had heard and he was disappointed. 'It got going much too early, so that interest flagged half-way: the sound and technical stuff well done but the German villain dialogue very obvious and a sad lack of visual description.' But Stephen soon got to appreciate McGivern's programmes: he wrote of one of them in 1943: 'Superb. Such drive – not a British modest cough in it (my style), not an understatement – all urgent and exciting. One of the best sequences I have ever heard was the man realizing he had to plan an aircraft factory in a fortnight.' McGivern was to leave the BBC after the war to get experience of films. He returned soon after as Controller of BBC TV.

A Potter–McGivern type of programme that Stephen made in 1941 was about the Royal Armoured Corps – *The Tanks Advance*. At their Training Centre at Bovington in Dorset, Stephen's reception was hospitable and most of the first day seems to have been spent on lunch at the Grosvenor Hotel, Swanage, followed by a dinner/dance there that evening. He was glad to have a work reason for getting back to his pre-war holiday haunt and contrived to spend a further four days there. All tank-related noises were recorded, as was the talk of the men and their parade ground drills.

He even tracked down some of the crew members from the earliest tanks in World War I and recorded their voices too (now lost). The officers were keen on the idea of the broadcast and helpful; and his guide Bill Allenby put across to him '"something of the sincere and tragic grief of the cavalry at being mechanised" … he speaks of "the joy of riding at the head of a jingling troop of horse, of the slow march to the fine tune of the 11th Hussars".' With only three days to go, General Martel, who commanded the Corps, recorded his contribution:

> 30 July. Martel records himself very well – then back to lunch at the Club. He tells me plenty more details about tanks, e.g. about the necessity of not putting the carrier pigeons out of the tank with oily fingers, as otherwise they might spend half an hour perched outside the tank making a full and deliberate toilet, even under full bombardment.
>
> 1 August. Doing my usual day-before hand-over of script to Roneo. Maurice Brown is in the room, which doesn't help much. Moray asks me if I will play croquet tomorrow morning and M.B. says 'tomorrow he's got his little piece.' Perfect Brownism.
>
> 2 August (transmission day). Today I produce my Tank programme and after it as usual feel splendidly worn out, and relaxed after happy effective action. Of course next day will come the usual incredulous discovery that half the world was *not* shaken by it, but that half a dozen people thought it was 'quite nice'.
>
> After this terrific day [he had described the production, marked by the unusually large number of records of music and of sound effects that had to be fitted in with the script], at 11 o'clock we have to go through it again, with 10 minutes cut out, for Empire. Actors tired of course. Half way through this second transmission two actors stop – a cut misunderstood – and *will* not go on. I have to, and read one of their lines at random to get it going again. Drive back Ronnie pleasurably and slowly all the way to Mobberley. I haven't had a full night's sleep for a week.

Stephen not only liked tackling a new subject, but went out of his way to do so. A new production by the Sadler's Wells Ballet, *Wedding Bouquet*, was to be shown at the New Theatre in a month's time. It was a choreographed version of Gluck's *Orpheus and Eurydice*, with the solo singers participating from the wings, no chorus and two pianos standing in for the orchestra. Stephen proposed a Feature following it through from start to finish – its conception, planning, rehearsals and production. 'Laurence likes the idea and I am looking forward to that unmatchable free pass which the BBC gives into the lives of other people.' He knew little about ballet, so read it up in a paperback on his train journeys to London.

27 May 1941. I go to New Theatre to try and beard Constant Lambert [Music Director], to whom I had sent an unanswered note. Not liking to appear to be hanging about waiting for him, I slip past the box office and watch him rehearsing. I nab him by the stage door and he says: 'Come in here, if you don't mind Helpmann being naked.' Helpmann was rubbing brown make-up on his shoulders and looked rather pathetic and skinny. They seemed to like the idea: and then Ninette de Valois comes in, like a very nice, competent female don, kindly but firm, and *she* seemed to like the idea, so I walked away pleased.

28 May. After breakfast I go off to see rehearsal. Alas it seems to me (although it may be their preoccupation with the coming première) that they have somewhat cooled off. They only say a word or two to me, don't ask me to have drink or offer me a seat for the show tonight.

3 June. Lambert half an hour late for lunch at the Club. I have had two sherries to tackle him and sit looking bluer and bluer. Prog. would have gone west if he had not turned up. He does, and starts badly by smoking in lunch room (I'm not a club man) but ends up playing snooker and being well pleased by that good Beaujolais. I soon spot that he and de Valois don't … etc. 'Ashton and I work very much more *together*,' he says.

Ballet First Night was transmitted on 23 June. It is one of the few Potter programmes that can still be heard today on tape and ballet historians might be interested to hear first hand the views and discussions of de Valois, Helpmann and Lambert. The tape also contains the backchat of the Corps de Ballet: as Stephen wrote, 'the three jokes are for the males to talk caricatured pansy talk; for them to caricature the singing of the soloists; and to say how gorgeous the latest pop songs are.' The programme was more of a 'miss' than a 'hit'. It was criticised for not conveying any sense of movement on stage. More reasonably, it was suggested that it was too elitist, even for the BBC. The only other possible listening at the time it went out was a military camp concert from Wales on the Forces (by now a full scale alternative channel). 'Which would the Durham miners choose?' asked a reviewer. Criticism which Stephen was prepared to take came from McGivern:

> 15 August. Drink with McGivern, who intelligently breaks down my ballet programme, which did not (as some of my programmes do) leave him with a warm feeling. It showed the thin, pansy side of it and not the fire, e.g. of Helpmann dancing. I said it was billed and intended as backstage, but there was something in what he said and his free, simple face and sincerity made me think of the old great days with G. B. Edwards. G.B. would have started in just the same way – 'I didn't like it.' [Edwards had for many years been Stephen's literary mentor.]

Black Market and Calais

Stephen undertook two further war-related programmes before moving his family South at the end of 1941. *Black Market* was mainly about the widespread evasion of rationing and had a plea by the Minister of Food, Lord Woolton, tacked on to the end of it. For this, Stephen planned a script based on two days in court listening to trials of 'spivs'. But when he asked the Ministry of Food for help on points of fact, they sent him a complete script of their own, which he could only adapt and modify.

While *Black Market* had been frustrating, the other programme, *Calais*, was a disaster. At the time of Dunkirk, Calais was still occupied by a small British Force. The fact that it held out there, in spite of being told by Churchill that it would not be possible to send ships to take them home, was later acknowledged by the Prime Minister to have been a factor in the success of the Dunkirk evacuation. Stephen was asked to write about this saga, mainly because one of the regiments involved was the 60th, the subject of his 1939 script for *The Thin Red Line* series. The *RT* gave the programme a big build-up:

> … Stephen Potter tells, for the first time, the story of an epic that will probably go down to history as one of the greatest delaying actions of all time. Only a handful of survivors returned to this country. It is from their stories that Potter will tell his…. These men themselves do not appear. Actors take their parts, for Potter

does not believe in mixing his casts – let them be all actors, or else all people who have actually done the job.

Unfortunately Stephen seems to have too readily succumbed to the hospitality of the Regiment:

22 July. The grand dinner at Tidworth with champagne. I listen to the stories of the survivors of Calais – their heads widening and coming together, double then single. Fortunately, an orderly was taking shorthand notes.

23 July. The next morning, a slight fading of charm and helpfulness, especially when I visit the HQ of the 1st Battalion and they don't talk to me, after all getting up when I come in. Then, after a decent lunch with Major Turner, there comes a moment after the prolonged slight strain when I realize I have gone asleep between two of his sentences. Relieved to be driven off to Andover.

For whatever reason – there may have been trouble over censorship – the programme was, despite the *RT* article, postponed. Later entries show that at the end of the year he was again working on it, this time with the co-operation of his friend at the Savile, Eric Linklater. 'The fearful Calais programme' was finally transmitted on 9 December.

Chapter 7
Literary Editor

'Director of Beauty Features'

That little more than half an eyebrow had been raised at the minority appeal of *Ballet First Night* is not surprising. Before the ratings wars began, a good proportion of Home Service programmes were unashamedly highbrow, even at this most dangerous time of the war. More popular programmes may have predominated, but the schedule was also filled with classical music, high-class drama, talks and poetry. The Reithian ethos still held sway and the educative and uplifting role of the BBC had not been forgotten.

Gilliam's *forte*, as an ex-journalist, was on the propaganda side. *War Report* was his particular responsibility and took up much of his time. He wanted to delegate some of his responsibility on the artistic side. In July 1941, after working all day on the tanks programme, Stephen dined with Gilliam at the Café de Paris:

> The upshot is that he wants me to have something to do with the editing of lit. Features – literary in the widest sense – 'Director of Beauty Features'.

Stephen's appointment as Editor of Literary Features resulted from the range and number of literary programmes he had recently written and produced. Those he wrote in the second half of 1940 have already been noted. During the first half of 1941, in addition to the one on Moore's Irish songs, he had also contributed:

The Wit in Rhyme, in which he presented verse epigrams.
Changes to the Moon: an anthology reflecting changing attitudes to the moon and the way poets write about it. Stephen: 'A two-hour rehearsal

for a 15-minute programme. Ah – when I have a fine idea and can give the line myself, how enjoyable the rehearsal.'

Hate I and Hate II, selections of poems and prose motivated by hate.

William Ireland's Confessions. This was a remake of a programme by the playwright Arthur Miller for the Columbian Broadcasting Studios (CBS), which Gilliam admired, referring to it as 'that enlightened emporium'. The subject was an eighteenth century fraudster who claimed to have found various original Shakespeare manuscripts and successfully sold them. He even wrote from scratch, and managed to put on, a 'newly discovered' Shakespeare play.

True Counterfeits. A series which started in June with readings from Wordsworth and Coleridge being mixed with parodies of the same two poets, leaving the listener to guess which was which. In July Tennyson and Browning were subjected to the same treatment.

'*This will never do*'. A long-running series proposed by Stephen on contemporary criticisms of classic works. The umbrella title was taken from the first line of a review of Wordsworth's *The Excursion*. The series did not escape the last minute crises that, through lack of adequate preparation time, so often dogged his productions:

> 25 April. Another programme to be dealt with today: *This will never do*, which I find is 20 minutes, not 10. Thos. Hardy no good as a subject because the attack on *Jude* needs too much research. Must finish with a good one, so choose What They said about Ibsen, and what Mr Bernard Shaw said about Them. Message gets back from Shaw that he wants to know exactly what quotes we are using from his great attack on the anti-Ibsenites because now he doesn't agree with everything he said then.

But the programme which probably did most to persuade Gilliam that Stephen should handle the literary side of Features was *Married to a Genius*, a programme in March 1941 on the letters of Coleridge's wife to Thomas Poole, a former neighbour at Nether Stowey. Following his editorship of the Nonesuch Coleridge and his biography, *Coleridge and STC*, Stephen had become an acknowledged Coleridgean and had been told about the existence of these letters, which in 1934 he had used for another book, *Minnow among Tritons*. The letters show Mrs Coleridge (the minnow) at sea among the Lake District 'Tritons' – the Wordsworths, de Quincey and Southey. They show her lack of empathy with her husband, e.g. 'Oh! when will he give his friends anything but pain? He has been so unwise as to publish his fragments of "Christabel" and "Koula(sic)-Kahn".' Now the book was used as the basis of *Married to a Genius*, over which Stephen took a great deal of trouble:

27 February. Then to the problem of the unappetizing canteen breakfast, then to the problem of casting my Mrs Coleridge programme, which is important to me, because I want in this to try my hand at the kind of thing that might lead to a stage play. It is next Thursday and I haven't got down to it yet. Choose a cast-iron cast – and hope for inspiration at the last minute as usual. But the comparative failure of Everest – best of subjects – rather hangs on my neck like a cold weight, damping down my invention.

The programme was transmitted on 6 March and was widely praised – particularly by the critics that mattered, that is by his wife at home that evening and by Mary Allen and the entire Features section at a debriefing meeting the next day, Archie Harding saying what an excellent thing it was that such a programme should be done in wartime. Herbert Farjeon (reviewing a later revival) urged Stephen to make a stage play of it – but he never did, probably because 'Priestley later tells me it would *not* make a play – no movement, unsympathetic central character.' The (unnamed) radio critic of *Penguin New Writing*, following a 1946 revival, wrote this:

… nothing is so easy to kill as the distinguished dead. Subtler writers and producers have realized this; the method they have evolved is rather to seize on one incident, person or story, and to treat it in such a way that it illuminates and comments upon a whole age, movement or branch of knowledge. The most brilliant example is Stephen Potter's programme. Ostensibly no more than a few incidents from the life of Mrs Sara Coleridge, it turns out to be one of the most sensitive and penetrating comments ever written on the particular mental climate of the Lake Poets, a work of scholarship, entertainment, and wit.

After *Married to a Genius* and the earlier successes of *Victorian Negative* and *Shakespeare Discovery*, Gilliam was inclined to let Stephen get on with his own literary programmes and did not interfere except to give his invaluable support, even when things went wrong. He sometimes called him 'LitPot', after Stephen's critique of the teaching of 'Eng. Lit.' at universities in *The Muse in Chains*.

Stephen now had more to worry about than just his own programmes. In a continuation of his entry on his appointment as Literary Editor he wrote:

The chief immediate object seems to be to help decide whether or not to have Stephen Spender at a B salary on temporary staff as a script writer. Neither Laurence nor me (I am still withered by his sneer when, three years ago, I said I liked Edith Sitwell) like the way he is coming in, meeting Ogilvie at dinner and saying he longs to work for the BBC – an interest that has not shown itself before.

Spender had earlier been sounded out at the Club:

4 June. Stephen Spender comes to lunch with Val and Laurence. He at 32 seems rather like a more effective and better-looking me. He is being at his best and started by saying he had years ago reviewed *The Young Man* [an early Potter novel] in the *Cherwell* – and liked it. He answers clearly; and has keenly expressed ideas – which inevitably many others have had before: how difficult to think of a *new* scheme for radio. At such key Savile lunches, it is sometimes necessary to keep in the background my dear Uncle Willie, who comes forward with one of his confidently voiced (really nervous) round remarks about the war.

He was taken on:

17 July. Preparing suggestions for Lit. programmes before going to see Laurence and having lunch at the Etoile. I spend the rest of the day explaining to Stephen Spender where his scripts are lacking. He is a nice clever charming sensitive sort of chap and he seems to take my suggestions pretty well. Will he and MacNeice and these young ones pillory me in some famous diary one day? I can't help wondering.

Curiously, Spender omits his time with the BBC from his autobiographical works. *World within Worlds* finishes just before the war starts and *European Witness* and *Journals* both start just after the war ended.

Was it the war years he did not want to write about, or was it his broad-casting work? According to Humphrey Carpenter, in his book about the Third Programme, Virginia Woolf had told Spender in the late thirties never to join the BBC.

In his new capacity, Stephen now also begins to see more of Louis MacNeice:

25 July. Spend rest of evening with Laurence and Louis MacNeice, in light fawn. He has good ideas and a clear head. I am launching this literary drive and am supposed to be getting in good new authors. But is my heart in it? Should I swamp my tender little efforts with tough newcomers? Feel a little low.
15 August. To Café Royal, where are Laurence and MacNeice. Laurence, when MacNeice is gone, apropos of the astonishing affair of Jack and Louis M. upsetting the Navy, says that he has a curious faculty of causing tension, working it up to the verge of a row, and then mysteriously passing away and seeming not to be of it. I think I saw this even tonight – one of those fearful lidded glances of his. It was when he brought up a very pretty girl and I sat enviously *vis-à-vis* her for some time, feeling that I had passed out of pretty-girl-land for good.

Describing another night-clubbing evening, Stephen wrote of MacNeice: '... he looks smouldering with internal comment and tends to dry off any exuberance that I may have.' He never felt easy in his company. In a long entry (September 1942) about the excellence of Evelyn Waugh's latest novel, *Put out more Flags*, he compares MacNeice to Parsnip and Pimpernel, two characters in the book who had escaped to America:

How nice to have that gloomy apprehensive weight of Parsnip and Pimpernelism lifted and the need for respecting it questioned. To me MacNeice has just the same lordly superciliousness and spiritual swank. Think of Keats. Surely there was no trace of P. & Pism about him.
[Stephen fails to mention that MacNeice had chosen to return to the UK in May 1940, the most dangerous time of the war.]

Another aspect of Stephen's new role was that scripts would be sent to him in the hope that they would be broadcast. He records that on

15 September 'Eric Linklater after lunch suggests he sends me his Dialogue about War Aims, set in the Elysian Fields, with a British Tommy coming in at the last moment. The whole thing is a perfect description of the least likely of all programmes that anyone would possibly accept.' However, Gielgud was keen on the idea and this premature dismissal of Linklater's work by Stephen led to its being produced by Drama rather than Features. The dialogues were adapted by Edward Sackville-West and broadcast as *Cornerstones* on 15 March 1942. Plato, Aristotle, Confucius and suchlike, including a contemporary airman, met in the Elysian Fields, discussed War Aims and sought agreement on good reasons for fighting Hitler. Gielgud, who himself produced the programme, thought so highly of it that he tried to persuade the army to give Linklater extended leave (he was a captain in the Royal Engineers) so that he could write more radio scripts. This was not granted, but he was posted to the Army's Directorate of Public Relations, who allowed him to write, from his home in The Orkneys, similar propaganda scripts, such as *Socrates asks Why*.

Eric Linklater

An indifferent climate

Stephen was an ideas man, not an organisation man. Departmental responsibilities remained a sideline, while he continued to come up with a stream
of new ideas for programmes. His enthusiasm for radio contrasted with the
lack of it among the intelligentsia and he felt bitter about the indifference
of his fellow Club members. A major production in which he was not
involved, but which he admired, was the serialisation in drama form of
War and Peace. It was at the time that the German armies had nearly reached
Moscow and the parallels with Napoleon were obvious. Compromises
were not made and once a week, on the same day, two one-hour episodes
were broadcast, from 3.30 to 4.30 and from 9.30 to 10.30. Gielgud said it
was either a splendid failure or a not unqualified success, attributing any
shortcomings to lack of rehearsal time, the multiplicity of characters and
the fact that the whole epic had to be rehearsed and broadcast from the still
unbombed Monseigneur News Theatre. Stephen felt that the BBC deserved
praise for its courageous attempt. 'If only the BBC had been smaller,' he
wrote, 'everyone would be saying "how plucky".' Yet Ralph Richardson, a
regular squash opponent, told him in the changing room that the BBC
doing *War and Peace* was like a barnacle trying to win the Blue Riband
by attaching itself to the bottom of the Queen Mary.

Reaction to radio among the critics was still minimal and what galled
Stephen was the lack of serious discussion, rather than adverse comments.
However, there were a few openly anti critics. Evelyn Waugh sneered at 'the
radio-ridden villas of the Sussex coast' and even as late as 1963 Cyril Connolly wrote in his obituary of Louis MacNeice '… it is a pity he wasted so
much of his time and talent on radio.' An Oxford professor had told Stephen
with pride that he had 'never listened to the wireless'. One Club member
'wished radio had never been invented – wished it was under the sea'.

This surprised Stephen, as he himself marvelled at what it could do.
On a sunny January day in his next home in Essex, where he had been
gardening and listening outdoors, he wrote: 'Beethoven piano sonata,
Mozart piano concerto, *War and Peace, Brains Trust* [experts such as Joad
and Huxley discussed questions from listeners] – O marvellous Radio.
Why doesn't someone say that, firmly?' There are many tirades in his
diaries against the negative cynics:

Last week there were one or two of the usual cracks against BBC –
it is depressing for us, not because we feel criticism is unjustified,

but because it seems to us that intelligent people do not do justice to themselves in producing stuff which to name 'criticism' would be to pay it an extravagant compliment. There was the Parliamentary comment that *Murder in the Red Barn* was bad for wartime because shocking tragedy was depressing (it was of course a burlesque melodrama). Stale old bromides about 'the emasculated announcer's voice' (complaints made, curiously enough, very often by people whose own voices would not be allowed on the air for two minutes). Complaints made about the absence of good music by people who on questioning are discovered not to have known that yesterday x was played, or the day before the first performance of y, at enormous expense.

He also defended the medium in public. One of his articles in the *RT*, in August 1943, begins:

'I'm afraid I never listen': those will be the last dying words, I believe, of the last dying Bloomsbury intellectual, superior to the end – Bloomsbury intelligentsia, as we used to call them. The Superior Man of contemporary London still repeats it: 'I'm afraid I never listen to radio.'
The Superior Man, of course, cares passionately for the arts. He lives by them. Music and poetry are his meat and bread. A week ago, I was producing a programme of French poetry and music. The programme was planned by Edward Sackville-West, the poems were chosen and described by Raymond Mortimer, the music was arranged, played and sung by Lennox Berkeley, Benjamin Britten, and Peter Pears; the poems were read in French, and then in translation by Valentine Dyall, one of the best for broadcast verse, and Peggy Ashcroft, perhaps the best verse reader of all.
I couldn't help reflecting how firmly and at what intense personal inconvenience my superior friend would have gone, say, to the Apollo League of Verse Rooms, Lisson Alley, for the chance of enjoying poetry and music chosen and rendered by such specialists and such connoisseurs' men as these. He would positively enjoy the stuffiness and the semi-inaudibiity of the back row at Lisson Alley. But sit in his own armchair, turn the knob, and hear the progamme broadcast – hear it effortlessly and in perfect conditions – never, never, never.

The reason is of course that our friend is a highbrow – the miserable word has to come in at last. Minority programmes, we always hope, are not meant for highbrows. The highbrow listens to the correct thing in the correct manner. Minority programmes do not cater for this. They cater for the discriminating listener, who wants the best.

Stephen's dislike of any suggestion that he was himself a highbrow stemmed partly from the unusual height of his forehead – see cartoon by Low. More seriously, he was proud of making such music and poetry more widely accessible. He welcomed suggestions that he was popularising the arts and over the next few years redoubled his efforts in that direction.

Stephen Potter

Low

Stephen was now a fully committed radio man, vigorously defending it in private and in public. Moreover he had decided – at least during this period – that he was better as a writer/producer than he was as an author of books:

10 September 1941. I should hate to be judged by my published books. I really think I am better than them. Some extraordinarily debunking, ungenerous person seems to appear as the author, who seems to be intellectually agile and observant but whom I do not like. I could write a splendid damning review of my books. Better in radio scripts.

Feature Soaps

Any proposal with a recurring format was usually welcome to the planners, faced as they were with the nightmare of scheduling programmes from 6 am to midnight every day of the year. *Mrs Dale's Diary* and later *The Archers* were ideal. For Features, other kinds of long-running series had to be found. One that had the additional merit of roping in stand-offish contributors was Mary Allen's *And so to Bed*. It not only occupied the five minutes leading up to the midnight news on five nights out of seven for fourteen consecutive weeks, but also brought to the microphone a succession of distinguished readers, very often from the Arts, each presenting their own favourite bit of bedtime reading. Another successful series was *Famous Meetings* by the poet Robert Gittings, who, like MacNeice, did not hesitate to write some of his best work for radio. The *Meetings* were imaginary reconstructions of what might have been said when, for example, Wellington met Nelson or when Stanley met Livingstone. Gittings had originally been taken on as an assistant for Stephen, who thought so highly of his script for the first in the series – *When Tennyson met Garibaldi* (they met at Tennyson's home on The Isle of Wight) – that he asked to produce it. He insisted that Tennyson should speak with the same Lincolnshire accent as was detectable when the poet recorded *The Charge of the Light Brigade* on cylinder.

As has been seen, Stephen had himself already come up with a number of series, such as *True Counterfeits* and *This will never do*. His two suggestions now were *Contemporary Portraits* and *New Judgments*. Both were hampered from the start by the hesitancy to accept radio as a worthwhile medium. One needed major modification after only three programmes; the other eventually became successful and outran Stephen's departure from the BBC in 1948.

Contemporary Portraits

Stephen took great care over his proposal for this series, checking it with Priestley before submitting it. If approved, he would enjoy working on it: he would be writing, producing and presenting the programmes and he would first be interviewing in depth his selection of the best contemporary poets, scientists, industrialists, or whatever – no sphere was barred. Here are extracts from his memo:

OUTLINE OF SUGGESTIONS FOR 'LITERARY FEATURES'
(Programmes which are neither directly propaganda
nor immediately concerned with the war)

18th August 1941

1. AUTOBIOGRAPHIES. For a long time there have been literary programmes dealing with the biographies of great men, great Englishmen of the past, particularly famous users of the English

language. Since the war these programmes have taken an important position on the ground that they remind us of our inheritance.

The merits of the past, in fact, have been emphasised at the expense of the vitality of the present…. The implication in 'heritage' prog-rammes is that we are fighting to preserve a tradition of past achievement, not a means of keeping the paths of expression free for the leaders of the present and the future.

I now propose biographies of the present – a series in which the lives of eminent contemporaries are re-enacted.

Treatment   If possible, the men or women chosen should … be capable of doing their own narration. Scenes should be made up less of personal recollections … more of reconstructions of stages in development, escapes from convention, intellectual crises, or the receiving of new influence.

Reaction to this memo was slow:

22 August. Laurence tells me he felt absolutely sick last night 'because of C(P)'s carefulness and nervousness about my autobiography suggestions'. There might be objections … political … keep it to popular microphone figures. But the slightest adulteration of my conception in the direction of anecdote will take from it its one good quality. I am somewhat damped by this yet a little exhilarated, as I am sure that by doing this I am doing something against what is worst in the BBC – the element often present of cheap facetiousness or cheap seriousness.

26 August. In London. Called up by Laurence to attend a meeting on autobiographies. I arrive but am crowded out and there is a great deal of waiting. Gielgud keeping me down a little. Then in evening hanging about while Laurence sees C(P), but C(P) doesn't want to see me. Has seen my memo. As usual, no contact with big 4. Contrast with so many jobs. My programme agreed with reservations. Am rather beginning to lose interest.

10 September. Laurence says autobiographies are OK'd by the Board. Ogilvie likes the idea. C(P) very cagey.

The series having been approved, Stephen had to look for suitable subjects. In his proposal he had suggested names from many fields and under 'Authors' had written airily that a choice might be made from

Shaw, Wells, Priestley and Compton Mackenzie. The possibility of a programme on either of the last two is not mentioned again in the diaries and Wells (although a member of the Savile!) had refused outright. With the 85-year-old Shaw, he had already made the first approach before the series was approved. Shaw was staying at Cliveden, the home of the Astors, and Joyce Grenfell lived in a cottage on the estate of her aunt, Lady Astor:

> 21 August. Ring Joyce Grenfell this morning, and get through in five minutes. She always frightens me a little – so clear and confident, without any diffusing barrier of cigarette smoke or drink to make the fearful contact of two personalities more bearable by buffering. The best happened. Shaw was to have come to tea today. She will get him to come tomorrow instead.
>
> 22 August. I catch 4 o'clock Paddington to Taplow, taxi to Joyce, where I have memorable tea with Joyce and Mr and Mrs G.B.S., which resulted in the attached signed photo. And then walk, first with him and then with Joyce, through Cliveden.

No photograph is stuck in the diary and there is no further record of the tea and walk with Shaw. Three days later he writes that 'Shaw is not oncoming' and later still he wished 'Shaw wasn't so implacably closed down against *personal* encouragement of radio.' The immediate reason for his non-co-operation was only revealed in Joyce's 1976 autobiography *Joyce Grenfell requests the Pleasure*. She had written to her mother: 'G.B.S. won't do the programme because he says he is too old, which, being translated, means his teeth don't fit and make rude noises that would be particularly exaggerated on the air and his vanity won't stand for such a thing.'

Another preliminary approach had been made to Julian Huxley, Secretary of the Zoological Society, on the back of discussions about a programme on the Zoo:

> 15 August. I go and see Julian Huxley at the zoo. Huxley's dry, yellow skin, sudden movements, mixed with relaxed bearing, and peaked eyebrows make him look like Mephistopheles played by an amateur actor. But although he was impatient at first and inclined to tell me shortly that A was different from B, in the manner of Joad addressing one of his mistresses, I leave him escorting me down the stairs and roaring with laughter at one of his own funny stories. Upshot – I'll try and get a talk for him in September, and have a full-length

zoo documentary in April; but, more important, my 'autobiography' idea is caught onto … he suggests as better than himself A. V. Hill [physiologist], saying why. Then makes additional suggestion that there are people like himself who are more or less humble reservoirs of inherited talent and he could for example talk about T. H. Huxley [his grandfather] and his memories of him. A good idea.

By 25 September 1941 Stephen was beginning to worry about the '… appalling lack of someone to start the *Contemporary Portraits* series.' He had arranged an interview with Mrs Sydney (Beatrice) Webb, but in a later entry on the same day he wrote:

Hear in the evening from Val that Mrs Sydney Webb 'is out'. This news stuns me. Not only disappointment – but my feeling of working for an organisation, never strong, nonetheless exists. And to despise the organisation makes me gloomy. Apparently the reason given is that she could be too political. Which means, of course, that *they* are too political. This near-saint, and great woman, who should be approached hat in hand by the whole committee is 'out'. Nevertheless I shall go and see her tomorrow, with the gloomiest feelings.

Extracts from Stephen's long account of his visit are quoted below, as they show very clearly what it was that the BBC was worried about – as well as showing the sort of lady she was and what sort of programme it would have been:

26 September. Down to visit the Webbs at Passfield Corner, Liphook. Mrs Webb was sitting at the end of the drive to meet me. She showed me in to wash, which I took time over, putting off the little ordeal (it wasn't, because talk was very easy). A low, comfortable but unobtrusive house in a comfortable but unobtrusive acreage and lots of very well cared for veg. for vegetarians. 'Here is an example,' it seemed to say, 'of the standard of life of the future. Here are optimum requirements for everybody.' Then in to tea and in comes, with rather tiny, old man steps (in sharp contrast to Mrs Webb's thin, easy, elbow-clutching stride) the Other One….
Mrs Webb talked readily about everything. 'Some other woman should be chosen … an actress … I am not dramatic enough … nothing about feelings in what I do, it is all thought. Not theory,

however, but the application of the principle of empiricism. I was the first person to study sociological problems at first hand. Going round the sweat shops. See for yourself. Objective. That of course is what I should want to do. I should want (laugh here, and very clear voice) to point the moral – of Russia, for example. A great example because, unlike what unsympathetic critics say of him, Lenin was always altering if the thing didn't work. Stalin's purge was necessary. No fifth column left – those generals were all pro German.'
'Shaw ought to do one of your programmes.' (I was not candid enough to tell her he had more or less refused.) 'He is much more of a figure: I should be so boring.' She showed me their books, all modern-looking, including Local Government in Japanese. Lenin translated the Webb books and she explained to me exactly to what extent he had incorporated which ideas of hers in the régime.
She seemed all kindness and openness yet anxious to maintain her purely *scientific* nature. In the end, she talked about her diary, how she did a lot of it, how it couldn't be published in her lifetime, how she had left it to the London School of Economics and how she depended on it, used it as a confessional, agreed with me that it took the sting out of the cause of a 'pillow-bite' because one became absolved in the act of re-creating it.

Further worry about the lack of suitable subjects followed: 'My literary programmes are folding up on me – owing to *my* inactivity and discouragement. A crisis is approaching.' However, there were to be three programmes in the mould he had proposed and the first featured Lord Nuffield, originator of Morris cars, whose first business, making bicycles, had been founded with capital backing of only £4. Here are extracts from Stephen's exploratory meeting with him:

29 October. Today I spend the morning with Lord Nuffield. I am bowled over by his informality and unbossiness, easiness, quietness and humour. And above all, his readiness to speak on anything. He hates anyone thinking he owes anything to luck. He is off to see 'Beavercrook – beg pardon, Beaverbrook. Will Churchill never see that he is out for publicity? But I suppose Churchill has to keep the right side of the press. I've worked for everything … never let up … I wouldn't do it again. When you've got something, you no longer want it.' How did he become a mechanic? 'Just grew … always was …

bikes into motors … everybody did it. I was asked if I would take over *x* and make Spitfires … at first I said no, but then Beaverbrook called me: did I realize Churchill had asked for me? Yes. Would I do it for the country? Well, that cut the ground … that did me. So I got it going. And then when just ready for production, Could Sir C. Craven of Vickers come and look? Yes. He came – at 4 o'clock, two hours late. Then I am asked: Would I hand it over to Craven, for the good of the country? Well yes, for the second time, I would. When he went round the factory he obviously didn't know the difference between a saw and a screwdriver (in fact he used two more technical terms). Nobody gets right how much I have given away. The figures are actually published – it's £15,000,000.' He has no sign of wealth – no wonderful quality cigarette case. Only 2 or 3 pounds in his notecase. Charming smile. Likes it, and laughs when I tell him he's 'under my orders' in the BBC. I order a drink – he suggests gin and light sherry.

In the afternoon of 13 November, between an interview with the Poet Laureate and visit to his old college Merton in the morning, and an interview with Lord David Cecil for *New Judgments* in the evening, Stephen squeezed in a visit to the car factory:

Thence to Cowley works, forbidding and vast and low in the rain. First, the little dentist's waiting room in the office block, with the famous names in the visitors' book. Then Mr Hobbs's office, so grand that there was nothing on the desk, only at the side a huge instrument which I attempt to be knowledgable about expecting it to be a wireless, but it turns out to be an air-conditioner. All goes swimmingly: we seem to be in agreement about what is dramatisable.

The programme was broadcast on 22 January 1942 but no record of it survives: it would be interesting to know how much of Lord Nuffield's resentment at being elbowed out of Spitfire production was left in the script.

The series had been launched in the *RT* in the issue of 16 January. Laurence Gilliam wrote: 'Stephen Potter will produce a series of radiobiographies, starting on Thursday. His programmes will do for Britain's present heritage what has already been done by this same producer for its past. Here are our Leonardos, our Telfords of today.' The same article suggested that among those to be featured in this way, after Nuffield, would be

David Low, Edith Evans, Paul Nash, Dobson (the sculptor), Lutyens and Masefield; but this turned out to be over-optimistic. Shortly after this *RT* puff, Stephen had taken a Mr Baber Smith with him to see Lutyens: 'In spite of B.S.'s good looks, taste, knowledge of architecture and respectful good manners, Lutyens is out of the series. He begins (apropos of Nuffield): "do you want *my* life to slow music? It'd bore me, make me absurd. Besides, I can't talk."' Nash too had been unresponsive. A review of the Nuffield programme made matters worse by forecasting a Portrait of Lawrence of Arabia – an almost certain non-starter. Other reactions had been muted. 'Nuffield pleased, and so on. But no real come-back. After all my attempts with these programmes, I see a memo from C(P) damning them with faint praise – and no reference to the paraphernalia of tact and awkward engineering and breaking of new ground entailed. Beat away at the stone wall, I suppose. Worry No. 1 is the difficulty, so close, of my Masefield programme.'

The Laureate's initial response had been positive, but when Stephen first drove down to his Dorset home in November, he found that Masefield was hesitant to talk about himself, insisting that the main part of his life had been too ordinary. He had, however, gone to sea (orphaned) at the age of sixteen and had worked in a carpet factory. These episodes he remembered clearly and would be less reluctant to recall them on the air. During a second visit, in February 1942, Masefield was still doubtful. 'Am I going to write about other bits of my life? At present they are locked up somewhere in my head. Maybe I shall draw on them.' Later he did, with *So long to Learn* in 1952 and *Grace before Ploughing* in 1966. Meanwhile he agreed that Stephen should go ahead with a script and the programme was scheduled for later in the month.

By the date of the next entry the Masefield programme was already billed on the front cover of the *RT*:

11 February. Today, in the middle of dictating my Masefield script, which I am to show him tomorrow at Burcote Bridge, the blow falls. I had pleaded against doing the Masefield programme so soon after Nuffield – but too late. The schedule couldn't be altered. Now he writes to say he won't do it in this short time. He seems to have misunderstood the date. Well – I sat stupefied for a time, with visions of a major loss of name and feeling that my little 'Lit. Department' was toppling. Feel like a maid having dropped a valuable vase. Where is Laurence? I appal him with suicide face. But he rose nobly to my assistance. Smoothed ways and found a substitute.

Masefield had not ruled out a later broadcast and Stephen went ahead with his draft script, sending it to Burcote Bridge for approval. On 25 February, Masefield turned this down.

26 February. In afternoon I reply to Masefield and show my letter to Laurence. He laughs. 'Written,' he said 'as if I was fingering the pistol by my pillow.'

As Heppenstall was to write later, 'Gilliam would always stand by any member of his department who had got himself into momentary trouble … would take everything on his own shoulders, which were broad.' Stephen was not so sure about Gielgud:

27 March. This morning's Feature meeting a bit of a Waterloo for me. Difficult to beat Val's technique to keep himself irretrievably up…. After complimenting MacNeice and Speaight, a series of slighting remarks on the Failure of *Contemporary Portraits* and the necessity of getting new names…. C(P) wants to strangle it … telling me what to do about it *at the meeting*. Above all, enlisting Speaight and MacNeice on his side.

Even before this meeting, Stephen had written: 'Decide to shelve *Contemporary Portraits* for the time being. Enough of knowing and meeting the great – now is the time *I* must do something.' But this was premature: by April he had recovered from the shock and was working all out on a *Contemporary Portrait* of David Low, the left-wing cartoonist employed by Beaverbrook on the *Evening Standard* and the inventor of the reactionary Colonel Blimp, usually depicted in a Turkish bath, fulminating against some new regulation. An exploratory meeting had already been held at the Savile Club the previous autumn:

23 September 1941. … his strong NZ accent makes him easy to get on with. 'I don't get up and flame out of the room at the idea … I'm not one who won't speak in the programme unless the Archbishop of York is billed in smaller letters…. I'm flattered, of course, but I don't get excited any more if an old lady in the bus whispers "that's Low".'

The broadcast was on 24th April. It was a model of what Stephen had intended for the series, showing how Low had come to be a cartoonist in the first place (at the age of 12 he had had a contract with *The Christchurch Spectator* to produce two cartoons a week) and going on to describe how he set about his cartoons. He told Stephen beforehand how some were easier to do than others: 'I have done Joad. He is a wonderful man to do because he caricatures himself – you can even hear him doing so when he speaks on the air. But I have to *make* the caricature of these wooden-headed, vegetable politicians....' He talked about the sources of his political beliefs. Stephen was struck by his extreme seriousness and his belief in the possibilities of his profession for good and evil – 'a conviction held, of course, with perfect simplicity and modesty.'

Low and Lord Nuffield did not constitute the string of glittering names that Stephen had wanted and at this point Stephen gave up. There was, however, to be one more. Sir Compton Mackenzie, it will be remembered, was one of the four literary figures that Stephen had originally proposed for the series. 'Monty' was a notable raconteur at the Savile Club when he was in London, but most of the year lived in Barra, an outer island of the Outer Hebrides. He had never joined in the chorus of sniping remarks about the BBC. On the contrary, he had declared in 1929 that 'radio gives the artist the greatest opportunity since Homer to express himself without mechanical barriers.' In 1942 Monty came South for ten days and had carried out, in the words of Tom Harrison (now radio critic of *The Observer*), 'a one-man commando raid on Broadcasting House. Within six hours last Sunday he had three different programmes on the air (and three more during the week) – surely a record?' One of these was a *Contemporary Portrait*, not of himself but of his sister, Fay Compton.

The programme went out on 31 May, with Monty playing the part of Monty and Fay that of Fay. Stephen was an immense admirer of her act-ing but had some difficulties during the final rehearsal and transmission: 'Monty's cold and his tendency to slow up. Fay sticks up for him instantly if I criticise. Monty also tries to edge in for himself, with anecdotes, more than is written. After it's all over – nothing since a quick lunch – I haven't enough money for the kind of restaurant that stays open 10–10.30 – to bed without supper. That'd surprise Fay.' Monty dealt with the occasion at length in *Octave 8*, the eighth volume of his autobiography:

This was composed and directed by Stephen Potter.... I have never understood why the film people did not bring him in as a film director. He would have been in the top rank and his gamesman-ship would have been too skilful for the most difficult star to resist.

Half way through, we were three minutes behind. Stephen speeded us up so that we finished exactly on time. The composition and direction were so good…. Of course, Fay and I both knew our job with a microphone, but to do that job one must have the material and that is what Stephen Potter provided.

This salve came later. Tom Harrison's review provided more immediate compensation for the hard work and lost dinner and usefully describes Stephen's techniques:

Feature programmes of this sort can be terrible and lend themselves to mutual boosting matches. This one was romantic without being artificial, emotional without being fulsome; alive. Potter loves to use the snatches of overheard talk, the small incidents of everyday life (the little girl Fay spitting on a visitor over the bannisters), building from selected trivia a pyramid of moods. He is not afraid to be occasionally obscure. It is a mistake to think that in radio everything has to be complete, comprehensive, and serially co-ordinated. The Potter programme succeeds, just as the Brains Trust succeeds in another way, by being informal, diffuse, random, while working within a comprehensible framework…. Some years ago Stephen Potter wrote a book called *The Muse in Chains*, attacking the unimaginative teaching in schools and universities. He has done much to loosen some of these chains by giving to the wide public, over a period of years, an imaginative form of radio literature. It is well we should recognize that in this he is doing something as truly creative and original as the poet or novelist.

That was the end of *Contemporary Portraits* – killed for the want of famous people willing to be spotlighted. However, the idea was to crop up again in a new, net-widening form. Describing the plans of his department for the coming season, Gilliam wrote on 21 August 1942 in the *RT*:

Stephen Potter is responsible for several interesting experiments, and in all of them the contemporary note is starred. The series 'Contemporary Portraits' is giving way temporarily to a succession of 'Professional Portraits', in which a doctor, a lawyer, a miner, a seaman and an industrialist reveal the fabric of their lives.

New Judgments

'Eminent contemporaries on their classical prototypes' was how Stephen described them. Writing about this new series in *The Listener*, he said 'The discriminating listener does not care for two columns of the Encyclopaedia Britannica set to music and put into dialogue to celebrate the bi-centenary of a minor poet laureate. In place of that old recipe they want a new one – an assessment by someone they can respect.' Although conceived, edited and produced by Stephen, contributors were being asked to write their own scripts and to present the broadcasts themselves. Possibly this is why he had less difficulty in finding participants. Whatever the reason, the formula worked and after a sticky start, *New Judgments* ran for many years.

The first in the series was by the recently recruited Stephen Spender and his subject was Walt Whitman (also a paragon for Stephen Potter):

15 October 1941. In morning, read Spender script on Whitman, which I have scarcely dared to do before because of agony that it might be bad and my first programme of the series be a flop. But I see a way in which it might be done – Spender's sane, emancipated attitude plus rather pansy voice might make an interesting presentation of the old by the new.

27 October. Spender in a fireman's suit, looking bold and fine. He slightly antagonises me by his confident assumption of poethood, but Link [Eric Linklater] says later this is all right and necessary. Spender agrees to everything I say about the script – no help. Talks extremely well about Whitman in the library but falls short on the acceptance of the 'true' Whitman. He thinks of W's sordid affairs with bricklayers round dim backyards, or his dope-taking, as some kind of 'clue'.

Whitman was broadcast on 2 November. The second 're-assessment' got bogged down. The presenter was to be Max Beerbohm, with whom Stephen had once had dinner when working as Henry Arthur Jones's secretary. Beerbohm's initial response had been encouraging. After some gallant words about their earlier meeting, he wrote: 'As to the BBC proposal, I have never fancied myself much as a critic of writing; I have always preferred myself as a discourser on things in general. But I think I might be able to be rather good on the subject of Lytton Strachey. I regard him as technically the best handler of the art of English prose in modern times. If the BBC would like me to speak about him, how much would they offer as a fee? Everything depends on that.' Beerbohm then invited Stephen to lunch with him and his wife at his home near Dorking:

11 November. A lovely heart-of-autumn sunny day. Bus to Dorking, cab, then walk second part of way to Abinger Church. Feel nervous and unwilling to enter the Beerbohm cottage. Must keep my eyes open. Have stiff drink at pub the other side of the church. Max receives me, opening the door. Lovely autumn woods outside.
His clothes: fawn suit, perfect spats, delicate green-stone ring. All clothes seem as if suspended from a coat-hanger, which takes the weight off his tapering legs. Lady B. has a nice quiet common sense presence. Easy, long talk (till 4.30), and just enough drink to keep right but not soporific. The main object of my visit fails. Music, he says, is so much more beautiful than the human voice – 'and how can I stand up to it if some of those angelic voices come in?' His line – the most mocking modesty.
He talks of the Abinger set and its members (R. C. Trevelyan, E. M. Forster). Of his cartoons: 'I never draw from life, only from memory. When I found they were becoming kindly, I knew that was the finish. But he shows me the Abinger magazine, with a good one of R. C. Trevelyan as the Scholar Poet, with knapsack and boots like tea-cosies. Says that he has also been asked by Talks to do something about eating and drinking. Seems he would prefer that to the Lytton Strachey.

Mary Allen had also failed to get Beerbohm for *And so to Bed*; and he had turned her down in a similarly fey manner. 'I myself am always in bed before midnight and shouldn't care to be out of it, even for a more than "nominal fee".'
As a substitute, Stephen now approached the critic James Agate, an authority on Hazlitt. He enviously compared his own modest output with that of Agate, who with his annually published diary (*Ego*) and a stream of reviews and articles seemed able to produce up to half a million words a year. Discussions began well on 14 November with lunch at the Ivy – one of those places like the Café de Paris or the Midland in Manchester where everyone seemed to know everyone else. ('Lilian Braithwaite comes in and Agate pops up twice to talk to her.') A *New Judgment* on Hazlitt was agreed in principle, but later Agate queried Stephen's ability to write the

dramatised sections. He withheld his agreement to letting him do so until the last possible minute, leaving Stephen to write those sections overnight. The programme went out on 7 December, to a lukewarm reception.

Stickiest of all was Philip Guedalla, the irreverent biographer of Palmerston and Wellington, whom Stephen asked to re-assess Froude.

21 October. Call on Guedalla at British Council. Will he do a literary programme? He is charming and wittily voluble, with a smart red rosebud in his buttonhole. And how about a programme on Churchill's life? [he had just produced a biography, *Mr Churchill*]. His comments: 'You won't want it too Johnsonoid?' and 'Padding about in a bowler hat – I think Churchill is modelling himself on Churchill for that.'

16 December. Lunch with Gittings and Guedalla, talking about Froude. Delicate stream of his conversation plays over it all. Amusing story I shall tell about this series later on – getting these eminences to do Features. How I have to sell it to them – not quite believing in it.

2 January 1942. A grand start to new year's work: a phone message that Guedalla has been ringing everybody up from the DG downwards to say that he won't broadcast at time allotted (10.38 pm on Jan 11). I ring him and he says firmly that he won't. Agate had the earlier time. I write a firm letter saying that the time can't be altered, that it would muck up the *RT*, etc.

3 January. Guedalla gets me to phone him – says he will do it if there is a guaranteed repeat. After consultation with C(P) via Laurence, I am commissioned to say we can't give him a *guaranteed* repeat.

5 January. Guedalla rings up to say 'this doesn't really take us any further, it seems to me' … and I see from his tone that a little buttering up and talking round will probably do it, so I go and see him ('anything to get your programme')…. All is fixed. We then find, after all, that by some lunatic mistake the *RT* has printed Cecil on Cowper [the *next New Judgment*] as coming at Guedalla's time.

11 January. Lunch Guedalla, and then start rehearsing for his programme. Guedalla's manner is pleasantly acid. Between rehearsals he stands me dinner at the Ritz. Goodish wine, but he cancels order for brandy because we were (only fairly) in a hurry. Programme meticulously timed by me, but closing credits did not go

out, as they were cut by a fatuous announcement giving advice on how to walk in the blackout. This programme has been dogged by misfortunes.

Thereafter things went better. In 1942 and 1943 alone twenty more *New Judgments* were broadcast. Stephen was overall editor. He produced most of them himself, while the remainder were put in the hands of other producers, including Bridson, Mary Allen and Gielgud himself. Stephen was pleased that the series had succeeded in bringing in established writers, such as Elizabeth Bowen (on Jane Austin) and Raymond Mortimer – arch-intellectual literary editor of *The New Statesman and Nation* – on Fanny Burney. Celia Johnson was cast for the latter programme and it was the first time Stephen had heard of her. He did not recognize her potential:

15 June 1942. … tall girl in glasses, good stage face. Read through very well but didn't impress. Too much nice old mum about her. A rasp-deep understanding note in her voice – altogether too 'nice' – wish I had got Athene Seyler.

Thomas Arnold, headmaster of Rugby, had died 100 years ago and Stephen asked J. T. Christie, headmaster of Westminster where one of his sons was at school, to do a re-assessment:

9 January 1942. Lunch at Club with Christie. A great talker, with the loose mouth of a parson, though not parsonish in talk. Has right ideas about his part in the programme. All goes well except that when he says 'I must go after this cigarette' I leap up with just 7% too much alacrity to cut in for the next snooker four.

Not content just to recruit re-assessors of a high standard, Stephen worried that they did not always give of their best. In an August 1943 article, Stephen wrote about *New Judgments* as follows:

The difficulty here has been that the contemporarily eminent tend to take radio too easily, as a thing anybody can do. Exciting exceptions to this rule have been Victor Pritchett, Lord David Cecil, Francis Meynell and Elizabeth Bowen – all of them discoveries for broadcasting.

Stephen was implicitly disparaging the efforts of the rest, among whom were James Bridie (on J. M. Barrie), Edith Evans (on Mrs Siddons), Professor Joad (on Socrates), and Rosamond Lehmann (on George Eliot).

If these presenters did not take their scripts seriously enough, at least Stephen was no longer able to complain about unwillingness to take part at all. Some even suggested themselves:

> 21 January 1943. Dinner Joad. Bike up there and meet his daughter, her doctor husband and Cyril Connolly. Joad very bumptious and sparky, having just had a good *Brains Trust*. He says no-one else had a chance to talk because he talked all the time. I find myself trying with Cyril Connolly, imitating the Religious *Brains Trust*, which later we turned on hilariously – and talking big about *New Judgments*. I find suddenly that he has turned my conversation into an invitation to do one, which I didn't give. Yet he talks against BBC culture because it means diffusion and he is an 'anti-diffusionist'. He is all taste and no principles, which is no good.

One of the few to decline an invitation to deliver a *New Judgement* was Kenneth Clark, then Director of the National Gallery and later the presenter on television of *Civilisation*. He did not spurn it. First he wanted to accept, but then wrote to Stephen to say that he was: 'ashamed to give a superficial picture of Ruskin and had no time to prepare a more profound one'.

David Low was again enlisted, this time to talk about his predecessor Gillray – 'the cartoonist of Hitler on the cartoonist of Napoleon'. Rehearsal and transmission were in the Grafton Theatre, Tottenham Court Road, which, like the Monseigneur News Theatre, had been converted into an emergency BBC studio. In an attempt to record what a production day was like, Stephen describes the ups and downs of this one in some detail. For this type of programme, rehearsal facilities were only made available for one day, the day of transmission. The original plan had been: '11 am – go over Prokofiev music records on office gramophone; 11.45 – drink with Low at Stag; 12 – rehearsal read-through; 1 – lunch Low at Savile; 2.30 – rehearse gramophone [music and sound effects?] in Grafton studios; 3 – continue with cast until all is set and timed, including at least one complete run-through. Final notes. Break for dinner. 9.40–10.10 – transmission.'

> 27 November 1943. Well, first of all, things going wrong. Low turned up at 12.10, so we were late from the start. Then John Laurie (he is

playing Gillray) just doesn't turn up: he rings from Victoria Station to say he has realized his mistake and what shall he do. The result is that I have to leave Low at the Club so that I can do the records. Thenceforth all goes well until run-through. This goes well but is 10 minutes too long, which means cutting about 6 pages out of a 22-page script. I hoped and wanted to cut 2. Feared 3 but did not expect 6. Nor did Low. At 6 pm we settled down to it. It is rather surprising that someone who was in every other way a model in rehearsal should have suddenly become stubborn about cuts. Maybe it was shock at the amount because he believed (I believe him, with a pinch of salt) that the timing was right. He had obviously taken great pains with it and said it was a closely reasoned thing, difficult to cut. But not so difficult really. He took his coat off and squared up in a boxing position – but there were moments when I was really worried. We ate at the Café Royal and P. turned up and she was quite dismayed. I had to keep pulling him back to the cut question while he started long talks about something else to P. and saying he must *eat*. He had at first left all the cuts to me – 'so that he could argue about it later'. And he did. There had been a bad bus journey to the Café and now it is 8 pm and there is an appalling bus journey back to Grafton, in inky night. The revised parts were finally handed out at a quarter to nine – a period of growing strain and tension!

So much on the wrong side. But on the right side, plenty. Low on transmission soon warmed up to exceptional ease, with delightful and spontaneous laughs: a really warm person with (as Laurence said on reading his script) 'a free mind'. I was in slight agony at the end for timing but with sympathetic help from continuity we did get it right. There wasn't a single fluff or music hitch except for one at the end (due to my attempt to speed up). The afternoon rehearsal had shaped up well – one saw at once that the 'colossal gamble' came off. A gamble because we had given him such large chunks to do. [And also because it was against the usual policy of using actors and Low had had no acting experience.] As he got into it, so his gift for acting his own personality emerged.

Before leaving the subject of *New Judgments*, mention must be made of the one on Dickens, when Stephen at last had the opportunity of working with Priestley. Like Dickens, Priestley dealt with social issues in his novels and was the natural choice for the programme. Mellower from yet another series of talks to the nation, he was keen to do it, and nowhere to be seen in the following entries is any of the curmudgeonly behaviour recorded earlier.

30 November 1943. Having heard that Priestley may be able to do my suggested *N.J.* on Dickens Christmas programme, I get on to him for Savile lunch. One of the occasions when I think he really is the most understanding, wise and amusing man I have ever met. When he sets out to be nice there is no-one like him. [He started off by talking at length about Att's paintings, analysing why he liked them.] He told me that Brendan Bracken [who back in 1941 had replaced Duff Cooper as Minister of Information] said to him: 'Now you do a lot of writing and very successful writing and you have a great power of giving pleasure. Now why can't you keep off social questions?' Like Dickens? Then: 'People say Dickens gets his characters just by exaggerating. Well, let *them* try exaggerating.'
As we were leaving the dining room and I was paying – Jack had gone on downstairs – Frank (the oldest and greatest of Club servants) said to me 'I've never enjoyed a book so much as *The Good Companions*.' So I hauled Priestley back and he was extremely nice to Frank.
9 December. After lunch Priestley rings up, comes up to Club, has big new ideas about casting. I am playing snooker and can't hit a ball after he comes in. I make a lot of sprawling notes on the back of last night's Gargoyle bill.
22 December [transmission day]. Spend part of to-day semi-consciously longing for 5 pm. Contrasted with tomorrow's production [*How to give a Party*], this was the pill before the jam. Why do I dislike it? The read-through in the morning, Priestley not present, all OK though damned if I know how to tell Trouncer to be Pecksniff, or Ralph Richardson Micawber. But when Priestley turns up, in spite of his determination to be nice (itself slightly alarming) things are a bit tense. He doesn't very much care for the music I have chosen…. The little burlesque Christmas sequence at the beginning isn't as smooth as it should be, isn't funny, isn't quite as good as I would have made it without Priestley being there…. But he *was* rather nice and made a great effort to be tactful, speaking to the actors…. I felt I had very little to do with this production, beyond the idea for the series and for this item, which Jack very brilliantly carried out.

Chapter 8
Savile Based
1942–1945

Toppesfield and London

By the time of the Dickens programme, the Potters had long since moved South. With Gielgud, Gilliam, Bridson and many others already based in London, Stephen had begun to feel isolated. He was influenced by the 'lively and debonair' composer Arthur Bliss, who joined the BBC in July 1941 and expressed surprise that Stephen had not moved nearer the hub. In the end two events on 14 November of that year persuaded him to make a move. One was the loss of Moray McLaren as a good friend and croquet opponent:

> The Moray news is that he is to leave the BBC. A sad and serious blow. So good at the job – born smoother-over and sincere sympathiser. A tactful and cultured boss…. Catch a glimpse of him in the Savile in the evening, softly, understandably, damply, nostalgically tight, of course. Linklater saw him home. The final straw, this, that makes me want to leave Manchester.

That very evening another Savilian, Leslie (Dick) Plummer (managing editor of the *Daily Express*) said to him 'What about Berwick Hall?' Dick lived not far from the Meynell house in Essex, where Stephen and Att had often been weekend guests. He ran a farm nearby and was offering the Potters the chance to rent the farmhouse. We moved there in December 1941 and stayed until just after VE day. Throughout this time Stephen spent weekdays in London, usually staying at the Club.

Berwick Hall was in deep country. The village of Toppesfield, with one shop and a pub, was only half a mile away, but walks or bicycle rides were needed to reach the Plummer or Meynell houses (both about three miles off) or the nearest station (five miles). Stephen struggled to grow vegetables ('digging for Victory') and develop a croquet lawn. On Sunday nights or Monday mornings he bicycled to the station, put his bike on the train and from Liverpool Street pedalled to the Savile or Broadcasting House, scripts fluttering from the basket.

> Monday, 4 January 1942. Bike after huge P. breakfast by waned moon and low line of dawn to cold train – stamping passengers on Marks Tey platform. The slow bike from Liverpool St, perpetually almost catching my overcoat tails in the spokes.

Stephen's healthy if spartan life in the country was compensated for midweek, when the majority of his non-Club meals seem to have been at The Gargoyle, The Ivy, The Aperitif and The Café de Paris – where Laurence Gilliam was usually to be found in the evening. But his main haunt was the Savile, which he increasingly used as his office. While Val Gielgud had belonged to the club ever since 1931, many more colleagues now became members, including Gilliam, Bridson, Pudney, MacNeice, Sackville-West and Stephen Spender. Most of the non-BBC writers that Stephen worked with, such as Compton Mackenzie and Eric Linklater, also belonged, as did many of the actors he used, including Ralph Richardson and (a bit later) Robert Donat. His programmes were devised there and candidate participants were lunched there. He developed a tendency to make his guests wait until he had finished his game of snooker and was sometimes over-eager to play again after the meal. Alan Keen, called up yet again to the Savile to discuss another book programme, passed the time while waiting in drawing on the back of an envelope a picture of 'the Savile sandwich': two hefty bits of snooker bread, with a thin filling labelled 'any BBC programme'.

London, however, brought no release from Home Guard duties and bombing. Even the weekly journey to Toppesfield was hazardous. The railway line was often bombed and twice Stephen found that the only way he could complete the homeward journey was by bicycling from Chelmsford, twenty-four miles distant. Fire-watching was now in Langham Place and on duty nights Stephen would sleep in his office in between stints on the roof of the BBC. The Club was never hit, but with its bedrooms on the top floor and the Hyde Park ack-ack at the end of the road, it was not a particularly safe place to be. Overseas member Ed Murrow, CBS's UK representative, who made himself famous in America with his regular 'Britain can take it' broadcasts on the hardships of wartime London, did not trust it and took a room at Claridges.

Stephen's account of one raid suggests that Londoners were not prepared to take it much longer. The following is about one of the last conventional raids, before the onslaught of V-1s and V-2s.

24 February 1944. Drinks with P. and the F.s at Café Royal. We then pop in and out of strong buildings during tonight's nightly raid. Back at the club after the all clear I move out with Link to see the fire. We get through a couple of cordons (American soldiers) and see many Goya scenes in Old Compton Street – men at last getting the blazing gas main enough under control to get at the quadrant and turn it off. Under a flattened pub are doubtless many casualties. Churchill had turned up to watch this one – apparently his geniality, cigar and a.d.c. daughter didn't go down too well, with the casualties still buried close by. 'Churchill was loudly cheered,' said each bulletin stubbornly next day. But my informant says – silence. Not even a 'good old Winnie'.

Actually people seem slightly more nervy about this slightly less radical Blitz series. I feel more inclined to dodge, myself. Is it because one's nerves are more worn? I think not. It is a combination of a) guilty conscience about our own raids on Berlin, b) fact that life seems to have more future now than then and c) the general desire not to be the last man killed.

In June 1944 the 'less radical' raids gave way to the buzz bombs, or V-1s:

Friday, 30 June. Desmond MacCarthy explaining to me in the Stag at 12 that he never felt anxiety *in the midriff* for bombs, only intellectually. But the buzzing overhead makes me want to get on the train home. Then, on the way back to Broadcasting House, a great crack and a mass of dust rises slowly in a shape like a castle. That was Tottenham Court Road.

On the same day, Stephen learnt later, Glasshouse Street, the Air Ministry at the bottom of Kingsway and the house next door to the clinic in Vincent Square where Doyne was working had all been hit. Everybody felt the strain:

Wednesday, 5 July 1944. Ronnie's bomb 30 yards from his home. The whole street uninhabitable. Joyce knew four of the 60 killed when the Guards Chapel was hit [in Birdcage Walk, on 18 June]. One looks at friends with curious, new friendly eyes. The Savile has never been better and one hopes intensely that it won't be bombed.

One day when the buzz bombs were at their worst, *The Evening Standard* reported that '70 were killed last night in the City of Westminster'. This, according to Stephen's Civil Service informants, counted as a 'good' night.

At the beginning of August that year Stephen wrote of a rumour 'that a rocket bomb has fallen on the suburbs, leaving a crater the size of a swimming pool'. On 8 September there was a similar explosion at Chiswick, which was said to be caused by a faulty gas main, 'but Howard [Marshall] still thinks it's a projectile'. The V-2 rockets proved to be the most unnerving of all, as there was no defence against them and no warning of their approach.

However appalling the bombs, Stephen's feelings about the war were gradually changing from the fearful pessimism of 1940 to a feeling of 'deep and excited hope'.

A difficult employee

Stephen's attitude to the BBC varied with his mood swings. He continued to scorn the bosses. On 9 November 1943 he had an hour's interview with the new Director General, William Haley. 'He did give a lot of his views which were sensible enough, of course, but not very profound. He has only known broadcasting for five days. Why the outside man brought in?' He could not accept the idea that the BBC always had to be managed by people with no radio experience. Invited on a later occasion to dine with a new Chairman of the Governors, he found him also intelligent and amiable but quite ignorant of radio. Afterwards Stephen learnt that when being sounded out for the job, this Chairman had asked: 'Does that mean I will have to listen?'

Never slow to lambast others, Stephen was also aware of his own limitations and knew why he would never be in the running for an executive job. For a start, he hated meetings, where he was easily put down, reacted badly to criticism and doubted his own debating skills:

28 September 1941. Listen to the *Brains Trust* with amusement and delight. It is as if Joad was in the room, so well do I know what

expression of face is behind what tone of voice, and so unchanged does his personality come through. But … I feel a little jealous of all this impromptu skill, which I fear I am deficient in. And yet I feel, because occasionally the entangling knot is unloosed, I can do it very well – if conditions are perfect. But anything like an attack shuts me up.

He disliked routine office jobs – or anything to do with an office:

3 January 1944. Plunge into an officey day. Piddling memos, walking up and down my room. Does secretary A get on with secretary B? Shall I get Miss H. in a row by revealing her lies to Streeton? Then the discovery that Larry [Olivier] has been offered £25 and Donat too has been offered £25, going against what was said. I have to sort that out in the evening. Just lately I have hated the office – a new motive for being a War Correspondent?

Stephen's last-minute-itis was made more dangerous by the paring down of rehearsal time, in order to save money. For the same reason, the BBC repertory company, which was working well and saved producers having to explain the basics of how to act on the air, was being over used, so often actors would find themselves in up to three productions in a single week. This made for tension. They did not appreciate it when scripts were delivered so late that there was barely time for a read-through. Stephen realised the importance of a dependable image:

March 1941. [apropos of the suspension of Michael Redgrave for belonging to the People's Convention] … it was not Ogilvie but the Chairman of the Governors that was responsible. How do such people get into such positions? The perpetual question. I always think they are given to the one who, in some undefined way, gives the impression of being dependable. That is why I shall never get an executive job. But what I say to myself is that when given the chance, I could drop the undependabilty character and combine dependability with constructive ideas.

Probably Stephen would not have accepted an executive job if it had been offered. His great pleasure was to read up a new subject, make sure with the help of experts that he was *au fait* with the latest developments and then turn his new-found knowledge into a programme. The job he was doing suited him perfectly and on good days realization of this surfaced in the diary:

22 July 1942. Here was I, in the 10 o'clock to Marks Tey, jogging along in what seemed like a trainload of the doomed – all the young men and women in uniform have a glum look because of the bad luck for them of the war – 90% not doing what they want. Yet here am I, at 42, happy and thankful for the pleasantness of my life.
30 July 1942. In talking over my programme suggestions with Laurence the question comes up once more – which do I want to do, and I am reminded of my fortunate position in being able to take my pick of the programmes I most like. It is really a tremendously lucky position and a great chance, if I can bring to bear the necessary application.
13 October 1943. A very nice lunch given to me by Victor Pritchett. He tells me about his slog at home – 9–1, 5–7.30, 8–12 – writing government booklets in order to get his 'freedom' from e.g. BBC office hours. How much more freedom I feel I have.

Output

Between club life and fire watching, Stephen wrote and produced prog-rammes in bouts of extreme hard work. When a deadline had arrived and a script had to be finished by tomorrow, Stephen might still play a couple of snooker frames before getting down to it, but he would then retire to an armchair in the library, where he would write all night without book-ing a room. Over the next day or two he would work flat out at rehearsals, with little regard for meals or sleep. During transmission he was on a high and it took him some while to simmer down. Sometimes he would go back to the Club and fill ten pages of diary, describing not only the performances of each actor in the programme, but also his thoughts on the progress of the war, his recent snooker scores and, on one occasion, eight pages of comment on a book and two articles in the Encyclopaedia Britannica that he had read that same night.

Stephen wrote and produced many more programmes than will be mentioned in this book. A one-off programme not dealt with in the diaries was *The Nelson Touch*, broadcast on Trafalgar Day 1942. The picture opposite is of a read-through with Olivier on the extreme left, Richardson

two away with Stephen standing behind him, Leslie Banks (smoking) and Michael Redgrave on the extreme right. Such stars made no difficulty about giving their time to patriotic programmes of this sort. Of the recurring series, *Professional Portraits* had replaced *Contemporary Portraits*. Like *New Judgements*, these became a successful standby and gave Stephen the chance to immerse himself in other people's jobs. For the one about a Test Pilot, he chose Michael Daunt, who took him up in a new version of one of the fighter aircraft. The one about a Doctor was a second collaboration with Doyne, whom he shadowed for three days, writing in his diary everything Doyne did and said. Thereafter Stephen always considered himself a knowledgable amateur, acquired a library of medical reference books and diagnosed his own and other people's illnesses. Similarly, he spent many hours with Gerald Barry at the *News Chronicle* for his portrait of an Editor, thereby gleaning enough knowledge to be offered the editorship of a national magazine a few years later.

These Portraits are now lost and forgotten. Better remembered were the 'How' programmes he wrote with Joyce Grenfell. These, together with the Natural History programmes he wrote with ornithologist James Fisher, did not peak until after the war and will be covered in later chapters. Stephen's most remarkable wartime achievements were his literary programmes and, later, his success in winning more airtime for poetry.

Chapter 9
Arts Unswamped

Dual role of Features

While at the beginning of 1939 Features was still a nebulous appendage of Drama, from the end of 1941 it could lay claim to being the flagship of the BBC. It flew two flags – and most producers waved both. Patriotic programmes still took up a substantial part of the schedule. Olivier's film *Henry V* was later to stir up nationalistic sentiment; and this had no doubt also been the idea behind Stephen's Trafalgar Day programme on Nelson (also with Olivier in the title role). Sturdy programmes on various branches of the armed forces and their bravery in battle boosted support for 'our men at the front' and made the bombings and the privations at home more bearable. However, the danger in the summer of 1940 that these 'relevant' programmes might squeeze out entertainment and culture altogether had passed. Just as Kenneth Clark strove to keep the visual arts alive by appointing over 300 'war artists', just as CEMA* promoted live entertainment, so the BBC helped music and poetry by giving a generous amount of airtime to both, and by commissioning new works. Shakespeare's King Henry V had called Peace 'nurse of the Arts'. Peace was a long way off, but the BBC did its best to stand in.

Arts afloat – Poetry

Although Stephen remained Literary Editor, his administrative role was minimal. His contribution was creative and he continued to provide the BBC with a stream of ideas for literary programmes, including two new series: *This Correspondence must now cease* and *How it was written*. The first was the reading of letters between well-known adversaries, e.g. Coleridge

---

* Council for the Encouragement of Music and the Arts, which in 1945 became the Arts Council.

vs. Lamb, Johnson *vs.* Chesterfield and Dickens *vs.* Thackeray. He considered that the literary value of these was such that all the actors had to do was to read them clearly. As a critic put it: 'Mr Potter avoids the temptation to allow the speakers to fiddle about with diapason and vox humana and all the other phoney stops in the organ.' The other series began with how *The Pickwick Papers* was written: how it was issued in monthly parts, how sales multiplied as more and more characters were introduced, and how it was affected by the suicide of Seymour, the illustrator, half way through. Stephen's later 'biographies' of literary works included *Robinson Crusoe, Kubla Khan* and *On the Origin of Species.* This last was not far from being a biography of Darwin himself, since he had spent most of his life conceiving the book, and then withholding its publication. Stephen considered it his best programme, but it does not survive.

But it was poetry that took up most of Stephen's time. Although more of a back-room job, and although not always well received, he set himself the task of getting more poetry on the air and regarded this as his most valuable wartime work. In an April 1942 article in the *RT* he had suggested that more people were listening to poetry programmes because 'we are re-learning something which has been forgotten – that most poetry is written to be spoken.' He went on to outline his plans for more verse on the air, promising four new rotating series, each to be produced once a month. All these would be in addition to one-off programmes, while *And so to Bed* had now been reconstructed by Eddy Sackville-West, who had taken it over from Mary Allen. In due course, most of these plans came about. One of the monthly series was readings of narrative and dramatic poems. Ernest Thesiger read the first of these, *The Rape of the Lock.* Stephen also went for bigger names:

Tuesday 11 August 1942. This evening I had prevailed on Peggy Ashcroft to read Spencer's *Epithalamium*, which she did with marvellous youthfulness, delight and rhythm-in-the-blood in her voice, and the learned little remarks I had mugged up to say as suggestions rather went by the board. Plummers, with many winks, saw me dining with her at the Café Royal.
Friday, 16 October. The great pleasure was hearing Larry [Olivier] get hold of *Maud*, improving it through the day. Two lovely moments of perfect fitting of voice and music: 'Come into the garden' with *Songs without Words* No. 18 and 'See what a lovely shell' with No. 35. I have never felt so inferior and superfluous as a producer in that

such an enormous proportion of the ideas and thoughts about it are his. He takes up about half of my very small suggestions. Afterwards, alone in the big No. 1 studio, I play the Mendelssohn on the good piano. Then down to feed with L.O. at the Midland. He is very silent, but signs autographs for waitresses. In the train, later, he goes through his career – first, *Macbeth* in modern dress and then Noel Coward. Rather dull, with remarkably few successes. But he says: 'It's much better to be an actor than anything else – when I look at these other chaps.'

Other poetry series that Stephen devised and introduced were:

(i) Groups of poems round a single theme. *Rhythm of the Line*, for example, was an anthology of railway poems. *Air Poems* were all by Flight Lt John Pudney, he who had first got Stephen into the BBC. Stephen had again persuaded Olivier to read them: 'Have to be up at 7.30 to be at 200 Oxford Street to rehearse Pudney's poems going out first over Red Network [overseas]. L.O. had not been to bed at all. Very undissipated, brown and well-looking.' One of these poems – 'Johnny head-in-air' – became widely known and was also read by Michael Redgrave in the film *The Way to the Stars*.
(ii) *New Voices*, which were poems read by amateurs with no previous microphone experience. He was overwhelmed with the number of people wanting to participate. Every three months he had to arrange auditions of up to 70 would-be stars, from whom he would choose six. Assisted by Eddy Sackville-West, he insisted on unaffected and intelligent readings rather than theatrical plumminess.
(iii) Personal selections, loosely based round a theme, called *What the Poet sees*. Stephen chose and presented the early ones himself – '*Phases of the Moon*', for example. Later, his friends took on some of them, Eddy presenting '*Landscapes and Cloudscapes*' and Francis Meynell '*The World in a Grain of Sand*'. This series ran until after Stephen had left the BBC in 1948.
(iv) Poems from abroad – US verse in October 1942 and Russian verse in November.
(v) Features on famous poets. Stephen produced two by Eddy in 1942, on Byron and Shelley. Other writers carried on from there, the next being by Robert Gittings on Pope and Clare.

One-off programmes usually celebrated an anniversary – and the fiftieth anniversary of Tennyson's death in 1942 clearly demanded one. It was decided to mark it with a 'Tennyson Week', organised by Stephen. On 6 October (the date of the poet's death) he was to produce a biographical Feature, written jointly by himself and Robert Gittings. Stephen collaborated aimiably with Gittings over a weekend at Berwick Hall but was irked by the advance publicity in the *RT*:

Friday, 18 September 1942. I was talking about Tennyson on the phone when S. P. B. Mais came in. 'Ah – *you* can give me the stuff…. Why didn't they tell me? The *RT* editor rang me for a front page article, at 12 hours notice, on Tennyson.' I gulp. Why? And why not in conjuction with me, since I am doing the Tennyson week. How can they know who knows about T.?

1 October 1942. Having received a letter from Charles Tennyson quite rightly objecting to the stinkingly chatty and cheap references to his forebear in the *RT* – it is old-fashioned, 'snappy', journalism at work again – I ask him to lunch apologetically but he takes me to a good one at the pleasant United Universities. I show him the script and he distinctly likes it, thank goodness. He makes references all the time to *Memoir* [written by Tennyson's son]. It is a fascinating, jumbled mine of a book. All our 'superior' ideas of Tennyson are wrong – e.g. who would think of him trying to compose the best 'Wordsworth' – meaning banal – line?

Friday, 2 October. Hard day getting Tennyson script done. Manage to get Celia Johnson all right: I have been very extravagant with the cast.

Tuesday, 6 October [transmission day]. What richness of pleasure from Gittings, the actors, the Frank Bridge music, my own work (I was in good producing vein).

Wednesday, 7 October. This morning P. tells me how Harold Nicolson, stranger, not knowing my number, rang her up suddenly last night at Toppesfield to rave about Tennyson – astounding and lovely news.

A Governor of the BBC, Nicolson had himself written a book on Tennyson, published in 1923. The next day Stephen received a letter from him: 'Even from the outside, I should imagine it would be regarded as one of the best features that the wireless has ever had. But to someone who knows the details as I do, it was doubly impressive as showing such knowledge and understanding…. I will of course cite [at tomorrow's

Board meeting] your handling of the whole Tennyson anniversary as a model of how these things should be done.'

Encouraged, Stephen set about arguing for still more airtime. 'Why doesn't anyone answer my splendid memo about More Time for Poetry?' he wrote on 28 November 1942. He had pointed out that although the listenership figures were *comparatively* low, the research indicated that as many as 450,000 people tuned into poetry programmes. Still more listened to good music and his target was to achieve a similar level for poetry.

Nicolson's intervention

There is no record of any response to Stephen's request for more airtime. It was Nicolson who, as a Governor, got things moving. In a letter dated 6 January 1943 to the joint Director General Sir Cecil Groves he complained that the BBC's literary output was 'too small, too ill-timed, too unintellectual and too second-rate … although possessed of the finest literature in history … we take no real pains to convey knowledge of that literature either to our own people or to the peoples of the world. The only literary contribution of real value, namely *And so to Bed*, is squeezed into five short minutes when nearly all listeners have in fact gone to bed.' Nicolson ended this depth charge by saying that he was sending a copy of it to all his fellow Governors so that the Director General could report back to the Board as a whole.

Groves reacted slowly. He sent a copy of Nicolson's letter to all departmental heads. In due course he got lengthy replies from all of them: mostly they conceded that there were aspects of Nicolson's letter that ought to be attended to, but claimed that it had not given due weight to the quality of some of the programmes that their departments had put out. Moreover, the intensive listening period on which he had based his comments had included the Christmas break and had not been typical. Episodes from *War and Peace*, for example, had been deliberately excluded from the festive season. It was some time before a meeting could be set up to discuss what should be done. First Groves got 'flu and then C(P) succumbed to the same bug. Eventually all agreed that a committee should be set up (so much had already been suggested in Nicolson's letter) with Stephen Potter in the chair. To begin with, its only other member was to be the poet Geoffrey Grigson, from Talks.

Potter and Grigson were told of this on 9 April, but they had not yet been shown Nicolson's letter, which was thought to be too confidential.

Harold Nicolson in 1945

The Board of Governors ruled on 14 May that they should see it. They were instructed to draft the BBC's response as soon as possible and they completed this on 31 May. Their report was sent *in toto* to the Governors on 22 June, but with a covering note from Foot (the other joint Director General), C(P) and Sir Richard Maconachie (Controller of the Home Service) saying that they agreed with it subject to reservations. These were that the committee should be joined by a weighty expert from outside the Corporation and also by someone to represent overseas broadcasts; and that the committee should have no executive authority.

Stephen's Literary Committee first met on 28 August, with Ivan Smith for overseas broadcasts and the literary journalist Desmond MacCarthy as the outsider. It continued in being until well after the war, but became increasingly ineffectual. Early on, it did lead to better liaison between departments (e.g. on how the BBC should handle the anniversaries of famous writers); and to more poetry.

The first positive response from management to Nicolson's 6 January memo filtered through in September, when Stephen was urged at a Features meeting to say how he would expand the ratings for poetry. He proposed a) inserting verse readings in the middle of popular programmes, b) using famous actors, and c) monthly presentations of new poems.

13 October 1943. Poetry meeting with Val. I have got everything I wanted – return to the ABCD type anthology, of which new poetry will be one – also the editorship of inserts into Variety, with more time: 15 minutes of 'popular' poetry and prose.
Much hard work for me, alas.

Stephen invited poets to a meeting to discuss these ideas:

Friday, 15 October. A long-by-me-planned meeting this afternoon – the young poets, to get their views on broadcast poetry. Present: Laurie Lee, Day Lewis, frantically sensitive and civilised, quiet but helpful. Louis [MacNeice], smiling not ungenially nor unhelpfully down his nose. Dylan Thomas, high blood pressured young man, coming in late with a muttered '*I'd* write for the Plumber's Gazette.' *Enfant terrible*, not quite sure which side he's on. Spectacled, keen Alex Comfort. Tense nervous talkative Kathleen Raine. Sane clever Geoffrey Grigson. One argument started, exactly what one would expect but still even now, 30 hours later, makes me exclaim Christ! K. Raine obviously came with an unclear idea of sticking up for a principle and chose the evils of patronage – commissioned work – commissioned work not having been mentioned.

After more such consultative meetings, bringing in more poets, Stephen wrote in the 3.12.43 issue of the *RT* about his plans for poetry in 1944, backing them up with the views of the poets themselves. On the subject of new work for radio, he first gave their reservations, such as: Must the poem be comprehensible on one reading? Are not lyrical and ballad poems best for the medium? Is not the summons to write likely either to sterilise the talent of the young poet or to produce just that kind of generalising and impersonality which is least suited to radio? (Desmond MacCarthy's opinion.) Others were more positive: Surely the Elizabethan poets were stimulated by the necessary limitations of poetic drama? (Day Lewis) Is not the adaptation to a new medium a useful exercise? (Spender) Stephen settled the matter by quoting a long letter from Laurie Lee, from which:

Musicians can exploit the qualities of the microphone; the poet would be a crass conceited isolationist not to attempt the same thing. Of course he would have to make concessions – why not? It would have to be stronger in image, simpler in treatment, wider in experience: but I dare say it would be none the worse for that.

9 December 1943. NEW POEMS. I at last produce the start of this series, one of the 'good things' I claim to have done for Lit. Some most effective ones, and well chosen.

New Poems, often read by their authors, was broadcast on the first Thursday of every month and continued at least until 1945.

Vaudeville

The other novelty, the insertion of poems or prose into the middle of more widely popular programmes, was carried out with the co-operation of the producers of *Vaudeville*. This peak-time Saturday night broadcast grouped together 'famous stars of Variety, Music and Drama'. It would now include a 15-minute pre-recorded cultural insert, edited by Stephen. For safety's sake, only widely accepted pieces would be presented; and the readings would be interspersed with, or even mixed with, music – ever since the 1930s Features had mixed verse and music, as had been done with Mary Allen's Mosaics. The first such insert, on 10 December 1943, was Fay Compton reading *The Lady of Shallott*. This came between a turn by Beatrice Lillie, known for her solo sketches on stage, and Gillie Potter, the comedian. Stephen thought the music chosen by Eddy fitted well, but was worried by 'Fay's slight tendency to sing the last word of each line', which was parodied behind the scenes by Bea Lillie.

For subsequent Vaudevilles, it had been agreed that Stephen should attract listeners by going for top names from the stage. Busy with several other programmes at the same time, for the next 'cultural insert' he had miscalculated by a week the last possible date by when the *RT* needed to know the name of his chosen presenter; which meant that somebody had to be found within a few hours. 'I am struck almost pale with consternation … must be a famous actress … where's my list of names … Edith Evans, where's the phone.' Luckily she accepted at once. 'It's the kind of thing I like to do, and I've just finished a play.'

Robert Donat, for the third *Vaudeville*, was equally quick to accept, wanting to read *In Memoriam*, backed by a full chorus singing Parry's *Jerusalem*. 'Back at the office I ring up. Have you got a full chorus we could use? (3 to 1 against) Yes, we have got a big chorus. Me: I suppose it wouldn't be possible to switch them to Parry's *Jerusalem*? He: That's what they've been hired to sing. One of my best coincidences.' The Aeolian Hall was hired for the recording of Donat and the choir:

Monday 20 December. A mike was set up and screened off in the gangway. To get the balance, I had to constantly vary his position relative to the mike, getting him to come in when the light was low.

Thereafter, Stephen had a series of meetings with the stars to discuss which poems they should read. This was often over lunch at the Ivy, where he invited first Ann Todd and then Celia Johnson. Early in the New Year Vivien Leigh consented to perform. On her first visit to his office, her appearance and poise knocked him off balance:

4 February 1944. Back to office where Vivien Leigh comes to see me about what poems shall she read. I last saw her in riding breeches ('ah, do you get a chance of riding?' I think I said, indicating nostalgia for the sound of galloping hoofs beneath me) but now she was in full rig – fur coat, dark lipstick and a black hat so smartly battered looking in its wavy brim that it looked organic – and I was struck. I was back in 1922. My hands were big and I greeted her grumpily. Where is my easy attentiveness and relaxed alertness from which arise not wit, but real humour? I felt absurd sitting at the desk. She upset her bag of books and I picked up one while she did the rest. And why for God's sake when crossing the road with her do I dither about a car and make a dash for the pavement while she walks calmly on?

Tuesday, 8 February. I had a BBC lunch with Vivien Leigh at the Ivy and then recorded her reading some odd poems. She had the same black hat and wore old gold globular earrings. We talked pretty hard from 1 to 2.30, interrupted about three times by Angela Baddeley and other actresses coming up to chatter briefly. I explain to her my dilemma – to leave the BBC where I get my own way and am badly paid, or go to films where I am better paid and a stooge…. There is not the slightest attempt on her part at a line, nor at being feminine, or actressish, or woman's wiles, or impressive, or conscious of the power of her beauty, etc. 'What I should like,' she said, 'is a small port.' 'You're just an old woman in a pub,' I said. 'Port and lemon,' she said.

Monday, 14 February. I recorded Larry Olivier reading *Ancient Mariner*. His suggestion, but he came knowing very little about the poem. Wanted to read it all, but got bored with it. I had just read it today, trusting to having edited it in 1935 … had some ideas, which he was ready to take. He kept making mistakes, just at the end, so that we had to keep re-taking. Vivien came too, fur toque for hat. I had the pleasure of taking them both in for mutual drinks at the bar of the B.H. canteen.

This last and most blatant attempt to interest the public in poetry was too much for some purists. 'Val Gielgud writes a snooty memo about film-stars reading verse. Stung by all the praise in the press, perhaps.' Barbara Burnham, with Mary Allen one of the first two women producers, said that Donat's reading of *In Memoriam* had been a disgrace. Even Mary carped (to Att, but not to Stephen). Not only the *Vaudeville* insertions, but Stephen's other poetry programmes were also criticised. 'Geoffrey Grigson's schoolmasterish memos on "the dubieties of the Wednesday readings", which sting me to a frenzy. It looks as if some have been taking the opportunity to put me forward as a phony populariser of poetry because of three *Vaudeville* programmes, i.e. three out of 156 on which I work.' Haley himself suggested that some of the fifteen-minute poetry readings should be cut back to five.

An additional criticism was the use of music. A *Listener* article in January 1944, headed 'Don't say it with Music', complained that because of it only one word in three of Olivier's reading had been heard. This was followed by a long attack in the next issue by the poet Alex Comfort, maintaining that 'the introduction of music before, during or after any poem is indefensible'. Commenting on Donat's rendering of *In Memoriam*, he wrote that 'neither *Jerusalem*, nor any other extraneous noise, should be affixed'.

None of these attacks mentioned the producer's name, but fingers were clearly pointed at Stephen. He felt that Alex Comfort's criticisms may have been suspect as he had only just rejected his work for *New Poems*. But the comments were disheartening and from now on there is very much less in the diaries about poetry and the number of poetry programmes was reduced. Stephen wrote '… my attempts to proselytise poetry by getting famous voices have been only half successful.' But overall he had at least been successful in getting more poetry on the air. His hope was that it could now be heard with such frequency, and in such a variety of ways, as to make it more widely understood and appreciated.

Arts afloat – Music

Throughout the war and until the birth of the Third Programme in 1946, the BBC Home Service played its part in keeping interest in serious music alive and in providing work for composers and performing musicians. The BBC Symphony Orchestra, under Sir Adrian Boult or his deputy Clarence Raybould, played concerts on the air, live, at least once a week.

Classical music predominated but there were also prime time performances of many new works, such as Tippett's *A Child of our Time* or Shostakovitch's eighth symphony. As regional broadcasting was still off the air, the BBC Scottish orchestra and the BBC Northern orchestra (to name but two) were also kept going with frequent performances on the Home Service. Still more work was provided by the commissioning of incidental music for Features and other broadcasts, and composers such as Britten, Alwyn, Walton and Lutyens did not hesitate to write it. Whatever its limitations, at least such music enabled both composers and players to carry on with their professions.

The BBC's music committee was until mid-1944 chaired by Arthur Bliss. He had joined the BBC in July 1941 and was promoted (at his own insistence) to 'Director of Music' the following March. There he fought for as much airtime as he could get for music of a high standard and against any suggestion of what today would be called 'dumbing down'. He was an impetuous and inflammatory talker and Stephen often records his comments at the Club:

9 April 1942. … Come in late [for lunch]. Bliss is talking to Bridges-Adams [the theatrical producer]. He 'shoots his mouth' whenever he speaks. His face definitely shows from physical signs of muscular development that he is a tremendous talker … loose, easy-swinging lower jaw. He is talking about the timidness of C(P) before the Governors and how they mean nothing to him. He gives examples of the Governors' schoolboy fatuity and becomes annoyed when we suggest that Nicolson is intellectually a cut above the rest. A schoolboy too, he says. Deficient in character, not in brain. Well, says Bridges, if he is a schoolboy, that suggests that *we* have gone back to the *womb*. Bliss, white and unsteady, walks out of the room in dudgeon.

Stephen's first music programmes were two biographies. One celebrated the life and works of Arthur Sullivan on the centenary of his birth in May 1942. Stephen had been brought up on Gilbert and Sullivan and was happy to pay homage. For the music, he had at his disposal an orchestra of 70 players and 30 choral singers, who played and sang musical excerpts live during the course of the programme. He managed to co-ordinate this without a hitch – '… to me a most valuable experience. I am now to produce Elgar. Good … but alas – the weight of work!'

147

Stephen also knew Elgar's music and often played it on the the piano. But the programme was scheduled for 2 June, only two days after his *Contemporary Portrait* of Fay Compton. On the day in between he wrote:

The day when I couldn't think of tomorrow's programme, utterly precarious as it is, because yesterday's kept bursting into my head.

At first Stephen had been warned off the programme by Bliss, who had said: 'Elgar impersonated? Don't. Sacred name to many – many remember him.' Yet Stephen had been asked by two musicologists to see what he could do with their own first attempt at a script. He had found words and writings of Elgar's that could be usefully incorporated and saw how the script could be put into shape. He thought it would take him about four hours. His deadline was the 12 o'clock train to Bedford the next day (2 June), where Boult was as usual using the Great Hall of Bedford School for rehearsing and performing with the BBC symphony orchestra. Transmission was that evening. The following is from the diary entry for 1 and 2 June:

… Then I realize I can't get the fitting together done until dinner. Ring Dale [secretary]. Could she come to the Club after dinner? She says she would slightly prefer to come very early in the morning – then it could be stencilled by her and rolled off in time to catch the 12 o'clock train. I relax. Exciting reminiscenses of yesterday keep pushing up into my mind, like waves still perturbing after a storm. Also, Monty [Mackenzie] comes up and says he has a marvellous new play and wants me to produce it. After dinner I have exciting bridge … I will do it midnight to 3 am … I will leave the light on. Wake up – broad daylight outside – 6.25. Maybe I can just do it. Panic puts me wide awake. I have finished half by 8 and the last pages are duplicated at 20 to 12. Catch the train with minutes to spare. But what would Sir Adrian Boult think if he knew that on the same day all his orchestra were turning up for an unarranged, uncopied script?
Boult most amenable – almost too pleasant. Not at first interested in my careful, tactful script, which I am determined should be incidental to the music, instead of strongly the other way round, as in Sullivan.
The great shock was the music. The huge orchestra in the huger hall, with no audience allowed. Listening in the gallery, with the

great music bursting up like intoxicating air, so that I had the feeling of strength and exultation which kept me bounding about till 4 pm next day.
At The Swan afterwards the actors do turns and I do my whistling and humming. [Stephen could whistle a tune and simultaneously hum the bass line.]

However casual and badly timed Stephen's work on Elgar may have been, the programme could not have been disastrous. In September Gilliam wrote to him: 'we are to take over the writing and production of music features. C(P) is sending us a list of subjects. Please do a list too, in consultation with Sackville-West and Maurice Brown.' Later in the month Stephen wrote: 'I am summoned to C(P) who talks to me about a title for Adults' Hour and tells me that music Features are being put "under" me.' He thereafter sat on Bliss's music committee.

The appointment also resulted from Stephen's enthusiasm as an amateur. He had more and more been selecting music for his own programmes rather than relying on the experts, such as Maurice Brown. He made a point of getting to first performances, writing accounts of the new music in his diary. He went with Eddy to the Wigmore Hall for the world première of Britten's *Michelangelo Sonnets* ('I can't quite adjust to the new wavelength required, but I am sure they are good'); and on his own to Tippett's *Variations on a theme by Handel*:

Music acrobatic and gutty, no obvious connection with the splendid theme with which it opened and closed, which seemed to hold the young musician's delightful antics in a gigantic palm of the hand. Interesting to see the composer at end of my row, two places off, his tenseness, hand clasping, his smiles and chatter with companion, his broken-up, sensitive face. He is liable to be put in prison for being not only a C.O. but refusing to work on the land.

Bliss invited Stephen to rehearsals of his new works:

Monday, 9 March 1942. ... feeling honoured to be listening to a first performance, as it were. A. Bliss was hearing it for the first time. The proof reader handed me a score and discussed it. It was not difficult to follow – a lovely thing to be happening in wartime. Bliss with hair and personality standing on end, sitting in his chair with more physical energy than most use jumping a five-barred gate. Second movement a fascinating time 6/8 + 2/8 – awfully difficult not to repeat to oneself in 9/8. All the quartet were in RAF uniform. Ist violin: 'we *can* do it at that speed – but it is very difficult – especially the pizzicato for the cellist. Cellist does his bit by heart, looking at me as he does it. At end of movement No. 1 pretends to faint and No. 3 fans him with his viola.

Monday, 25 January 1943. This morning I went at Bliss's request to hear records of *Checkmate* played over. A.B. gives me a piano score, with the action written in. I – liking the music and Bliss and feeling flattered at being asked in on this – go all out to say the piece should not be broadcast in a fortnight's time at 3.30 but in two months' time at say 9.20 with full words written in the *RT*. It is a new art form.

As with literary programmes, the Savile Club was the nerve centre of BBC music. Elgar and Delius had both been members and now Bliss, Walton, Vaughan Williams, Alwyn, Malcolm Arnold and many more had all followed their example. Bliss usually discussed work at the Club rather than the office. He does not seem to have had a high regard for radio in relation to the spoken word:

22 October 1943. Bliss's way of being tight was to say to us: 'Now I see through everybody. I see through you, Doyne … full of fine feelings and motives – but frustrated. I don't see through you, Eric. You are opaque. (100% barium meal, says Link.) I see you, Stephen, as an artist … yes, entirely an artist … but condemned to do hackwork.' He can't see radio as anything but hack.

When discussing another of Gittings's 'Famous Meetings', about when Beethoven met Goethe, Bliss told Stephen: 'Don't Hollywoodise Beethoven.' He was equally caustic about music for films, which according to Alwyn he saw as a 'way of earning easy money by dubious means'.

Britten was not a member of the Savile, but on 31 July 1942, shortly after his return from America, Stephen wrote:

… lunch at Savile today with Eddy, Dallas Bower [producer of the film *Henry V*] and Britten. He has just reached a new landing in his upwards career with his symphony. He completely lacks affectation about it and is nice, ordinary, intelligent and young (28). He makes a most warming impression on me.

Stephen met Britten again over *The Living Spirit of France*, a compendium with music chosen by Lennox Berkeley and readings by Raymond Mortimer:

29 June 1943. A very good lunch at Les Gourmets. Raymond Mortimer's mass of hair, looking more distinguished than ever, and the probably more distinguished B. Britten, looking if possible less distinguished than ever. Britten is delightfully ready to talk eagerly about music. He doesn't like Bliss's. We arrange the French readings.

This all-French compendium was the second item on the agenda at a music committee a few days later:

Friday, 2 July 1943. … I said I wasn't happy to have Herbert Howells for my Professional Portrait of a Musician. 'No,' says Arthur, 'you want someone who has been about a bit.' Now *he* went from Hammersmith to the Royal College. That's a twopenny bus ride. Bliss did a pretty piece of Blissing. Coming to the *RT* proof of my anthology *The Spirit of France*, he says: 'Peter Pears and Benjamin Britten?' Then a tremendous 'Really!' (because Pears and Britten are C.O.s). 'This does *not* sound right … and two of the songs by Debussy and Poulenc? *Les Six*? If not actually collaborationists, they represent the France of the 20s – niggling, charming art-for-art-sakers. Where is the true France – Berlioz – musicians of the barricades – something big (splendid gesture) – Rabelais?' Hereupon Laurence, having fallen over himself in admiration of the super-Laurentian title 'music of the barricades', does nonetheless point out that Bliss, as Head of the Department, was entirely responsible for the selection and had seen the names coming up through all the preliminary discussions.

The Living Spirit of France, produced by Eddy and Stephen, was broadcast the following month.

At another committee meeting Stephen argued for and got a new version of Purcell's *King Arthur*, which he produced for St George's Day, 1943. Henry Wood was the subject of Stephen's next *Professional Portrait*, in

June 1944. The programme was linked to the 50th anniversary of his Promenade Concerts and Wood himself conducted the music. (The actual anniversary date of the first Prom was not until 19 August; but the conductor died on the tenth of that month.)

Stephen's other music programmes during this period included a biography of Mendelssohn, a feature on Liszt (written by Eddy) and two programmes on the mechanics of organising a concert.

Eddy Sackville-West and The Rescue

Sackville-West had been called up, but failed his medical. Wanting to do something to help the war effort, he tried various civilian jobs and eventually landed up with Features in December 1941. He had wide knowledge of literature and music and, like Stephen, was able to make contributions in both. On the music side, he was a near professional: he was a fine pianist and his biographer De-la-Noy writes that he could sight-read a piano score before he could read words. Later he was to edit with Desmond Shawe-Taylor the Record Guide, which gave him one of the largest collections of LPs in the country. An aristocrat and an aesthete, he is supposed to have been the model for Uncle Davey in Nancy Mitford's *In Pursuit of Love*.

Stephen, writing about Raymond Mortimer's *New Judgment* on Fanny Burney, describes Eddy and his hand in the programme:

> Monday, 15 June 1942. … I am much helped by Eddy's music, with Fanny saying her verses before a background of the Cadenza from *Il Re*. His device (not new, but well done) of cross-fading piano into harpsichord for passage-of-time backwards … but E. slightly gets on my nerves, because he gets in a pansy flap and agonises over a detail … I wanted him to say an Italian line and he said 'O no really – I can't' and at the rehearsal came down three floors to tell me so. I, already irritated by being kept waiting 15 minutes for a circuit, shout at him. A strange high voice comes out of me – 'for God's sake go upstairs and read a line. That's all I want you to do.' Also, he is inclined to take the line of keeping an eye on my possible excesses, with a sharp wince and an 'Oh no.' Also, there was a slight feeling of myself *vs.* the *New Statesman*. [Eddy often contributed to Mortimer's periodical and they were life-long friends.] This cast a slight displeasure over part of the show, for me. But Raymond M.,

welcomed by me to sit at my side at the panel, made many suggestions, some helpful and all went hitchlessly in the end.

Later that year Stephen wrote: 'Eddy says that he never wants to be a
producer, but to be a producer's assistant. Yet he doesn't assist enough. He
is a cut above this. He half gets round one by a more or less conscious
charm, half does not.'

Eddy remained wary of a producer's work and most of the programmes
he wrote were to be produced by Stephen. In other directions he made
distinguished contributions. In addition to his Features on Byron, Shelley
and Liszt, he continued to develop *And so to Bed* and did the adaptation for
radio of Linklater's book *Cornerstones*. He persuaded his friend Elizabeth
Bowen to write a *New Judgment* on Jane Austin. He gave a series of talks
on musical appreciation, which achieved a wide listenership, perhaps just
because they made no attempt to hide his aestheticism or compromise
his intellectual standards. He became the main authority on the choice of
incidental music and 'maintained an unbendingly perfectionist view' on
this, always arguing that the music should be especially performed for the
programme and, if possible, especially composed.

Stephen often describes him. At a weekend when they were both guests
in the same house he wrote:

6 November 1943. Eddy is there and a very good person to have –
a) he plays the piano here, b) we talk about the job (on a cold walk
along the railway line), c) for his complete lack of vanity and his
ancient calm wisdom (so entirely belied by his office voice), d) for
his lack of self deception and absence of moan about his many
bodily weaknesses. He talks about Knole [the home of his father,
Lord Sackville]. The 24 weekend guests, with never less than 12 guests
in the house. 'If you have 20 servants they eat so much that the
guests don't really make any difference.' When he inherits he will
have occasional house parties at Knole and enjoy them.

Earlier Stephen had been invited down to Knole for the day, where
Lord Sackville at once challenged him to a round on his private golf course.
While Eddy caddied for his father, Stephen borrowed the head gardener's
set of clubs.

The radio work for which Sackville-West is chiefly remembered is *The
Rescue*. This was a translation from Homer and covered Odysseus's return

to Penelope. It was broadcast in two parts, each one-and-a-half hours long, in prime time on 25 and 26 November 1943. The music was by Britten and a special feature was that there were no sound effects: the music served for them, suggesting the mood and the movements in time and place. Soliloquies accompanied by orchestra were intended as a new kind of aria. Eddy wrote that it was 'an attempt to unite speech, song and symphonic music in a form which only the microphone can manage.' He told Britten 'The music surpassed my highest expectations.'

Another novelty was the colloquialism of the translation. Eddy tried to get away from 'the unreal vocabulary of academic translations and to present listeners with characters and situations which do not seem remote.' This was also the aim of E. V. Rieu in his 1946 translation of *The Odyssey* and of other translators of the classics since then; but in 1943 it came as a surprise and helped listeners to relate the drama to contemporary events.

Stephen gradually came to see *The Rescue* as a classic:

18 October 1942. Read Eddy's new Homer masterpiece and find it fascinating.
3 September 1943. After lunch Val tells me, rather abruptly, that John Burrell is to produce *The Rescue*. I have angled for this….

There was uncertainty about the conductor. Boult, disapproving of Britten and his music, had refused to conduct and Bliss would not allow Britten to do so ('Ben thinks the whole world of music revolves round him,' he said in the Club). In the end Raybould did it, but not after a derogatory remark he had made about C.O.s had nearly caused Britten to withdraw. He consented to finish the score out of friendship for Eddy, but took no further part in the production.

23 November 1943. After nice snooker lunch, up to Maida Vale to listen to first run-through with orchestra of Rescue. I expect a really dramatic little situation – Raybould conducting with Britten listening and not liking it, Burrell producing and Eddy also on the panel, not approving of Burrell. [In the event Britten had 'flu and Eddy's comments were not disruptive.]
John sits back calm, gloomy, unsmiling – no matiness is his line, obviously. No friendliness. Good. But I could never keep this up. I run a production, someone once said, as I run a party. The orchestra are not too Bolshevistic. These scraps of new music by a young

composer often using only a very few instruments are hell. There are some grim smiles and a big rush for tea. 'Yell of pain from the orchestra' is one of the stage directions in Eddy's script. If any of them troubled to read the script – unlikely – what a joke for them.

Stephen listened to Part I on Friday 25th on his own set in London: 'Listen attentively and admiringly, to some extent looking for faults.' His wife (P.) had been listening in Berwick Hall and clearly made him listen more receptively to Part II, which they heard together on the Saturday:

'Nothing much to record this week' – but something real tonight – from the most unexpected quarter. A poetic drama on a Homeric theme by a super-highbrow with a fretful voice. Part II of the Rescue was a thrilling poetic and artistic and dramatic experience. Part I last night I listened to critically. But this time, influenced partly by P.'s boundless enthusiasm for it, I listened without script – and was completely carried away and moved to complete silence for 10 minutes after it was over. Staring at the fire, I *saw*; in the nice warm bedroom I thrilled – I prickled. Much of the time going to bed – and much of next morning – my thoughts whirl. A feeling of thankfulness – pride in the medium Radio, thus honoured, some bitterness that I had neither produced nor written it, but in the main, excited pleasure.

There follows a draft letter of appreciation to Eddy, from which:

… making use of the best radio techniques, and adding something in writing words to music, it is *the* best work of art to date. It is imagined … for two evenings I was away in the world you had created. It was written for the sight, as radio should be. All the time I was seeing – 'the statue's eye turned inward' – I saw Penelope watching from behind the pillar alone … saw Odysseus as an old man in the entrance being led forward, saw the profile of his shadow. At each stage of Odysseus's approach I thrilled – which means a curious blow from the centre from which nerves come, which makes the touch ends tingle….
And the production? A very strict and clear interpretation of your intentions. But – ah – better I believe than I could have done it – that bit more graveness and solidity and care and unwasted effort.

The Rescue got mixed reviews but was acknowledged by both Val Gielgud and (later) the Director General as a classic and was re-presented many times in years to come. Eddy never again attempted anything on the same scale for radio, despite many invitations to do so. He left the BBC at the end of 1944 on grounds of ill health and wrote to Stephen regretting 'the dissolution of our partnership', saying that the last years had in many ways been the happiest, and certainly the most interesting, of his life. He now became radio critic of *The New Statesman*, but in 1945 wrote freelance for Stephen a 'How it was written' on Madame Bovary and in 1947, for a new Potter series 'Return Journey', he wrote about and broadcast his memories of Knole.

Chapter 10
The Course of the War

Between the return of Features to London and the end of the war, the bulk of Stephen's programmes were on the Arts side. His remaining war work consisted mainly of his 'Army Week' programmes at the beginning of 1943; his training as a war correspondent in the run-up to the Normandy landings; and his VE day profile of Churchill.

The Army

The BBC had scheduled an 'Army Week', starting on 28 February 1943. Over fifty programmes relating to the army were planned. The three main ones, which were to be broadcast simultaneously on the Home and Forces programmes, were to be called *The Building of an Army*: Stephen was to produce the first two and write them in collaboration with Linklater, whose book on the subject, *New Army*, was already in draft. The first, on the period from Munich to the abortive landings at Dieppe, was to go out on 1 March. It would give the facts about Munich, conscription, the British Expeditionary Force and its exodus from Dunkirk. The second, scheduled for 3 March, would tell of the over-stretched attempt to man the island against invasion and go on to describe the development of the much larger, new army that existed by the middle of 1942. Such details had not in fact been decided in January, when Stephen attended his first Army Week meeting. It was chaired by AC(P) (Assistant Controller Programmes) and attended by two representatives of the newly formed Army Broadcasting Unit: Lt. Jack Hargreaves, ex Radio Luxemburg and later to become famous as a TV personality on fishing and other country matters; and Eric Maschwitz, playwright until recently under contract to MGM, ex-editor of the *RT* and future head of light entertainment on TV:

Wednesday, 6 January. Army Week meeting to discuss lay-out of week – two War Office representatives and two of their 'liaison hand-out chaps', Maschwitz of MGM and Hargreaves. I am very unused to such meetings and am therefore fairly dumb. Laurence, as usual, takes charge of our side of it with great efficiency – but after half time begins to shut up. Young Hargreaves and Maschwitz have obviously got together to put some life in the old stick-in-the-muds and are full of ideas – e.g. Reveille and 'Come to the Cookhouse Door, Boys' should be played through the week. AC(P) in the chair looks clever, darkly cool, but does not take a firm hand ('weak chair', says Laurence afterwards). Director General Foot comes in and seems like a delicately grave and beautifully-voiced older man, like best sort of general talking to his men, not knowing much about it but obviously weight-carrying – knows all about difficulties of getting hold of P.M. C(P) also makes a whimsical appearance, sitting on the arm of the chair and eating digestive biscuits….

Wednesday, 3 February. One of the Army Week meetings in the morning. Various programme organisers speak out about their plans. First of all Val, in chair, asks McGivern, editor, to summarise. Then Val: 'The danger is that the whole thing is likely to become a bore – if it becomes routine.' Looks charming and quizzical. McG., with a worried look, gives dependable, serious impression. I describe my prog. and suddenly for no reason, almost dry up – then just at the end save myself and talk about 'the technique being studio' – fairly irrelevant. Yet I start a red face and a sweat drop. Barnes [Head of Talks], with nice young donnish voice, does know something about the art of speech, and so my God does the handsome Snagge [chief newsreader], very precise, his well clipped moustache, fresh skin and wide serious eyes seeming to contribute to the general lack of fidget and unnecessary detail in his plain voice. Ah – I don't come out especially well in meetings, there is no doubt.

Having caught Val's whimsical eye, I disappear (aided by pre-arranged phone call from Betty), dash off to play squash with Ralph [Richardson], who swamps me.

Sunday, 13 February. How many of the jobs listed below shall I be able to do *this* weekend?

Army Week
> Read through 9 books and booklets. Find *the* one to help save
> this threatening prog.
> Read Battle School literature in preparation for Monday.
> Get bits of script expanded.

'Army Week' was just one of six subheadings listing the things to be done that weekend. On the Monday he was to spend two days with Hargreaves at the Durham Light Infantry's Battle School at Barnard Castle. Later Hargreaves commented on how fit the 43-year-old smoker Stephen must have been to have done all of 'that fearful assault course' at Barnard Castle without any training – the long description of the visit in the diary makes no mention of this feat. It starts off inauspiciously:

> Our introduction was not good. The whole art of approaching the Services is the long build-up – introduction from the DG – importance of the BBC, with special act that 'here is our key man, do what you can for him', which invariably results in Generals and an almost embarrassingly elaborate special committee laid on for the occasion. To arrive under the wing of a member of a suspect and new War Department Broadcasting Committee [Hargreaves], to arrive under its most junior member, a subaltern, who though helpful and intelligent in himself had none of the necessary deferential manners with the CO and who besides being extremely junior in rank, was a radio advertising man – a fact which he was far from anxious to conceal – meant that my visit was clouded from the start.

Luckily Stephen soon discovered that the Brigadier in charge was squash champion Val Wilson, who had been particularly helpful to him over his pre-war programme on the 60th at Tidworth. Wilson spent much of the rest of the visit explaining the thinking behind the modern army's training and tactics, giving Stephen invaluable material for the programme.

> Sunday, 21 February. Work all day on Army Week programme.
> Sunday, 28 February. Never get down home this weekend at all. P. tells me it is a grey day down there but I learn later this wasn't true – said to cheer me up. Work all day, apprehensively, in the Savile

library – oh I shudder to think of this day (writing 9 days later) …
then to dinner at Hargreaves, and already tired and sleepy, work
with ever mounting wakefulness till 6.30 am. Impelled by what force?
I think chiefly pride in standard of Potter programmes.

Monday, 1 March [transmission of first army programme]. We are
much rushed for rehearsal time and all go nobly without food – get
a bite at Adam and Eve, 9.15. Most effective use of Vaughan Williams's
F minor symphony.

Tuesday, 2 March. Beginning to feel now that great surge of relief
which will mark the end of these programmes. The recordings
of yesterday are excellent…. Get down to work on Dieppe and
'this modern army' sections. Work once more, after dinner, with
Hargreaves … beginning to be tired. Bad patch at 2 am…. At last,
at 5 am, I begin to take an extremely long time to answer Hargreaves's
remarks. (On Sunday night it was he who gave out first – and he is
only 30.) I went on swimmingly to 6.30, when I had a shave.

Wednesday, 3 March [transmission day of second army prog-
ramme]. I felt I had done one of my best and cleanest jobs and was
thinking clearly all day. But it had a very bad start. Round at
Jack H's flat we had put in a call for 8.15 – but we slept through it.
Jack rushes in on me at 9.45. I was due at 9.30 at the office, with
script. Ringing the office, learn that Betty's down with 'flu – only
she can read my writing. Jack follows me to office and interprets
my handwriting to efficient Miss Davis. The last part is typed by
12, not quite right, then come 5 phone calls from 4 different
censorship HQs, including Combined Operations. And half an
hour before run-through, a request for a 'purple passage' speech
about the wonderful delaying actions of our armies in Greece,
Crete, Abyssinia, etc.

Well, I am 25 minutes late for the actors, but things go well, the
script seems good. In the afternoon I spend 2 hours with the
sequence of recordings taken at Barnard Castle – which are fine.
Rehearse the rest in the evening, never really getting to grips with
the final 5 minutes of Dieppe. On the final run-through but one
(I never did another), again that strange experience of instinctive
timing, as it was 29 minutes dead – i.e. correct to a second. An air
raid started as we began, which put the actors on their toes, and gave
a pleasant electric feeling, but unfortunately prevented London from
hearing the programme [probably because when bombers were

approaching a city, the BBC transmitter for that city was switched off, as otherwise the Dorniers could home in on it. Other transmitters could still be heard, only less clearly].

At Broadcasting House afterwards, a glimpse of high-ups drinking in their special room. Not wanted! I think of Priestley's treatment and then see him in the pub, but can't bear to listen when he starts talking about what is wrong with radio Features, feeling that I am in a position, at this moment, to know something right with them.

On my way back to the Club I see the street strewn with mortar and glass from a shell burst on a top flat and promise myself to go straight downstairs from my top room if the raiders return in the a.m. They did, for two hours, but in spite of sirens and full Hyde Park guns I never heard a sound and slept right through it.

Thursday, 4 March. Last night's raid caught the main line in the middle. [A train had dived into the crater, killing the driver and his mate.] Have to bike from Shenfield to Ingatestone and then from Marks Tey home, through the Colne Valley. Rather tired in the legs but full of relief for work done. A cold, promising, brisk March day.

Find there was a really bomby raid round here which, on the phone, P. never told me about. She nestled among the logs alone and could hear little of the programme.

The two army programmes are perhaps my best job to date, considering the difficulties – and liked by most. Val wildly enthusiastic.

There was one other armed forces programme in 1943: *Fit to Drop*, about the Airborne Division. Stephen insisted that he should participate in a practice drop from a glider. A week before this was due, in June 1943, he wrote a loving valedictory note to his family in his diary, together with a request for Bach at his funeral. However, at the last minute this drop was disallowed and Stephen had to get what flavour of the real thing he could by jumping from the practice tower at Ringway airport. While researching this programme, he was again accompanied by Jack Hargreaves, who quite possibly had some kind of watching brief from the War Office or even the MoI. If so, it was unobtrusive and Stephen appears to have been unaware of it. Again, the absence of direct interference from such authorities – except for the unco-ordinated and amateur last-minute telephone calls just before transmission of the Army Programme – is remarkable.

Maybe the answer is that Stephen was not lacking in feelings of patriotism and was happy to extol the achievements of the Forces and exult in any successes – all in the sort of terms that would have met with the approval of the MoI. Later these programmes would no doubt be regarded as MoI-inspired propaganda; but they did not feel like it at the time. Bridson writes that the BBC kept him from being called up so that he could write propaganda: yet he insisted that he only wrote what he felt.

War Correspondent in waiting

Towards the end of 1943, with the Allies half way up Italy and with one-and-a-half million troops massing in England for the invasion of France, many of Stephen's colleagues began looking outwards, hoping to extend the scope of their work outside their until now besieged island. Stephen himself determined to become a war reporter.

The arbiter of this was Club member Howard Marshall, who had become known before the war for his running commentaries on cricket. Stephen, in a *New Judgment* on W. G. Grace, had got him to fabricate a running commentary on one of Grace's innings. With the war, Marshall had moved to the Ministry of Food, but after three years there as Head of PR, Lord Woolton had been persuaded early in 1943 to let him return to the BBC as Director of War Reporting:

> 26 January 1943. Howard Marshall tells me all about it – how Foot came to see Woolton and pleaded for him (rather nice!). He is to get £3000 p.a. plus expenses – well up on Min. of Food pay – starting in Tunisia, scrounging back our recording apparatus from the Americans.

Marshall's dispatches from North Africa soon became as famous as his earlier commentaries on cricket. His first attempt to involve Stephen came in October, when he suggested that Features should 'pluck the apples in from BBC correspondents abroad and make programmes from them.' For example, Stephen could make a Feature on Rome based on recordings of, say '… bells … a thanksgiving service … an Italian soldier who wants to get back to his job as a waiter in England or America … "now it can be told", the story of Poggi, the news vendor, who kept up underground anti-fascism.' This all came to nothing, but on his return from North Africa, Marshall was put in charge of recruiting and training a team of war reporters to go out with the invasion forces on D-day – six of them with the ground forces and five with the navy. He asked Stephen to be one of them:

24 October 1943. Howard Marshall has been telling Dick that I 'have left production' and joined his war reporting unit. Dick: 'was he shooting a line?' I am not, never will be, a member of anybody's BBC unit. Yet feeble to say no: sounds as if I don't want action … yet that is just what I want.
16 November. Another job-full but essentially frittering day at the BBC. Linklater to Gibraltar by air tomorrow. Doyne with his plan for advancing behind the second front line to save European children. What am I doing? Shouldn't I damp down slight restiveness at working 'to' Howard and go in for War Reporting?

Stephen soon dropped his reservations. His feelings of guilt were made worse by the fact that, as well as being just too young to fight in the the first world war, he was now just too old for the second. Moreover, although not cushioned from danger, he had been cushioned from any real hunger or hardship and had been having an interesting and often enjoyable war. He accepted; and at the beginning of January 1944 went on a 3-day course with seven others and 'two brilliant stars, old hands in the commentary sphere – Godfrey Talbot and Richard Dimbleby.' The morning of the first day was spent in being lectured in tips on how to do it '… and then after lunch some of us go to Westminster Bridge, some to Trafalgar Square to do a 3 minute commentary on what we see.'

5 January 1944. Today we hear played over our yesterday's recordings. Mine comes first. In my first effort I dried up – I had started with some badly thought-out mental notes and nothing on paper. For my next attempt I found to my surprise that I had got into the gear and inflection of Howard Marshall, which my croak didn't suit at all. It is rambling and dull because it is not me at all. Top marks should go to commentaries that express the character of the speaker; one wants to see the thing through the eyes of a certain person.

On the third day Stephen came in to listen to the recordings he had made at Waterloo Station. Standing 'on a throw-yourself-over ledge' he described the crowds – 'the station trot, that ugliest form of locomotion.' Unlike his recording the day before, which was listened to in silence, this one elicited 'roars of laughter'. He felt he was getting there.

The next step in Stephen's training was two days on a divisional exercise in Kent. He did this together with Louis MacNeice:

Monday, 21 February 1944. Spend the morning buying War Correspondent clothes. Quite a well-fitting battle dress, £2.5s.11½d, off the peg at Chelsea Barracks, 2 pairs of khaki socks, 2 shirts, 1 cap, 1 pair of gloves and a well-cut and handsome looking mac. Coupons and money for all this on the Corp.

At 3, down by car with Louis MacNeice to Ashford. 'Captain the Marquis of Ely' was to have taken us down, but he was ill. Lt. Col Tufton, CO of this PR unit, had said 'Someone must go down with them.' 'Is it necessary?' I said. 'It is just a question of depositing us, surely, at The Saracen's Head, Ashford.' 'Absolutely necessary,' said T. 'You see, you couldn't give orders to the driver, for one thing.'

22 February. It could never be said that Louis was the ideal companion for military work. These junior officers (we were very much among B mess today) make jokes and expect responses. Louis looks sourly down his nose, getting paler with cold as I get redder. Occasionally, at the wrong moments, he springs to a quick little salute, mistimed, with a little toy soldier click of the heels which makes him overbalance.

Today we are with the HQ of the 61st Infantry Division 5 miles N. of Ashford. Through a snowstorm, we are shot round to office after office, ending the morning in a drinkless B mess of bored young officers. Chief topic was whether tomorrow's exercise, surely, wouldn't be cancelled. Our guide was due up at five a.m. and it was freezing cold. The weather was beginning to let up and at every break in the sky he groaned. They all keep up a general joky background except when they are talking about the job, when all look very serious and speech assumes a deliberately anti-pompous but serious tone, like a school captain to his eleven before a match.

23 February. First half of day Louis and I are taken up onto a hill to be shown a skeleton exercise. A division is supposed to have landed at a beachhead (grave faces and anxious thoughts of Anzio when this word is mentioned) and is to advance up from Folkestone, one brigade in reserve and the other two along parallel roads. They have all been up early and drink cups of very strong tepid tea. Slit trenches dug first thing with clean yellow earth sides. Vehicles scientifically dispersed round edges of fields. Windscreen

covered and every vehicle quickly camouflage-netted as soon as it arrives....

Stephen's long account of the manoeuvres continues to read like a running commentary – he was getting his hand in.

The BBC now began to have doubts as to whether they could afford to release Stephen for the assignment:

18 and 19 April. Spent these two days in office jobs and trying to get decision on whether or not I am to be allowed to go on this second front assignment. I want to go for so many reasons … 30 service Features and never seen a shot fired in anger. A great desire to have something to do with it all, with this great great occasion. To see the great concourse of ships – I have already thought of a running commentary image: 'all drawn by one hand, like Gulliver pulling the enemy ships away.' I've been so much on the fringe of 2 wars without being in either. And a chance to get away from the office.

The matter was settled that weekend by a telephone call to Berwick Hall. The Director General, Haley, was not prepared to let him go.

The dynamic Howard Marshall and his team did a fine job, using improved but still awkward-to-use recording equipment. Marshall stopped at nothing to get the latest news back to the UK and, according to Asa Briggs in his history of the BBC, managed to upset both General Alexander in North Africa and General Montgomery in France. During the Normandy stalemate, Montgomery complained that his broadcasts were giving information to the enemy and put an embargo on any further transmissions from the front. Marshall went too far when allied troops entered Paris and he broadcast news of this before the fall of Paris had been made 'official' and even before the Supreme Headquarters Allied Expeditionary Force (SHAEF) had made transmission facilities available. For this transgression, SHAEF returned him to England.

Monday, 4 September 1944. Lunch with Hargreaves, discussing our army part in the Victory Week programme – and there is *Howard* back, looking a little sheepish but on the whole making a good story about his having been sent back by SHAEF for broadcasting from Paris without censorship – he had tried to cross streets under fire to find the censor, etc. The stuff was colour only, etc. Then at dinner I tell the story to Alan B. [Sir Alan Barlow, First Secretary of the Treasury], saying that after all, Howard knows as much about censorship as the censor. And *of course* being the Savile a faint repetition of this last phrase from my right reminds me that I am sitting next to Col. George ... the censor! *His* version is that no secrets were given away, of course; but it was letting down the other correspondents.

VE day

Stephen's two final war-related programmes, a summarised history of the war and a biography of Churchill, were both broadcast at the time of VE day.

Before then, there had been one political assignment outside the BBC which must have had some bearing on the choice of Stephen as Churchill's radio biographer. In November 1944, on Thanksgiving Day, a two-hour pageant was staged at the Albert Hall to mark Britain's appreciation of America's part in the war. It was sponsored by *The Daily Telegraph*, which invited Stephen to devise the event. The BBC was not involved, but the last hour was broadcast on the Home Service and the last half hour on the blue network, a string of 600 stations in America.

Stephen christened the event *To You America* and orchestrated the whole thing. With help, he chose the music:

> Having rung up Arthur Bliss, I come well armed with music sugges-
> tions. One of Bliss's ideas (at once accepted by Barbirolli) is the
> first movement of his own piano concerto. It is dedicated to America,
> A.B. is half American, it has a lovely first movement with a good
> bit of fireworks for Solomon [the pianist] for the unmusical.

Stephen also chose the actors and the passages for them to read, which ranged from chunks of speeches by various American presidents to verses by the American poet Walt Whitman. He wrote the linking script – several pages of it.

The Prime Minister, rather at the last minute, decided to attend the event:

> Churchill – it was my first sight of him ever – standing round and
> short and paternal, beaming. His entrance was miraculously timed,

walking the length of the centre aisle, but never in the centre, rolling from side to side.

Churchill spoke and Stephen's linking script had to be revised to build up to this. The whole affair went off well and Stephen got much of the credit ('my name as big as Barbirolli's on the posters outside').

Parallel with this, the BBC was planning what it would do in the event of victory. By August 1944 a 'Victory Week', rather on the lines of the Army Week, had been agreed and a six-day schedule drawn up. Features had been made responsible for the main programme each day, which was to be 'The Nation's Tribute': on Day 1, to the King and Queen; Day 2, to the Prime Minister; Day 3, to the Army – and so on for a further three days. The umbrella title for the tributes was *Their Finest Hour*. Gielgud referred to them in his book as 'the apotheosis of Features'.

On these early schedules, Stephen and Jack Hargreaves were down to do the Tribute to the Army, but no writer was allocated to the one about Churchill. Slightly revised schedules were for a short while produced weekly, but then petered out. Perhaps the German counter-offensive in the Ardennes and the impact of the V-2s made detailed schedules for Victory Week seem premature. On 2 October there is a short diary note: 'C(P) has snooped my very quick Churchill programme scheme to take to Colonel Ismay.' Ismay was Churchill's link with Chiefs of Staff and this was the first indication that Stephen was involved with the Feature on the P.M. as well as that on the army.

There is nothing more in the Caversham file until 13 February 1945, on which date, in a memo addressed to all those contributing to Victory Week, Gilliam informs them that the earlier proposals had *not* been approved by the Director General and C(P). He attached a new schedule, in which Stephen was down to write and produce a programme about Churchill for Day 2 'on the basis of the agreed synopsis'. He added that work on the new schedules should start immediately. The army programme had been relegated to Day 7, with no mention of Potter or Hargreaves. In the event, these two wrote instead a potted history of the whole war, which was broadcast just before the King's speech to the nation. An actual soldier (according to Alan Jenkins's biography) was used to do much of the narration. He was on leave before being posted to the Far East and was given £100 by Gilliam as spending money in London before going off to fight the Japanese.

The choice of Stephen to write and produce the Churchill tribute might seem surprising. However, at this time he had built up a solid reputation both for programmes on the armed forces and for Feature biographies – very different from his later radio reputation as a satirist and as the producer and co-author of nature programmes and a series on *The Canterbury Tales*. Moreover, Stephen had a particular interest in the Prime Minister in that he had written the BBC's obituary. Every time Churchill became ill, Stephen had to drop everything in order to make sure that this was up-to-date. He had become a fan. There are many references to this in his diaries:

Ralph Richardson (Churchill) posing with S.P.

10 February 1943 [on question time in the House]. What style!
What confidence. Fancy ad-libbing not for a momentary *Brains Trust*
but for the permanence of history.
6 November 1943. About once a month I or one of my friends says
fervently – isn't it extraordinarily lucky that at this moment a great
man, C., is on top, and then we go on to quote from a speech or from
a Parliamentary report.

If Churchill himself had any say in the matter, which in view of his close-
ness to Ismay is not impossible, his acceptance of Stephen as writer/producer
may have been connected with the success of *To You America*. The P.M. had
apparently enjoyed the occasion.

The nation's tribute to the prime minister, *His Finest Hour – Winston
Churchill, the History of a Reputation*, was broadcast at 9.30 pm on 9 May
(the first day on which all of Europe was at peace). It is one of the few
programmes that still exists on tape. Ralph Richardson read from Churchill's speeches and writings and Robert Donat was the narrator. It was a
biography, from schooldays to the roaring crowds outside Buckingham
Palace. His youthful craving for active service was treated in full. Difficult
episodes such as the Dardanelles were not glossed over. For his twenty
years out of office he was constantly referred to as 'The man below the
gangway'. In the circumstances, the objective tone of the programme is
slightly surprising, as at that particular moment an unadulterated eulogy
might have been expected.

Chapter 11
Joyce Grenfell and 'How'
1942–1948

Passages by Joyce Grenfell in this chapter are either taken from Joyce Grenfell
Requests the Pleasure *(Macmillan 1976), or from her half-hour tribute to
Stephen that she broadcast on the day of his death in 1969.*

Pre-Joyce

Stephen's first How programmes were in a different mould to the
Potter–Grenfell Hows that developed later. Although nothing he wrote
was ever po-faced, early Hows were educational, aimed at a discriminating
minority on the lines of How Things Work in the Arts. 'Potter invites
listeners to step back-stage and inspect the Arts in the making', ran the
billing. The How of a stage rehearsal, of a cutting room in a film company,
of voice training. 'Also,' wrote Stephen, 'How to read Poetry and, I fear, how
not to – we were getting our own back for weary hours in the audition room.'
The first was in November 1942. It did not come across well: 'A little disappointed with playback of How. As usual, only a tiny squeeze of gloriously
entertaining day got through the armour. It is the less enjoyable programmes which gush from the instrument clearly and fluently.'
  The second combined 'How poetry readers are chosen' with 'How actors
are cast for dialect parts'. It featured an audition of poetry readers, where
Stephen himself, Eddy and Joyce Grenfell were the assessors. Joyce did
not allow this to become solemn. Stephen wrote:

> … But the great pleasures of the day were Olive Groves, not quite
> able to 'take' correction, even in a demonstration lesson, and above
> all Joyce, untroubled and unhurried and as funny rehearsing as she
> is in transmission.

Joyce gave her own (quite different) account of how she was first involved:

> I didn't work with Stephen until 1942 and at that time he had begun a serious series on How Things Worked – Intercom, Running an orchestra and then one on selling and he asked me to contribute on *How to Persuade* and another on *How to be Interviewed for a Job.* The bits I did were illustrations of how these things were done – and more often how they shouldn't be done: and that's how our collaboration started.

The Potter–Grenfell Hows

The first all-satire How, and the first to be jointly written by Joyce and Stephen, was broadcast on 8 June 1943. *How to talk to Children,* which was of course largely how *not* to talk to children, contained sketches which Joyce drew on later in her stage monologues. To summarise one of them from her autobiography, she 'played a Nursery School teacher, with an unnatural brightness in her voice. Her confidence fooled no one, particularly the children. One four-year-old wrecker, Sidney, always managed to get the better of her.' The children had no speaking parts, but 'Don't do that, Sidney!' became a well-known ingredient of Joyce's sketch on stage. In Stephen's case, the sort of satire he developed in these Hows changed the course of his career to the extent that thereafter he was always known primarily as a satirist. The programmes contained many ideas later developed in his -manship books.

The Talking to Children programme was a huge success. 'We listen to a really brilliant feature by Stephen Potter about how to talk to children,' wrote Harold Nicolson in his diary. Lady Violet Bonham Carter, another BBC governor, wrote to him at length picking out the bits she had enjoyed. She added: 'It was without exception the most brilliantly amusing programme I have ever heard on the air.' But it still did not wrench the series from its original, instructive purpose. On 2 August, for example, came *How to arrange a Concert,* based on a paper by the musician Hubert Foss and executed with the co-operation of Sir Adrian Boult and his orchestra. In September Stephen wrote the second all-satire How in conjunction with his old friend Professor Joad. Joyce, although she pre-recorded one short sketch that came in at the end, was on tour, so the programme had a different flavour. Joad through the *Brains Trust* was recognized as the

king-pin arguer: he usually opened his replies with 'It all depends what
you mean by...' and he became associated, in a mocking way, with this
phrase. The full title of the Potter–Joad programme was *How to Argue –
including how not to, how to make an argument lead somewhere, argument
for the sake of arguing, not arguing for the sake of peace and quiet.* Included
was a one-minute argument in the middle of a game of tennis, on whether
the ball was in or out. Joad succesfully intimidated his younger and more
sporting opponents and the scene was to be re-set at the start of Stephen's
book *Gamesmanship.* Yet Stephen was still not satisfied with the tone of
his series and Laurence, at a literary committee meeting the next day, was
strongly anti. But for good reviews in the *Manchester Guardian, The News
Chronicle* and *The Observer,* the whole idea might have been dropped.

The second Potter–Grenfell How was on 23 December 1943: *How to
give a Party.* Joyce was at the top of her form: she had just returned from
entertaining the Women's Land Army round the UK and was about leave
for a tour of military hospitals in the Middle East. 'Party' firmly established
the pattern of the series:

21 December. Hurried to the afternoon first rehearsal of Party.
I was put out and cowed by the shadow of tomorrow [Priestley on
Dickens], which makes me feel disappointed with the script, which
seemed all the time too thin and I imagined that Joyce was popping
in with her comments too often. I half, and feebly, told her off.
23 December [transmission day]. I very much like this returning to
a production after a day away from it. I was in good form production-
wise, clear, with a really good shape in my mind. I get nearly ecstatic
pleasure from this kind of thing – the script, God knows, doesn't
look much (if any reader were to check up) – but every line is from
one's own remembered Chiswick party just before the war and is
an attempt to be funny but true. Furthermore each line is written –
and herein lies the futility of reading such a script – to fit the small
scale but definite range of character-creation which I know to be
in the range of each actor. When Gladys Young is introduced as
'Miss Treble' she corrects it as Mrs Trübel so that one instantly sees
a rather ratty Austrian refugee dame and laughs. Norman [Shelley]
too in excellent form and I think the best use is made of Joyce –
first straight (as hostess), then a most amusing [name of friend]
character, a grim lady, Ouspensky-ite, who says what she means.
Ronnie came in for some good lines as Freddie, the very intimate

old friend. As for me, almost every moment of the production was scrap of delight after scrap of delight.

In a later article, Stephen wrote: 'From the beginning we decided that we must never *try* to satirise. The lines people thought funny on the air were not invented. We merely repeated what we had heard. We have continued to work on that principle.'

Joyce was mainly responsible for the scripts for some of the characters – such as Mrs Trübel, 'who lived in Golders Green and spoke of "ve Britischers"'; and Fern Brixton, 'vegetarian lover of Beauty and weaver of her own clothes'. Stephen developed 'a guide-compère, known as the Listener's Friend; Len, the technically keen radio-buff with his [cockney] talk of baffle and woof; and the Practical Man ("I always carry a two-foot rule")'.

It would not be possible to make fun of such characters today. Even as long ago as 1976, Joyce recognized that How humour was dated. She wrote:

> … the points of view from which we satirised some of the attitudes of the day are no longer mine and I don't think they would be Stephen's. Or is it that I have become more self-conscious of the crime of being patronising? … I still find it impossible not to observe differences in speech and thinking, but now one is no longer supposed to notice that there are differences…. There was a brief time … when any sketch I did in cockney or rustic accent was criticised … for being patronising to the 'lower classes'. The fact that eighty-five per cent of my sketches mocked the upper classes was not noticed.

And 'p.c.' had not been invented when that was written! The fact is that all Joyce's sketches were completely devoid of malice. She entertained troops on her tours as well as West End audiences without letting go of her inherent goodwill-to-all nature and without ever being snide about or running down the characters she was making fun of.

Both Stephen and Joyce described their method of work. Stephen: 'My wife and I inveigle Joyce down for a week-end. Having decided on a theme, we walk it and talk it and act it at each other. (I can't act but Joyce understands my mumbles.) Then we rush to paper and write it all down in illegible longhand written at shorthand speed and only decipherable by my secretary, who is miraculously able to reduce our muddle to some sort of clarity. And there, in one day, are the bones of a half-hour programme.' Sometimes a stenographer was present, as described by Joyce: 'High speed shorthand-writers came to Stephen's office and there, in cold blood, we improvised scenes. It was not easy to forget the presence of the shorthand-writer, head down, painstakingly recording our hit-or-miss exchanges.' Other extemporising sessions were held in Joyce's Kings Road

A 'How' broadcast with Ronnie Simpson at the mike, a bearded Derek Guyler and S.P. on the right.

How 'How' was written. S.P. and Joyce at work in Stephen's Harley Street flat.

flat, in the Potters' flat in Harley Street (see picture opposite) and less successfully in Kew Gardens, about which they left conflicting reports:

Joyce: I provided sandwiches and coffee and we sat on remote benches, surrounded by sheets of paper. Stephen's enthusiasm for botany kept luring us round just one more corner in search of what might be blooming in the long grasses ahead of us.

Stephen: Lunch with Joyce at Kew. Joyce notices so many things and changes the subject so many times that it's like visiting a calm spring day on a switchback railway.

The writing was a joint effort, but Stephen was always the producer (although the early, more serious Hows and *How to Argue* had been jointly produced with Douglas Cleverdon). The small group of actors played a large number of recurring characters. Roy Plomley (later the long-term host of *Desert Island Discs*) in one programme played nine different parts. Stephen referred to them as 'the gang' and Joyce wrote of the feeling of re-union as each new How came up. Soon they were officially billed as 'The How Repertory Company'. Joyce records that Stephen 'never corrected us publicly over the intercom; he came into the studio and quietly explained to the actor the changes he wanted made. This may sound the obvious way for a civilised Director to behave, but they are not all like that.' Sometimes Stephen took a small part for himself, which was always a duologue with Joyce. He admired her ability to play a variety of characters in quick succession, each time not only getting the accent exactly right, but also the demeanour and thought pattern. They made each other laugh, as well as their listeners. She wrote of him:

We used to spark each other off. He was a really brilliant improviser. I remember working on *How to Woo* and he was in turn Young and Ardent; Polished and Sinister; Inarticulate and Helpless. I did the appropriate girls and women and this shorthand man would take it all down, breathing heavily.
At the read-through Stephen allocated parts to the cast sitting in a half-circle round him. He indicated how he wanted the character to be played and was so good at this that I wished he would play in the programmes more often. No one knew better than he how the parts should be acted … there was always a good deal of Stephen

in what he had written, just as there is usually something of me in my monologues.

Later, he wrote of her (describing a lunch):

No sloppiness, no off days permissable with J. As usual she reproduces one or two voices heard today on her way here, on the top of a bus – usually one of many varieties of cockney. It is so exact that the whole mouth and larynx of the bus passenger seem to have been transplanted into Joyce by plastic operation. I don't laugh: but listen with the pleasure given by reality made more real.

A new How batch began in April 1945 with *How to Blow your own Trumpet*, about which Eddy Sackville-West, now radio critic of the *New Statesman*, wrote: '[S.P. and J.G.] are in a fair way to becoming the *enfants terribles* of the BBC…. When next somebody accosts us with "How lucky you are to find time for reading *in the morning!*" how satisfying it will be to reflect that he is only trying to blow his own trumpet.' *How to move House*, in April 1946, was mainly based on Stephen's own experiences when the Potters moved from Berwick Hall to a flat in Harley Street the previous year.

The high point of all Hows came at 6 pm on 29 September 1946. It was then that the Third Programme first went on the air and *How to Listen* was the inaugural broadcast. It was a 'special double number by Stephen Potter, with selected examples by Joyce Grenfell' – the *RT* way of saying that Potter wrote most of it, maybe in this case because Joyce was performing on stage in Noel Coward's *Sigh no more*. Although it was clearly going to have an exceptionally wide listenership, with habitual non-listeners tuning in to see what the Third was going to be like, there is curiously little about the making of it in the diaries. Even retrospectively, Stephen's only comment came at the end of the year, when he wrote that it had been a tremendous success and had already had two live repeats.

Fortunately the programme was well covered by various BBC historians. Asa Briggs, in *The History of Broadcasting in the United Kingdom*, wrote: 'Stephen Potter's script on the very first evening pointed the way…. [His scripts] were to be one of the few real attempts to initiate explorations, and they soon influenced broadcasting as a whole.' Humphrey Carpenter, in *The Envy of the World*, quotes verbatim the opening half page of the script, in which fun is made of the non-listening or half-listening public ('Could we have the wireless down a little, please? Difficult to concentrate on the bridge.') and goes on to describe how every cliché of stock radio programmes is guyed. John Drummond also listened and, in *Tainted by Experience* (2000), claims he can still recite by heart every word of its cod biography of Wordsworth.

Altogether there were 29 How scripts. They petered out after Stephen left the BBC in December 1948, but later attempts were made to revive them. *How to Broadcast*, in 1951, mirrored *How to Listen*. The last diary reference is 12 January 1956: 'response to three Hows this year not good enough to do another.' The best tribute to the series came from Bridson, who (modestly omitting his own contributions) singled out the How programmes, *The Last Crusade*, MacNeice's *Columbus* and Sackville-West's *Rescue* as the key programmes that had proved the ability of Features 'to engross and entertain'.

An unlikely partnership

The Potters had been introduced to the Grenfells soon after Joyce's useful *Observer* article about Stephen joining the BBC at the end of 1938. He then helped her, in a still more striking way. He arranged for Herbert Farjeon, the writer and promotor of revues, to be present at a party to which he had also asked Joyce. As has already been related in a number of auto-biographies, he then called for silence and asked Joyce to do as a party turn one of her imitations of a lady addressing a Women's Institute meeting on How to make Something out of Nothing. The upshot was that Farjeon invited her not only to submit a script, but to act it as well in one of his revues. It was the start of Joyce's stage career.

The two continued to exchange professional favours. Stephen's meeting with Shaw at her house has already been mentioned. In October 1941 Joyce gave her first solo performance on the air – four sketches in twenty minutes. Stephen produced it, and invited Eric Linklater to listen with him at the control panel. They both laughed so loudly that they could be heard in the studio through the wall – and also on the air. Once the How programmes got under way, they worked closely for the next five years.

Yet there was usually some tension between them: perhaps it was this that gave a special quality to their joint programmes. In character they were opposites. Like her aunt Lady Astor, Joyce was a non-smoker, a teetotaller and a Christian Scientist. She was a 'do-gooder', as exemplified by her war-time tours to entertain the troops. Privately as well as publicly she was always on the look-out for people and causes she could help. She was tidy, punctual and well organized. She described herself as a 'planny-Annie': 'I have always been haunted by any writing job I have to do until it was finished' and 'I have been known to set the table for a dinner party twenty-four hours or more ahead of zero-hour.... It was not like that for Stephen.' The contrast with him will by now be apparent to any reader of this book, without having to quote the deficiencies that Joyce went on to list. Stephen's private thoughts about Joyce are written up copiously. Fundamentally he looked up to her, but as usual, he is sometimes more critical in the diaries than he ever was in what he said. Much has been written about Joyce that stresses the saintly side of her: this may be somewhat de-sweetened by Stephen's occasional astringency.

> 10 December 1942. Then I rush Joyce to the Savoy and give her a BBC lunch at the Grill, where I have never been before but will certainly go again. We discuss my good idea for her participation in How.... She says her monologues don't go down with the troops except for RAF – and she refuses to broaden them. We talk about integrity. What does it mean? The question of communication comes into it. Also private means.
>
> 12 June 1943. [They were co-guests at a week-end in Essex.] Joyce of course the perfect week-end person, singing, imitating and being always amusing. Her one fault is that she is so accomplished that she thinks she is fully accomplished in everything – e.g. serious knowledge of music. She has *not* got this, although she is one of the most naturally musical people.
>
> 27 February 1946. This evening went to the Embassy Theatre, with Joyce as partner. The new Sean O'Casey. Joyce is the world's most perfect audience, receptive to every point, laughing often and repeating the line very quietly to me with pleasure. Afterwards I paid her compliments and was a pretty good male attendant to her, in the way she is always bullying me to be. We parted at the tube.
>
> 22 July 1946. Bay and Joyce to lunch. ['Bay' was Alex Kilroy, the future wife of Francis Meynell. At this time she was the most senior female civil servant.] Joyce at her worst. She talked about America without stopping. Start on *How to Listen*, the first programme on C.

'C' (for Cultural) was the code for Third Programme. Despite three more pages on this day alone, the above is the sole reference to the making of the best known of all the How programmes.

2 January 1947. Nice lunch with Joyce where we talk, as usual, bang-bang-bang at her seat at the Aperitif. We don't talk business until the end and then it is not too cheerful. Our last week's programme: a new version of our old Christmas How. Like most repeats, this doesn't seem to have come off – though we enjoyed doing it as much as ever, and admired ourselves. But the criticisms have been tepid. I realize that working with Joyce intensifies my talent for social satire: it also intensifies a weakness, an apparent superficiality and domestic nice-ification in the 'serious for a moment' bits. I am not able to get a deeper feeling in my work and so am tied to being pretty caustic, and to the funny detail of observation.

14 February 1947. The Potter party was today. It was a success in so far as the jabber-jabber noise was warm and loud, without any drunks. Joyce (with whom I've not seen eye to eye lately), not asked to do turns and not wanting to either, thought it was 'too grand' and 'got better when it thinned out'.

24 March 1947. Go to J. for lunch and stay all afternoon to talk about a Shakespeare How and about Gamesmanship inserts in her new revue [she was working on *Tuppence Coloured*]. I get the impression that she is not really very keen on my submitting anything.

On 19th December of this same year Stephen wrote an account of the astonishing success of his book *Gamesmanship*. He could hardly believe the sales figures and his good fortune. He then reverted to the latest How, *How to be Good at Games*:

But on the strange rule 'the Lord giveth, the Lord taketh away', there has been a petty undermining of my pleasure. Today's programme, recorded for Christmas Day, was not pleasant to produce. Joyce got right across me and I felt that just when I had been given the peakiest time (after the 9 o'clock News, Christmas Day), it went wrong. Translating *Gamesmanship* from book to radio was difficult. [He lists various things that went wrong.] And then there was Joyce. She 1) said when I asked her, eagerly, yes, she wanted to be in it, there were several things she could do then 2) didn't do anything, so I said 3) 'By me. With inserts by you.' She agreed. 4) Inserts came, unbelievably skimpy. 5) I screwed one or two things out of her, wrote one or two more. 6) Not being the star of the show, she *much too subtly to pin down* played against it in production, by obtrusively

STEPHEN POTTER AT THE BBC

writing letters, complaining about my cigarettes, making the photographer feel awkward, being bored, being a *bit* nasty when dear old Ron suggested putting in the line 'Doesn't Uncle George look funny in that hat' (which of course I faded down). All very slight. *Trying* to help, and not making many constructive suggestions.

Finally, she rings up after Christmas, without the shadow of guilt or apology – because why should she, this was supposed to be *my show* – to say not good, not Christmassy enough, wanted more women.

20 little points. I haven't the faintest idea whether it is thick-skinnedness, over confidence, malice, or annoyance with the success of *Gamesmanship*. Or just not caring, because I am not attentive enough to her; or because she wants to mark the fact that *she* has got on so well … or genuine friendly frankness.

On my side I must admit to touchiness because she is my psychological boss.

The moral mentor aspect of Joyce was described in a different way by Richard Hoggart in *An imagined Life*. Both he and she had been members of the Pilkington Committee on the future of broadcasting. 'Her pertinacity and honesty,' he wrote, 'became the litmus paper of the committee's own sense of honesty.'

Joyce could be as critical of Stephen as he was of her. As became apparent in her account of Stephen's life in the Dictionary of National Biography, she disapproved of the concept of Gamesmanship and of his dependence on sequels in later years: 'For Potter the joke was played out, but for the rest of his life he found it difficult to write or speak naturally, so accustomed had he grown to the jocose gambits and ploys of his own invention….' Joyce also disapproved of Stephen's divorce in 1955, after which they rather drifted apart, although there were to be a few more radio collaborations. Her broadcast obituary could not have been more generous. Their working relationship had been fruitful and, in most cases, undertaken with enjoyment and gusto.

Chapter 12
Features on the Third

Features post-war

Early in 1945, Features nearly ceased to exist. Gielgud had suggested that Features should be disbanded and most writer/producers transferred to News – after all, Gilliam had started as a journalist and his own programmes had always been on current affairs. Bridson, McGivern and Dillon should also go to News (presumably in their capacity as documentary writers) but 'the output of Potter, MacNeice and the like should remain as part of the Drama Department'. This first attempt to wind up Features failed: William Haley said 'I have a completely closed mind against Features being allied to the News Division'; and those Feature writers whom Gielgud had wanted to retain resisted the attempt to blur the distinction between Features and Drama. Features emerged in a stronger position than before, as a Department in its own right. From July 1945 Gilliam was made its Director and no longer reported to Gielgud.

Drama and Features now developed in different ways. The main emphasis in Drama was still the adaptation of stage plays. Ian Rodger, in his book *Radio Drama*, calculated that in 1946 only three new plays were especially written for radio; in 1947 one, and in 1948 two. Features on the other hand became more uninhibitedly highbrow and experimental. As if to accentuate the distinction, Heppenstall describes how the two Departments even congregated at different pubs at lunchtime. Features went across the road to 'The Stag', where Heppenstall himself, Bridson, Dillon and MacNeice were regulars. This group was enriched by outside visitors such as Auden, Orwell, Dylan Thomas, C. P. Snow, Angus Wilson and many more. 'Stephen would never have more than half a pint and a sandwich, before going off to the Savile to play snooker.' Gilliam would stay longer: although also a member of the Savile, he was a pub man rather than a club man. Drama went to 'The George', where they drank less but cultivated a more stylish line in clothes – 'nobody could afford to do both'.

An unsettling factor was the impending return of television. It had been put on ice at the start of the war but its reintroduction was now being planned. Viewers might before long outnumber listeners, so would it not be prudent to learn the new techniques required? Gielgud, as has been seen, had made a start at it before the war. For those without that advantage, the obvious way in was to get experience in films. Stephen made continual attempts to do so, partly to gear up for TV and partly because films paid much better than the BBC. There are many references to a man called Baxter, who appeared to be luring Stephen into that medium with encouragement, flattery and vague promises. Nothing lasting emerged. Stephen did spend several days on set, trying his hand at minor jobs. He hated the slowness of pace, when days would be spent on a few short sequences and large numbers of extras and studio hands were kept hanging about at the whim of some dictatorial Director.

He was not alone in these worries. Even Gilliam spent 1949 away from Features, working with BBC Television. He found this did not suit him and he returned to radio. Perhaps he felt he was now too old to make the change. Only Cecil McGivern got it right. He left the BBC for a film company in 1945 and 1946, but was welcomed back in 1947 and appointed Head of BBC Television. In fact the cloud of TV proved to be more distant than had been feared. When it restarted in June 1946 it was allotted only a few hours each evening, reception was bad, range restricted and not many people had sets. It merited only three pages per week in the *RT*. Features continued to flourish in the fifties, well beyond the time span covered by this book.

A dividend of peace was that the Features Department no longer had to worry about propaganda. As Sackville-West pointed out in *Penguin New Writing*, its educational role had been sullied by its propaganda role. '… the two greatest enemies of education are noise and propaganda. Feature programmes have zoomed with dive bombers, rattled the dice box with Bren and Sten and crumpled the ear with high explosive….' As has been seen, MacNeice declined to do any more war-related programmes well before the war had ended, while Stephen had firmly shifted the main burden of his work to literary subjects.

Most positive of all for Features, and more than off-setting the pessimism about TV, was the introduction of the Third Programme. Some Feature writers had misgivings. Heppenstall wrote that one of the consolations of his work was that '... one communicated with a large, mixed audience, whom one might induce to accept what it would never have sought, an audience which, after all, had accepted Louis MacNeice's *The Dark Tower* and Stephen Potter's extremely sophisticated 'How' programmes. The Third Programme would separate off and spoon-feed just that part of the audience which was most capable of procuring its own artistic pleasures.' Yet once the Third had started, such doubts were quickly forgotten.

The New Channel

As a 'supply' department, Features theoretically provided programmes for all channels. In practice, almost all of its output had hitherto been for the Home Service: now it was nearly all for the Third. Its writer/producers felt they were released from the danger of being too elitist and were encouraged to experiment as freely as they liked. It is almost as if the new channel had been designed as a vehicle for their work, as is exemplified by the use of a How programme to start it off.

The Third Programme has only recently been comprehensively and lucidly dealt with by Humphrey Carpenter in *The Envy of the World* and his work will not be duplicated here. However, the author's introductory remarks about the BBC's output before the Third started do no justice at all to the seminal role of Features. The whole of wartime broadcasting is dealt with as follows:

> ... during the war the Home Service put out schools programmes, *Children's Hour*, drama, talks and light music, as well as news, with some orchestral concerts. The tone of both channels was relentlessly cheery.

In this summary, neither Features nor any of its efforts on the cultural front are mentioned. This omission contrasts oddly with Gielgud's assertion, in his 1957 book *British Radio Drama*, that 'It can reasonably be claimed that without ... Feature Programmes ... it is most unlikely that the Third Programme ... would ever have been thought of.'

Carpenter goes on to quote a wartime letter from Harold Nicolson to Lady Violet Bonham Carter on 'the BBC's unerring instinct for the second rate'. Nicolson set high Reithian standards and, as has been seen, was indeed critical of the BBC's treatment of English Literature. But that neither he nor Lady Violet thought all BBC programmes second rate is attested by their letters quoted on pages 140 and 172, respectively. The fact is that Features did constitute an embryonic Third Programme and that from now on producers and writers such as Cleverdon and MacNeice wrote for that channel rather than the Home Service. Their wartime output may have suffered from shortages of money, studio space, actors and above all time; but nonetheless they had managed to keep a high level of cultural programmes going, despite competition from propaganda and government information programmes.

George Barnes, formerly Head of Talks, was in charge of the new channel, assisted by Leslie Stokes, a producer from Drama and Features, and Etienne Amyot, a pianist who had injured his hand during the war and who had for a time been running the BBC's African Services. Stephen had been miffed that he himself was not one of the planners:

20 February 1946. About now have to decide whether or not to apply for the job of being No. 2 to Barnes on the new wavelength. In my view (this is my message to posterity!) I feel that I should have been *asked* to be connected with this, and if I had, I believe I should have made a great thing of it. As it is, I didn't even apply because a) I am not ambitious in the BBC, because I want to have my own real fling at creative writing in the next few years and b) I know the 3rd Floor are a bit agin me. Nevertheless this probably means that I am irretrievably stuck, from now on…. Some day the BBC will discover that I am only doing 20% of my wartime work and output.

14 July 1946. Who is this new second to George Barnes, chosen by him? He is an ex – presumably failed – pianist, who knows music. Surprise was a) that he was very positive and assured and b) that he was bow-tied and Raymond Mortimerish in polite dogmatism and air of francophilishness. Inclined to make statements which one was assumed to agree with and then wonder afterwards whether they ought to have come from him and whether they were in fact true. E.g. 1, that all Features using bits of recorded music must be bad; and 2, that Shaftesbury Avenue is the laughing stock of Europe, in every capital of which superb plays, e.g. *Huis Clos*, are to be found.

He also made a remark at which we all laughed – that I might remind Arthur [Bliss] to look to Britten's new scoring for 12 instruments only in his new opera – as a tip for Arthur's own radio writing.

But I was considerably calmed down in my uneasy rebellion by the big way I was asked to figure in the early plans. *Start* with a how – *How to Listen!* And *Moby Dick* (I admire and like Henry Green's adaptation). Laurence held his end up pretty well against Barnes and Amyot – but 'wanted a drink badly' afterwards.

Did Barnes ever consider Stephen as a henchman? Stephen was now 47, Barnes 42 and Amyot and Stokes 37 and 36. Barnes may not have wanted an older, more senior producer working under him. In any case, although Stephen had a good record as a fertile originator of programmes, he had none at all as an executive.

For Gilliam and Stephen, the situation was not comfortable. In effect, a new layer of authority had been interposed between them and C(P). The same was true of Drama. Gielgud had gone on record as saying that Sartre's *Huis Clos* was 'pretentious bosh of a decidedly unpleasant type'; yet Amyot had insisted on its being included in the first week of Third Programme broadcasts.

A major innovation of the Third was that it lifted the taboo on using recordings of programmes for repeats. Even before the new channel had opened, this ban had begun to crumble. Gramophone records may have led the way. Increasing use of them was made to fill off-peak music slots, although peak-time concerts were still live. Economy drives might well have further eroded live music if the musicians' unions had not stuck out against excessive use of 'needle time'.

Next it came to be accepted on the Third that recordings of spoken as well as music broadcasts could be used, as long as the original broadcasts had been live. It was only programmes that were pre-recorded before being broadcast at all that were still frowned on. Yet once it had been accepted that for repeats it did not matter if the audience was not listening to words at the same time as they were being spoken, how could anyone object if even the first performance was pre-recorded? The answer is that pre-recorded programmes were sloppier. When *The Critics* went out live, there may have been one or two garbled words, coughs and ums and ahs; but when it was pre-recorded, never less than 100 'edits' were needed. Stephen thought that for How programmes, it was essential for the actors to know that their efforts were being heard by millions at the very moment of performance, in order to get them keyed up. In her book, Joyce Grenfell disagreed: 'He [Stephen] had an innate sense of rhythm and pace that gave the programme something of the freshness of improvisation....

Immediacy was supposed to add quality and excitement.... But not for me. A performance is always a performance as far as I am concerned, and I find the necessary concert-pitch tension at a recording as stimulating as a live show.'

The Third used recordings for repeats years before the other channels. This may have been partly to save money and to encourage contributors with the lure of repeat fees; but the reason given was that listeners needed more than one chance to assimilate new and difficult works. When the BBC at last accepted the use of tape, editing became easier and pre-recording became the norm. The longest to stand out against it was Val Gielgud. According to John Drummond, in *Tainted by Experience*, Gielgud was still advocating live broadcasts when Drummond joined the BBC in 1957.

As feared, the effect of the Third was to deepen the distinction between highbrow and lowbrow. Classical music and poetry were no longer 'forced' on Home Service listeners; which is the very reason that Reith and others had argued against the new channel. Consumer choice was not yet king, but a step in that direction had been taken. Most listeners chose to stick with the Home Service and they far outnumbered those who switched to the Third. At first, no one seemed to worry about this. Writers and producers in Features were not instructed to popularise their work. The coming of the Third, taken together with the severance from Drama and the release from propaganda, presented Feature-makers with new opportunities.

More time

The hectic pace of wartime became a slow march. Gilliam took on more writer/producers and before long there were fourteen of them. Also, there were many more contributions from freelance writers, whose resistance to radio had largely been broken. Potentially, Drama benefited from this more than Features. Peter Shaffer submitted his first play (rejected) to radio, not the stage; Alan Ayckbourn began as a radio producer; Robert Bolt's first published script was for *Children's Hour* and Tom Stoppard's first play (fifteen minutes only) was for radio. For Features, outsiders such as George Orwell, Dylan Thomas, Laurie Lee and Elizabeth Bowen all contributed. At the same time, more studio space became available and three to four days were now allowed for rehearsals. So each writer/producer had fewer programmes to prepare and enjoyed a luxurious amount of time.

Stephen took advantage of these easements to take on more work elsewhere. He became the dramatic critic of the *New Statesman* and took on the weekly book reviews of the *News Chronicle* (the BBC accepted this last on the condition that he did not have a contract). In 1947 he wrote *Gamesmanship*. He seems to have played golf most days of the week and snooker every day. He wrote a play on a medical theme with Doyne Bell but failed to get it on the stage. He continued to cultivate various one-off jobs and links with the film industry, none of which developed. Some wondered how he managed to spend any time with the BBC at all.

He was not alone in spreading himself. Gilliam took on a series called *This is Europe* for the American-inspired Economic Co-operation Administration (ECA), based in Paris. This was to do with the distribution of Marshall Aid and the programmes, each about one of the recipient countries, were for broadcasting in the States. For a while, this took up most of his time – and the BBC accepted it as an extracurricular activity. Heppenstall, who devised some of the best post-war programmes, took advantage of the lack of pressure to stay at home. He says, in *Portrait of the Artist as a Professional Man*, 'I left home as late as possible in the morning or even in the early afternoon, and returned home as early as possible in the late afternoon or early evening.'

With so much more time and talent available, it was no longer necessary for each writer/producer to be able to turn his hand to any subject that came up, so they tended to specialize. MacNeice continued with verse plays, less easy to interpret. The best known, *The Dark Tower*, would have been ideal Third Programme material but came in January 1946, nine months before the channel opened. The hero is on a John Bunyan-type quest, the nature of which is largely left to the imagination. Reviewer Philip Hope-Wallace commented favourably on how little there was in it to help the listener get a visual picture of what was going on. This did not go down well with Stephen, who always maintained that good radio had to be written for the mind's eye, so that listeners could 'see' the events. Hope-Wallace, on the other hand, suggested that MacNeice had deliberately avoided visual images, so that the mind and ear could concentrate without that distraction. MacNeice had sent in the script suggesting Anthony Hopkins as composer, but Gilliam, perhaps sensing another *Rescue*, arranged for the music to be written by Britten. MacNeice dedicated his printed text to that composer, so pleased was he with the result. Response to the broadcast was at first mixed – either 'ecstatic or virulent', according to the author. *The Careerist*, written for the Third and broadcast in October, was still more obscure than *The Dark Tower*. As Carpenter describes it, it 'presents the life of a modern Everyman, James Human, largely through different voices inside his own head'.

Nesta Pain, who had joined Features in 1942, wrote largely on scientific subjects, such as a series on Archie MacIndoe's revolutionary techniques for skin grafting on burnt pilots' faces and hands. She specialized in big scientific or social subjects and made an hour-long documentary on atomic energy. She was an early version of today's investigative reporter, upsetting the complacency of those in charge. Her programme on Milk met with official attempts to suppress it, more dictatorial than any such intervention during the war:

> Tuesday, 25 February 1947. Laurence very excited about what really is an extraordinary affair about today's Milk feature. Nesta Pain was absolutely third degreed by the Milk Marketing Board, and Sir Donald van de Peer, Permanent Secretary, Ministry of Agriculture, tried to get Haley to stop the broadcast. In other words, vested interests (farmers), represented in both Board and Ministry, attempt to stop this broadcast, approved by doctors and by Ministry of Health. 2000 children die yearly from non-pasteurisation of milk.

Douglas Cleverdon had started with mostly Potter-type programmes. Indeed he had been co-producer with Stephen on the earlier, non-Joyce Hows and had gone on, confusingly, to produce non-satirical Hows on his own, such as, back in 1943, *How to look at a Town*, written and presented by John Betjeman. Now he produced a *Professional Portrait* and a *Return Journey* and ventured further into Potter territory with *The Minstrel Boy*, about the tenor McCormack. Later, some of his programmes became treasures of the Features department. Most notable were his collaborations with scriptwriter Henry Green, which began with a satirical series on twelve-tone composer Hilda Tablet, making near-the-knuckle fun of both Britten and Elisabeth Lutyens; and which later included such classics as Green's radio adaptation of Hardy's *The Dynasts*. Cleverdon was also the producer, in January 1954, of Dylan Thomas's *Under Milk Wood*. Over many months he had downed pints of beer in the company of the poet, in order to extract a script.

Rayner Heppenstall was a successful post-war recruit. It may be remembered that, like Stephen, he had been encouraged by John Pudney to try his hand at radio before the war, his first commission being on the subject of frozen meat. Having served in the army for the duration, he joined the BBC full time. His attitude to his work was in some ways similar to Stephen's. He thought his true métier was to write books and that he was only doing BBC work to scrape a living. In fact, like Stephen, his years at the BBC were his most productive and he created a range of imaginative programmes.

An early Heppenstall success was *Telepathy*, in October 1945. An investigation into whether there could be such a thing, it involved a mass experiment in which listeners were asked to participate. It was the first in a series *Is there something in it?*, which went on to cover witchcraft and other dubious phenomena. In January 1946 he persuaded George Orwell, with whom he had once shared a flat in Kentish Town, to write about Darwin's odyssey in *The Beagle* – this was for a new series, *Voyages of Discovery*. A third series he devised was *Imaginary Conversations*, rather along the lines of Gittings's *Famous Meetings*, except that the meetings as well as the conversations were imaginary. It was a good formula, as the number of imaginary meetings was inexhaustible: he was to produce and edit thirty 'Conversations' between 1946 and 1953. His main difficulty was finding good writers to invent them. He was successful with Rose Macaulay, C. V. Wedgwood, V. S. Pritchett and many lesser known names, but recorded in his autobiography, in a passage reminiscent of Stephen's efforts to find subjects for *Contemporary Portraits*, his more frequent failures: T. S. Eliot 'seemed disposed to accept, but… '; Graham Greene 'seriously toyed with the idea of writing a conversation between Henry James and Edgar Wallace'; Rosamond Lehmann 'proposed but never got down to' something else; and he 'had tea with Edith Sitwell at the Sesame Club … but nothing ensued'.

After listening to Heppenstall's *Professional Portrait of a Ballerina*, Stephen wrote:

21 March 1947. Beautifully written, beautiful atmosphere, etc. Ring up Rayner Heppenstall to congratulate him, knowing his troubles and remembering mine on the same subject. He has done his *far* better. Constant visual description. Haven't really liked a programme so much for months.

Stephen's contributions

Stephen was to do only one more music programme; and it provided his first real ear-opener to the music of Britten. The BBC had for many years been giving the composer a generous amount of airtime. They had broadcast early works in the early thirties. They had over a long period

191

commissioned him to write a great deal of incidental music. In 1945 they had broadcast *Peter Grimes* and in 1946 had commissioned *Festival Overture* for the opening night of the Third Programme. In October of that year they had presented a studio performance of *The Rape of Lucretia*. When they learnt that another new Britten opera, *Albert Herring*, was to be composed for Glyndebourne in 1947, it was decided that the première would be broadcast and agreed that Stephen should put together a programme about the making of that opera, to be broadcast the night before.

Britten was always wary of the media, and it could well be that his earlier meetings with Stephen, on the tennis court, at the Savile or over their more minor professional collaborations, helped him to accept this programme. The first reference to it is on 5 June 1947:

At Glyndebourne, spend night with Crozier and Peter Pears at Bishopstone Manor. John Piper is also there and Mr Lee, who takes down our talk.

Glyndebourne very cold, with harsh wind. Piper shows us a wonderful pub on the coast corner West of Seaford – beautiful decorations of boats. They are all deeply enjoying themselves. The music is most insinuatingly pretty in a lasting way. Ben is the complete boss, without slightest pomposity or hardness – just because he is working very concentratedly. As with the ballet programme, they are polite to me but I am obviously a queer fish to them, so utterly removed from their world.

Piper is the nicest. No drinks till 6 and then they *do* make moderate use of the cocktail bar. Ben's old open Rolls used for transport.

Christie, in a white jacket, rather avoided by everybody, which seems a shame. But he is alleged to be a little bit of a boring buttonholer, and he did so to me, asking me to take care over the balance between orchestra and voices. 'We work for months to get every detail exact, you see.' I thought Christie, rather unspoken to in the canteen, a sad figure, for all his wonderful possessions and enlightened use of them.

Monday, 16 June. Recordings, in morning, for opera programme. They all come up. Piper – I like his dry voice. Crozier – too incisive and well educated and clear. Britten – sounds, as he says, like Noel Coward. He improves under production (not so Crozier). 'I suppose there's a lot to be learnt about talking into the mike,' he says. He likes the records.

Thursday, 19 June. Fitting together extracts from rehearsals, studio discussion recordings, Glyndebourne recordings, James McKechnie's narration – all into a 44-minute programme. Very much enjoying the music, once more.

This jigsaw went out that night and the world première was broadcast live the next evening.

If Stephen was only doing 20% of his wartime output, that was by no means negligible. In addition to his How programmes, his specialization took the form of branching out into two new fields: fourteenth century English literature and Nature. But the more traditional Potter programmes also persisted. In his new series, *Return Journey*, writers talked about their childhood haunts: the first was in October 1945, with Eric Linklater on the Orkneys. Victor Pritchett revisited the Fells; the Lehmann siblings, John and Rosamond, returned to their family home in the Isle of Wight and Eddy Sackville-West (as mentioned earlier) described Knole. Francis Meynell, talking about his family home in Bayswater, showed up the hazards of live broadcasting:

14 July 1946. In spite of exact cutting, programme is *faded out* before the last four lines. This is a blow. Afterwards I share the delightful cold feast which P. has prepared for us and Doyne and Bay – but I cannot bear it. I fear I am partly to blame, though undoubtedly the major cause was the fact that F. lost a page of his script and ad libbed during it, very well, but time-takingly.

Eddy's programme went well:

Wednesday, 9 April 1947. … of course he chose particularly brilliant music; and he has so perfectly got the basic requirement of radio – writing for the eye, the mind's eye. Eddy did the narration and there again he was good because his voice passes the essential test, it is self-characteristic. Like his face it seems washed and worn by the waters of wisdom and feeling.

Another new series was *This Correspondence must now Cease*, readings of famous postal battles, such as Johnson *vs.* Chesterfield. Stephen arranged, edited and produced the first four; but this series, as well as *Professional Portraits*, *How it was Written* and *New Judgments*, were gradually taken over by others, who no doubt gave them fresh impetus. The last *New Judgment* produced by Stephen was on Cervantes in October 1947. He makes clear his lack of enthusiasm: 'Cervantes is to me one of those big classics about which all my life I have been handicapped with a vague smattering of literary education, which to me is like a wad of cotton wool plugging the orifice of learning and discovery.'

One-off Potter programmes included a hastily prepared tribute to H. G. Wells following his death in 1946, put together with his and Wells's fellow Club members Priestley and Pritchett. Another was a last collaboration with his friend Francis: a celebration of the centenary of his mother, Alice Meynell the poet.

For a talk he wrote and delivered on Wordsworth, Stephen underwent the new experience of being produced by someone else:

On the first run-through, Basil Taylor says I am declaiming too much. 'Talk to one person,' he says. And I realize it's all true. Isn't it incredible? This is the first rule of broadcasting, chapter one of all my writings. So I slacken up very much, and whisper into the mike, telling myself to keep slack and calm. P. says I sounded as if I was sprawling over the table. Boys say I got a bit passionate towards the end. One after-comment: 'How to do a scripted talk as if it was unscripted.'

The more creative aspects of Stephen's BBC work always took precedence over other responsibilities. His Literary Committee, set up at the instigation of Harold Nicolson, was not a success. The 'third floor' had never intended it to have any executive power and now with the Third Programme triumvirate doing the planning, it became superfluous. But it dragged on. As the non-BBC member, the ageing Desmond MacCarthy was gradually replaced by the unpredictable South African poet Roy Campbell:

20 February 1946. Lit. Com. in evening. Desmond has 'flu. Present: Geoffrey [Grigson] and Roy Campbell. I don't know whether it was because Howard Marshall had started me off with an enormous rum at the Club, but I found my company, except for Grigson, increasingly unbearable. I mean, really, Roy Campbell, that 'mad young man' Desmond provided for us. Wearing a wide-awake hat, he seemed to be constantly determined to live up to

some reputation of unconventionality, youthful intransigence, stark strength, South African bush, etc. 'What I like,' he will say, after two tiny whiskeys, 'is a real argument – you know, ceilings dripping with blood.' (To Geoffrey) 'You've got some real invective in you. That's what I like.' A little later: 'I'll open the bottle' (we hadn't got an opener) 'we used to do it with a biff like that' (with his bare hand). He then retired and took six minutes to get it off with the metal projection from the window, then darn me if he didn't say 'We used to bite them off.' He actually put the neck in his mouth, but in obedience to a feminine scream from the secretary, he repeated the same 6-minute business. I get stuffier and crosser and crosser.

So much for the committee that had been set up with such high aspirations. Stephen's value to the BBC lay not in chairing committees, but in the range and originality of the programmes that he continued to provide.

Moby Dick

Stephen's longest single production was *Moby Dick*, a radio adaptation of Melville's novel by Henry Green. It lasted two-and-a-quarter hours and was of a length that only listeners to the Third were expected to tolerate. Green had written it while working during the war as a cryptographer at Bletchley. Presumably he had a broadcast in mind, but at the time he affected to despise radio. He was converted by *The Dark Tower*. After hearing it, he wrote to MacNeice in January 1946, 'I have always thought your claim for radio's potentialities excessive; I now begin, reluctantly, to think you may be right.' Stephen had read Green's adaptation and promoted it: at a lunch with Barnes on 31 January it was agreed that he should produce it and that it should be earmarked for an early broadcast on the Third. 'Will Britten do the music?' wrote Stephen in July. As Melville's *Billy Budd* was later to be the subject of a Britten opera, his treatment of *Moby Dick* would have been of great interest; but in the event the music was written by Anthony Hopkins.

Hopkins later described his task, saying that as soon as Stephen Potter asked him to do it, he realized that it would require a full orchestra and that since so many players crammed into the studio along with the actors would be disruptive, the music would have to be pre-recorded. He had the knack of reading aloud the text while at the same time playing his music on the piano. This helped to get the length of each stretch right, but in case of overruns, he had for the first time used two gramophones. The music that accompanied the more meditative speeches was such that if the actor overran, the music too could continue, while the music for the next scene could start with the other gramophone whenever the moment came.

For Ahab, Stephen wanted Ralph Richardson, who just at the wrong moment went down with 'flu. Stephen managed to get the already scheduled programme postponed until January. He wrote to Gilliam:

> Only by postponing can we get Ralph Richardson for Ahab. He is far and away the best actor for the part: he has the exact right combination of earthiness, ordinariness and inspired fanaticism.... If he acted Ahab, it would make this production (provided I could play my part) one of the most successful and exciting programmes that the Third Programme and indeed the BBC has ever done.
>
> Thursday and Friday, 23 and 24 January 1947. Now I start to get going with *Moby*, in the biggest production I have ever had to do with. Difficulty No. 1 is *New Statesman* and *News Chronicle*. I have to go to *NC* in the morning. In the afternoon we do the music and I like the sound. But I have to prepare tomorrow's gigantic read-through with large cast, many of which I do not know. First horror – Ralph has 'flu (again!) and threatening laryngitis and must spend tomorrow in bed.
>
> After many more distractions, I really get going on preparing the script (87 pages) at eleven pm and have broken the back of it at 6 o'clock in the morning. This late night made me in what I felt to be tense and therefore bad form for the read-through at Langham.

The Friday read-through, scheduled for 10.30 am to 5 pm, took place without Richardson, although he was well enough to take part in the actual production. Because of its length, it was pre-recorded in four parts over four days of the following week and broadcast in two parts on the Friday. The cast also included Bernard Miles as Starbuck.

In line with the Third's new policy, a recorded repeat was broadcast on 18 February; and in September, there was a new production of the whole thing. Substitutes had to be found for Bernard Miles and two other actors, but Richardson was again Ahab:

Saturday and Sunday, 6 and 7 September. Two days full rehearsal of *Moby* so as to leave Monday, transmission day, clear. I have been dreading this; but in fact I have enjoyed it. Ralph is in superb form. He shows us a correction of a misprint: the sentence which spoke of 'our defective police force' should of course have read 'our detective police farce'. The gorgeous thing about these rehearsals is that Ralph, the monarch, treats me as if I was Prime Minister, and sends my stock up with all the other actors in consequence.

The programme was repeated a number of times thereafter. Green, as has been noted, became a prolific and admired contributor to radio. Nearly all his subsequent programmes were produced by Douglas Cleverdon.

Canterbury Tales

Stephen's last literary programmes revived his interest in early texts such as he had studied at Oxford while at the same time breaking new ground for the BBC. They were productions of works by Chaucer and Piers Plowman, using semi-modernised texts by Nevill Coghill. Coghill, an authority on this period, wrote that he had tried to make *Canterbury Tales* comprehensible to the modern ear while being as faithful as possible to the original, with 'no wanton changes'. To some extent the programmes succeeded in popularising Chaucer. The Third had seemed the obvious channel, but after their success on that, they were repeated on the Home Service. The texts were printed by Penguin in 1952 and became a best-seller. Later still they were used as the basis of a West End stage production. Coghill appeared to be just as enthusiastic about Stephen's productions as Stephen was about the texts. It was perhaps the only time that Stephen had unreservedly enjoyed producing works written by someone else.

Regional accents were used, as they were thought to be closer to the language as it was spoken in Chaucer's time:

13 March. *Canterbury Tales 6, Reeve's Tale.* Rehearsed in office in afternoon, recorded at 9.30. We got in Mawdsly for his Norfolk accent and Ian Catsford, the dialect specialist, to do Tyneside. Script particularly deftly treated by glorious Nevill, who has sent me a £3 book of Giotto reproductions. We have a lot of fun with the accents. (Later Billy Williams says in *The Observer* that we have 'taken the Eng. Lit. out of Chaucer'.)

Footnote. This programme utterly broke all previous records in my or any BBC experience for obscenity – totally wrong word. Should say broadness. (Ten days later still not a single complaint.) This is due mostly to the mysterious fact of the date making it OK. It is also due a little I think to the dialects. But it is principally due to Chaucer's complete lack of sniggering and his simple enjoyment of this kind of joke when it happens to come up.
Oh the luck, for me, of this Chaucer run!
16 April. Last number of the *Canterbury Tales*, alas. All pleasure and no pain for me, this series.

In line with the Third's policy of repeating 'difficult' programmes so as to give listeners the chance of hearing them again, all seven were repeated during a week in May, one on each day. There was also a re-run in 1949.
As soon as the Chaucer collaboration had finished, Stephen and Coghill began to work on a similar treatment of Langland's *Piers Plowman*:

Thursday, 13 May 1947. Plunge into mediaeval austerity and fanatical single-mindedness with the first number of another vast BBC series. Know at once that I am not going to enjoy this nearly so much as the Chaucer. Am made to realize how much the Chaucer pleasure was due to the lovely and beautiful geniality of Chaucer himself, who although in detail is somewhat impersonal, is in fact always present, like a generous, understanding and forgiving deity.
Thursday, 12 June. *Piers Plowman II*. Specially good translation by Coghill, who is in excellent appreciative form. Wonderful material. The thrill of realizing that this old monk was bold and original and imaginative enough to say some of these lovely, big or delicate poetical passages here in London in 1370. Excitement of this programme.
Monday, 7 July. *Piers Plowman III*. End of Chaucer and Langland programmes, which I most deeply regret. It has been my best break in broadcasting. Only I know how little the great, even historic series has been due to me, how much to Coghill.

In fact at the start of January 1948 another Potter–Coghill collaboration started, this time on Chaucer's *Troilus and Criseyde*. Stephen managed to get Celia Johnson for Criseyde – a coup, as she was by now famous and much sought after. He also got Miles Malleson. Describing a rehearsal on 13 January he wrote: 'Miles Malleson came in late. He had studied his part carefully, and of course there was no more real chance of my producing him, this born and studious actor, soaked in knowledge, than there was of instructing a wild horse in grace and virility.' After producing two of this new series, Stephen succumbed to a prolonged bout of 'flu, during which his treatment switched from M and B to penicillin. Summing up his period of illness he wrote:

There were to be four more *Troilus and Criseydes*. Well, I never went near any of them, except to do a little casting of small parts from bed. Jennifer Wayne produced … the party was perfectly happy … and after at first making frantic efforts to be there, and feeling intensely worried about not being there, this quickly gave way to a thankful feeling that I was not there, and a general desire to keep away as long as possible.

Nature

In what seemed like a reward for their overwork and confinement during the war, some writer/producers were given assignments that took them abroad. Bridson, for a series *Window on Europe*, spent three weeks touring Norway in November 1945, with similar tours of Czechoslovakia and Yugoslavia in the following two years. Gilliam gave himself three weeks in Denmark. Stephen, whose enthusiasms were anchored in the UK, had a different kind of break. For four consecutive summers he toured the remoter parts of Scotland and Wales in the company of bird and plant experts to make Natural History programmes. He was able to combine his knowledge of wild plants with his work; and he took the opportunity to expand into other fields, such as geology and birds. The pleasure of all this was enhanced by the fact that he would be driving. Before the war he had driven everywhere. Now, as late as 1947, petrol was still rationed and he could not in any case afford a car. So, getting away from blitzed London with a BBC car and unlimited petrol, he felt released.

Stephen needed a professional to help him write the Nature programmes and for most of them he collaborated with James Fisher, the ornithologist. When he and Stephen had first worked together, in July 1944, Fisher was in the middle of a four-year study to determine whether rooks should be shot for the harm they did by eating crops, or whether this was outweighed by the good they did eating pests. (In the end his advice was to let them be.)

The 1944 programme had been to mark the centenary of the final extinction of the Great Auk – that bird's last egg had been broken 100 years earlier. Fisher came down to Toppesfield to discuss it. Indoors, he always gave the impression of being still out in the open:

> Monday, 10 July 1944. … impossible not to be a bit irritated. Muddy boots, not helping to clear away, bringing no rations, only speaking to P. if he feels like it, generally uncouth manners. He does a fine imitation of the three main sea-birds of St Kilda and a fine description of the island.

Fisher had also supplied some of the material for Stephen's programme on the writing of *On the Origin of Species* in December of the same year; but their first motorised expedition was in the summer of 1945, when Stephen was invited to join him and Julian Huxley on a tour of Northern Britain to research the populations of fulmars and petrels. Using maps to keep as far away as possible from roads, they identified 101 species in the course of eight days. Stephen learnt to spot a bird 'by its flight, gait and occasionally silhouette; hardly ever by its colour.' In his programme *The Watchers Watched*, he tried to pass this on to those frustrated by not being able to identify birds from pictures.

The Watchers Watched was followed in 1948 by *The Botanists Botanised*; but neither really set the pattern for the major Potter–Fisher collaborations, which began with *Finding Alpine Britain*, in July 1946. In an article in the *RT* Stephen wrote: 'Those of us who were kept at home during the war are longing, more than ever before, for a glimpse of a new country. But the best place to see a variety of wild life is *here*.' As an example of this, he wanted to show that even alpine flora and fauna were to be found in Britain – even as low as 2000 feet above sea level, if one went far enough North in Scotland.

The expedition to research the programme had begun at the end of May, when Stephen and James had driven first to Skomer, on the West coast of Wales, to study seabirds. Stephen made copious notes. On the sound of the shearwaters he wrote:

> … a generalised effect of an undulating, seething coo, against the background of which the nearer birds fly past repeating the word

'Lo-pokova' in a voice which, though basically tender and cooing, is half strangled by asthma.

From Skomer the two drove several hundred miles to the Cairngorms in Scotland, where they were to look for the dotterel, one of the official purposes of the expedition. They climbed Carn Ben More, with Stephen noting which plants grew at which heights. They then drove through the Highlands to Cape Wrath, 'the highest precipice in Britain overlooked a perfect sandy bay.' In the late, cold evening Stephen found a few plants that were new to him, including Mountain Avens (Dryas octopetala) – 'the wonderful sensation of seeing a truly new plant.' (There are no other UK species in the genus.) At midnight, he noted the long line of Northern sunset.

From Cape Wrath they went along the coast to the North East tip of Scotland; and thence by boat to The Orkneys, where they stayed with the Linklaters, whose home was on the island of Hoy. Stephen described 'Link' as playing the part of 'the grim, lone, serious man of talent – the grand old man of Hoy' – this after he had ventured to play some Scots songs on the piano, and Linklater had stomped out to sit in another room, in the dark.

The next day was spent visiting, in freezing conditions, Muckie Green Holm, a tiny and uninhabited island three hours North by boat, so that Eric Hosking could photograph the birds:

Sunday, 16 June 1946. Those cliffs made the wild life seem on top of you. Suddenly coming face to face with the sack-like mouths of three or four hobbledehoy cormorants – with a new young one, absolutely naked, lying with horrible helplessness in its black, plucked bird skin at their feet. The young shags are a little pleasanter – they dart their beaks forward not to attack, but for food. The whole cliffside was as stale and untidy with this wild life as the bustickety drifts under a London railway bridge are with town life. Stale with stink and droppings. Terribly shorn sheep above … gulls always alone, gulls' nests open to our feet – no bushes, just grass and thrift and scurvy grass and spring squill.

The three hours in the boat back to Hoy were just as cold, and pretty rough. James had done a good job counting fulmars. We see stormy petrels and black guillemots. I was a little melancholy, at the end of my trip.

Notes such as these were the basis for *Finding Alpine Britain*. It was broadcast on 7 July. As Stephen did the narration, he was rehearsed by another producer, who told him he sounded like a WEA lecturer. In his notes on the production, Stephen wrote: 'It didn't really click with the cast. Polite interest only.' For once Stephen had decided on a straight-forward, narrative style, which was slammed as 'wordy and almost wholly unevocative' in *The Observer*.

Although reactions were muted at the time, *Alpine Britain* was followed that October by *The Natural History of Salcey Forest* and in May 1947 Stephen and James went on another expedition to the Highlands, to write about Inverpolly Forest, north of Ullapool. For the third year in succession, their Highland hosts were Tom and Charmian Longstaffe. Tom, an astonishingly active septuagenarian, had been a full-time mountaineer and President of the Alpine Club. He persuaded the party to go on a climb, difficult enough to qualify as true mountaineering. Stephen got to the top, managing to suppress his fear of heights, but not before getting stuck in the wrong gully, from which he had to be rescued with ropes by James. On the way home they were again the guests of the Linklaters, who had now 'moved South' to Nigg, near the Firth of Cromarty.

Ten days after the Inverpolly programme in July, Stephen set out on yet another expedition:

Saturday, 27 July. 6.30 pm from Euston for Stranraer Harbour [west coast of Dumfries and Galloway] with nine naturalists, including James and photographer Eric Hosking. Object of the trip: to satisfy various people's comprehensible lust to fly over Rockall, deep-in-Atlantic outpost of Europe, 400 miles West. We were also to undertake, with government backing, a seal count, flying over *all* the hundreds of islands in Britain above the latitude of Pembrokeshire. God bless the BBC – they sent me as their nature Feature expert and insured my life for £2000.

No sleepers, of course. Arriving at 5.30 a.m. frantic for breakfast, we get it at last in the RAF mess at Wig bay. But the trip was a failure – for me. As we were driven down to the Sunderland that was to take us on our 1700 mile journey, including the Hebrides, St Kilda and Cape Wrath, a thunderstorm broke, visibility disappeared and the Met vetoed our departure. Most stayed to do this trip, but I had to get back.

In fact the whole thing was postponed until September. Whatever its scientific value, it resulted in only one programme, *The Natural History of St Kilda*.

It was George Barnes and his successor, Harmer Grisewood, who encouraged Stephen to continue the series. He was persuaded at a meeting of all three in November 1947 to make the programmes more 'featurised', with less narration and more in line with his normal type of work. More expeditions ensued, resulting in *The Natural History of Winter*, *The Natural History of the Red Kite* (already then on the danger list) and a programme of bird song recorded by Ludwig Koch. Koch was an undeterrable believer in the potentialities of disc recordings. In an attempt to catch the voices of seals in a sea cave on the north coast of Scotland, he had had to cut 120 discs, before getting 12 that were usable.

Most enjoyable of all for Stephen was a five day break in April 1948 in the Grosvenor Hotel at Swanage, to make a programme about the Isle of Purbeck for an Overseas series on different parts of Britain. He took the whole family with him, which stretched the capacity of the small BBC car – if the weight distribution of the four persons in it was wrong, it began to sway. His diary notes about the plants, birds and geology of the area are mixed with comments on the family games of ping-pong and billiards played in the hotel.

The Potter–Fisher Natural History programmes helped to generate the now widespread interest in Nature and were the best that radio could offer to meet the demand that today is so much better met by television.

Chapter 13
Goodbye

Stephen was now on the brink of departure – a good time to summarise his techniques as a writer/producer.

Perhaps the most striking thing about Stephen's programmes is their diversity – Nature, Regimental Histories, Poetry, Satire, Ballet and so on. He had learnt how in a short time to become sufficiently knowledgeable to write a programme about any subject. With a didactic streak that would have been pleasing to Reith, he believed that once the jargon had been stripped away, it was possible to explain to listeners the latest developments in any field of study.

The subject matter varies, but there are recurring characteristics. On the production side, although early on he had used recorded sounds and interviews, notably in *Undergraduate Summer*, he later used actors rather than actuality; and would not mix the two. Accents were usually imitated by actors – his use of Cornishmen in *The Last Crusade* was an experimental exception. He also preferred the use of an actor even when the protagonist was himself available – the main exception here was the casting of the cartoonist David Low to play himself.

Stephen excelled at simulating reality, not in recording it. The background hum of conversation in *How to give a Party*, together with the halting and often interrupted conversations of those nearest the microphone, could have been mistaken for the real thing. Daringly, he encouraged his cast to ad lib, although this ran counter to the still strict rules about scripted broadcasts. This was particularly dangerous while programmes were still going out live. His aim in other Features was to make scripted discussions sound spontaneous. This artificiality eventually began to jar. Of John and Rosamond Lehmann's *Return Journey* to the Isle of Wight, one critic wrote that it was all too obvious that such 'impromptu' reminiscences were nothing of the kind.

How much easier Stephen's efforts with the Lehmanns would have been had he had the use of tape! The initial conversation would have been taped and then either edited and itself used for the broadcast, or used to write a script with a better simulation of spontaneity. Tape did not become available to producers until after Stephen had left the BBC in 1948. But it *could* have been. Invented by the Germans during the war, Bridson acquired it for his tour of Norway in 1945 – and so became the first BBC producer to experiment with it, just as he had been the first to experiment pre-war with capturing local accents on disc. Even after René Cutforth, a well-known reporter of the fifties, had used it to great effect in the early stages of the Korean war, it was (according to Rodger) locked away on his return to the UK and the invention was not generally taken up by the BBC until the mid fifties. Producers may well have been worried about the prospect of having to work with the new device – rather as surgeons may have quailed at being asked to switch to keyhole surgery. Gilliam wrote enthusiastically about it in 1950, but does not seem to have actively encouraged it. Stephen perhaps did as well as anyone with the traditional method of simulation, but had he stayed on, that would have been a dead end.

Stephen's attitude to the use of sound effects to some extent turned with the tide. To begin with, perhaps influenced by Lance Sieveking and his book, *The Stuff of Radio*, he was keen to explore their possibilities. He took his sons to the BBC to look at the store of sound-producing gadgets, such as a huge hanging sheet of metal which could be shaken so as to sound exactly like thunder. But the stock of sounds became clichés: if someone were to say, for example, 'I must go and get ready,' the listener heard the standard recordings of a door being opened and shut, the creak of stairs and the turning on of the bathroom tap. The idea gradually began to emerge that it was better to let the dialogue suggest what was happening, with music to indicate the mood – the rest being left to the imagination. Gielgud himself led the way. Early in the war he had produced *The Saviours*, a series of verse dramas on national heroes such as King Arthur and King Alfred, which relied largely on words and music. Linklater did the same with *Cornerstones* and Sackville-West took the idea still further: sounds other than words and music were excluded altogether from *The Rescue*.

Stephen was slow to follow this trend. In *Everest*, the clink of a pick on ice could be heard; in *Shakespeare Discovery*, the thud of a dropped book. In both he was stretching the listener's imagination not by doing away with sound effects, but by cutting out the narrator. But eventually sound effects came to be seen as old fashioned, and Stephen used them hardly at all.

A more unusual aspect of Stephen's programmes was their loose construction, which tended to the surreal. Quick cuts or fades from scene to scene were plentiful. A voice representing the protagonist's private thoughts would be gradually brought in over a conversation that at the same time would be gradually faded out. Key phrases encapsulating a character's aspirations would be repeated from time to time, as if from limbo. Grace Wyndham Goldie wrote of 'Mr Potter's frequent departure from any sort of reality of treatment'.

Such programmes were created to some extent in the course of rehearsals. Where more solid writing was required, Stephen again had a distinctive style. The 'hint of mockery' referred to by the reviewer of the 1938 *Guide to the Thames* was a constant element and, in the 'How' programmes, came to dominate. It first appeared in *The Muse in Chains*, in which he maintained that students reading English Literature were taught everything about it except Literature itself. With examinations in mind, they were taught 'Lit.', the shadow of the the substance.

Francis Meynell in his autobiography described Stephen as a 'supreme wordsmith'. Later several of his new words were incorporated in dictionaries: 'one-upmanship', 'ploy' and even gamesmanship itself in its present-day meaning were all invented by Stephen. Neologisms are always coming into the diaries, which is one of the reasons they are so difficult to decipher. 'Bustickety' has already been quoted as part of his description of Orkney cliffs.

The cliché was anathema. When ill in bed in 1941, Stephen had listened to the radio, recording his comments on everything:

> Yugoslav Folk Songs, sung well by Frederick Woodhouse and appallingly presented by him, in the fearful journalism used by the BBC. All the tired phrases roll out. A patriotic song is always 'a trumpet call to action' and so on. Should I write a memo about this? But who to?

Stephen believed the use of clichés was mere laziness and that it was impossible to express well an original thought or description with a pre-fabricated pattern of words. To write without clichés became for him the natural thing to do and they are difficult to find in his writing, even in his diaries.

Original in his use of language, Stephen continually came up with new ideas for programmes. *Contemporary Portraits* got away from the over-egging of our national heritage; 'How' provided a new formula for satire, and the bird and plant forays in the Highlands stimulated new interest in Natural History. Particularly valuable to the planners were the many new series that Stephen thought up. Twelve of these have been mentioned in this book. His treatments too were original, as when he hinged *Victorian Negative* on the reminiscences of Samuel Butler's ageing servant; or when he dealt with Home Front issues through the recalcitrant Mr Leversuch. It is as an ideas man that Stephen was most valuable to his employers.

An end to programme making

Stephen's new-found willingness to produce programmes written by others, mainly instanced by *Moby Dick* and *The Canterbury Tales*, did not signal his decline as a writer. His book and theatre reviews were more than a diversion from routine: they were a shift in the main focus of his attention away from the BBC. Although he was still producing a fair number of programmes, his diaries are now 90% about other matters. On 21 May 1946 he wrote:

> Today I really have finished the biggest spurt of writing I've ever been caught up in – feeling wonderfully exercised in the mind – just like the body after lawn tennis, clear, tired in a non-achey, non-sleepy way – words coming very quick to the pen. They include 3000 on Stratford for *Theatre Today*, 400 for the *New Statesman* and 4500 for *The Saturday Book*, on how I wrote the Doctor programme.

The very next day he writes:

> Mrs Milne of *Future* books comes and asks me to do something for them on Radio, about 5500 words. £30? No. £50? Yes. I feel quite flattered.

Stephen and Doyne had not been successful in getting their play accepted for the West End stage but he had achieved some status as a critic. In 1946 he undertook a long article on the state of the theatre in post-war Britain for *Penguin New Writing*. He accepted these jobs partly because he wanted to be poised to move on in one direction or another. He was working well and felt he was able to make a wider contribution than was possible within the confines of the BBC.

Also, he needed the money. His BBC salary had reached £1250, which was not enough for his style of life. His total income at the end of the year, including the outside jobs, came to £1990. This made a difference, but was still not enough. '... I remember my moneylessness, the daily pain of carlessness ... the lack of clothes, of decent summer holidays for the boys.' Bridson had complained to Director General Haley that his opposite number in the US was getting 25 times his own salary: only someone with Bridson's dedication would have stayed with the Corporation in such circumstances.

For some time Stephen had felt that the way ahead was blocked. In January 1948 he had been invited to an Ideas Dinner. He noted that everyone present except himself was initialled – C(P) in the chair, DFD [Deputy Features Director], ADF [Assistant Director Features], DT [Director of Talks], etc., etc. He thought his 'lowly status as a maker of programmes will never progress to the administrative class and the consequent tripling of salary.'

His bitterness about his pin-striped bosses, who although largely ignorant about radio hardly ever consulted those who did the real work, has been mentioned often enough already. To show that he was not the only moaner, here are a few comments made by some of his contemporaries and successors:

Joseph MacLeod, a newscaster and BBC writer during the war, was glad to leave in 1945 to make films in Scotland, where he found 'none of the sequestered softness of Broadcasting House, none of that effortless superiority and contempt for the masses'. In his book, *A Job at the BBC*, he says there was 'a cleavage between the convention-ruled officials and the talents of the many men and women on the job with a consequent universal sense of frustration in the latter'. He claims that Lord Reith's original plan was to have three adminstrators to every 100 programme staff; whereas in 1945 there were about 2000 administrators and 800 programme staff.

Gielgud wrote 'British broadcasting has always suffered from the tendency of the engineering or administrative tail to wag the programme dog.'

Priestley (admittedly a born grumbler) organised in 1947 through the Society of Authors a better deal for BBC writers by threatening strike action. He spoke of 'that contempt for authors and authorship which has always distinguished official life'.

Bridson, on the eve of his retirement, helped organise a petition against the dismantling of the Third Programme. 'Implicit in the protests,' he wrote, 'was the indignation felt by the signatories that once again the BBC management had taken upon itself to decide a matter of the greatest importance to BBC programmes without the slightest reference to people whose duty it was to make those programmes.' This complaint did not change over the years. As recently as 2002 *Libby Purves* wrote, in her *Radio: a true love story*: 'Programme makers – apart from a favoured few in television – were treated with arch contempt by not very talented managers.'

A related grudge of Stephen's was raised again in 2000 by *John Drummond* in *Tainted by Experience*. He wrote that in 1993 the top job in radio had gone 'according to the new pattern, to someone outside the BBC with no previous experience'. New? Even in the forties Stephen was being sarcastic about the policy that the top jobs in radio could not go to employees, lest their experience was too centred on radio. When Robert Foot in 1941 was brought into the BBC as 'No. 3 key man', with a view to his becoming Director General in the near future, Stephen simply stuck the press cutting in his diary, refraining from making any comment whatsoever. It read: 'Gas company chief joins BBC. Mr Robert Foot, 52-year-old manager of the Gas, Light and Coke Company, had been appointed....'

Troops always criticise the generals. Lord Simon, Chairman of the Governors from 1947 to 1952, pointed out that Gielgud and Gilliam had been left to run Drama and Features for twenty years and that at least the Governors should take some credit for that. But there does seem to have been an ineradicable malaise, which was a contributory reason for Stephen's departure.

In February 1947 the Minister of Fuel, Shinwell, had closed down the Third Programme for a fortnight as part of the economy measures during the fuel crisis. Lights were also dim in the snooker room and with snow everywhere, Stephen was hard put to it to get his usual quota of exercise. He took the opportunity to write *Gamesmanship*. It was so successful that even the BBC hierarchy noticed it – and commented:

> 28 November 1947. Alarming and irritating 'outside activities' memo this morning. I never asked permission to do *Gamesmanship*! Ye gods. What would *you* do? Stick on at the BBC at £1380 for life, providing them with prestige programmes, being given no responsibility for policy? Become a Lance Sieveking and disappear? Or what?

Shouldn't they *encourage* us to write other things?
However, my relations are usually pretty happy there.

The crunch came on 4 June 1948. Catching up on his diary the following August, Stephen wrote:

The Raison lunch at Jardin des Gourmets. Looks like being one of the most tide-in-the-affairs-of-men occasions of my life (though I have to say that in my experience these tides occur monthly, with the moon).

Max Raison had met Stephen before in the golf club at Aldeburgh. He turned out to be Managing Director of the Hulton Press, which owned a number of publications well known at the time, including *Picture Post* and *Lilliput*. One of them had been losing sales and money. He now said: 'We are dissatisfied with *The Leader*. My original idea, to which we want to return, was to make it educational. How much would you like to be associated with it as editor?' The salary tentatively suggested was £2500 and Stephen's first reaction was to indicate that he was very happy where he was. However, now began a long process of consulting with all his friends and listing the pros and cons in his diary:

My precious free time – my golf and tennis … a new régime would certainly be necessary, a new discipline such as I have never quite done – 10 am to 6 pm. On the other hand, haven't some of my recent programmes – *Botanists Botanised* and *How to play Games* – shown signs of staleness? The lack of encouragement and incentive at the BBC. Isn't it the famous burial ground, a Val-halla?

In the end, Stephen accepted an offer of £3000 on 11 August, undertaking to start on 1 November. His last programme as an employee was a new production on 12 August of Elizabeth Bowen on Jane Austin and he recorded feeling 'pleasantly sad'. As usual there were two pages on how each member of the cast had done. Of Celia Johnson, he wrote: 'She is at her absolute best. When she speaks a line, she mows a narrow path through the wildness and disoriented words of the text … she throws a lighthouse beam along the dim Roneo of the script.'

On 13 August Stephen told Gilliam he was leaving. A month after that he wrote:

My farewell to the BBC has been pretty well what I expected. Plenty of friendliness from the department, very bad on the formal side. First, a phone message asking me to put my carefully worded and warm letter to Laurence in memo form. Then, an interview with the D.G. who as usual does nearly all the talking having asked me to talk – to tell him, in fact, now that I have left, the pros and cons of working for Broadcasting.

1 October [his last day]. No regrets at leaving, in a way. Simply a profound depression. Why? Every available drop of my smallish productivity went into the job for years – years. Is it really all dropped like an old packing case, full of dusty old bits of paper, to the bottom of the sea – to leave nothing for the final ebb tide?

On 10 November he met a Club friend who still had not heard that he had left. ' "But you're the only broadcaster I listen to … I can't believe it…. Did they make no effort to persuade you to stay?" "No, none whatever." '

Rayner Heppenstall in his book wrote: 'Stephen Potter left, followed next year by MacNeice. The Department was thus deprived of its two brightest ornaments.'

It was the end of Stephen's career as a writer/producer; but despite his cool departure, he continued to work freelance for the BBC as a broadcaster. Douglas Cleverdon had devised a new series, *A Year I Remember*. Perhaps as a kind of leaving present, Stephen was asked by Gilliam to start this off and in December he talked about his experiences in 1925. Records at Caversham show that, including appearances in discussion programmes such as *The Critics*, Stephen made a further 144 broadcasts between 1949 and his death in 1969. In a last collaboration with Joyce Grenfell, the two started a quiz programme on classical music, *Call the Tune*. This evolved into Joseph Cooper's *Face the Music* on television – but this was without Stephen, who never got into that medium.

Stephen made a new magazine out of *The Leader* – more up-market and educational. But sales continued to decline and losses continued to mount. The job lasted a year.

Postscript

The Death of Features

The subsequent history of Features is well dealt with by both Bridson and Heppenstall. At first, Features in the Fifties continued to expand and flourish. In addition to those already mentioned, more outside writers contributed, including Ted Hughes, Olivia Manning, C. V. Wedgwood, Muriel Spark, Michael Innes and Pamela Hansford-Johnson. Features post-Potter shone more brightly than ever – and the Department was responsible for most of the programmes so well described in Carpenter's book about the Third Programme.

This scene was overcast in 1955, when the by-now-much-bigger cloud of television swelled with the first broadcasts of Independent Television. While BBC TV on its own had not had much impact on listenership figures for radio, the availability of a choice of TV channels, the willingness of ITV to give the public what it wanted and the improvement in the coverage of TV transmitters all began to have their effect. BBC management now began to think, like their ITV rivals, in terms of a competitive fight for audience; and this attitude spread to radio. The consistently small listenership for the Third was seen as uneconomic.

Endemic discontent with the bosses worsened with the periodic invasions of management consultants and outside accountants, whose criteria were more Thatcherite than Reithian. Heppenstall, writing of the late fifties, must again be quoted:

> The premises were invaded by creatures from outer space, cost accountants, time-and-motion-study experts and so on…. They invented new forms for producers and secretaries to fill in and, following processes not yet publicly divulged by C. Northcote Parkinson, themselves proliferated at an alarming rate, so that presently there were hundreds of them, each drawing his salary and all bent on establishing that in one or other production

department or technical section there might be a producer or a technician too many.

(This tone is no different from that used forty years later by BBC figures such as John Drummond and John Simpson – and by more lowly employees. When I myself was researching this book at Broadcasting House, I was told by someone in the Library: 'We've just had another big clear-out. We've only got Management Reports left on the shelves. You'll find Herodotus in the skip.')

In October 1957 Sir Ian Jacob, who had succeeded Haley as Director General in 1952, cut the number of hours per evening for the Third from 5½ to 3½. He was not swayed by furious and co-ordinated opposition from the BBC's programme makers, the only concession being that the channel would get six hours on Sundays. The net effect for Features was that its airtime had been cut in half.

Features never fully recovered from this blow. Laurence Gilliam, in his prime, might have faced out the calls for the dismemberment of the Department, which once again began to be heard. But now the weight of top brass he confronted was becoming too difficult to deal with. It has already been shown how soon after he had acquired unfettered control over Features he began to lose it, becoming subject to the new layer of authority represented by the triumvirate running the Third Programme. Then in 1948 new, broader divisions were created such as Entertainment and The Spoken Word, among which responsibility for the existing Departments would be divided. The title of Director was reserved for those in charge of such divisions: Gilliam became a Head rather than a Director and Features became part of the Entertainment Division. Instead of Features deciding how to fill their allocated slots, planners at a higher level would now suggest what was wanted.

Stephen equated the decline of Features with the decline of Gilliam. As early as January 1948 he wrote in his diary a three-page verbatim account of a planning meeting that included Gilliam and Harmer Grisewood, then Head of Talks. Gilliam was putting forward, bombastically, a proposal that the BBC should for once feature The Passion, telling the story in parts from a variety of European countries:

L: (quietly but with inner power): Here is this wonderful story – been told for centuries … inspiring generations … and *we don't do anything about it*. My idea is to tell the story with all the nations taking part. Switching from one to another, taking the music from each nation in turn. A bit of Bach from England, Verdi from – Rome, isn't it? Then Spain. Then Kiev – if we can get a landline there. It's an idea I've dreamed about for ages.

H: Yes, but is it a good idea?

L: It's an absolutely wonderful idea.

H: But it is not the policy of the Third to give musical works in bits.

L: Well, here's another good idea for you. Let it *be* the policy.

Years later, Stephen wrote of the meeting: 'Grisewood was just as tough as Gilliam, who never, in the end, got away with it. His idea was transferred to Home Service, where it was decently buried. Looking back, I see this as the beginning of Laurence's long, at first almost imperceptible, sixteen-year decline towards final extinction.'

The decline was indeed a slow one. At first Features seemed to be surviving the reduction in the Third's airtime, helped by MacNeice's return to the scene on a freelance basis. Yet gradually competition from television pared down the audience for radio. By the end of the fifties the numbers listening to the Home Service were only a tenth of what they had been during the war. And the figures for the minority interest programmes were of course much lower. The echelons of planners perceived a need for economies.

The boundaries of Features were still only vaguely defined and perhaps it was this messiness that doomed the Department. *Moby Dick* or *The Dark Tower* could both have come, perhaps should have come, from the Drama Department, while other Features could just as well have emanated from Talks. But it was not until 1964, ten years after the first ITV broadcasts, that Frank Gillard, Director of Sound Broadcasting, announced to the assembled Features Department that it would soon be dispersed to Drama, Current Affairs and other departments. He tempered this by saying that the change might wait until after Gilliam had retired. An early-retirement package was then agreed, but Gilliam, who had been ill for some time, died that year, still at work. As Heppenstall wrote, 'Gilliam died and Features died with him.'

Sources and Bibliography

Stephen Potter's diaries constitute the main source of information for this book and, apart from the passages quoted, much of the rest of the text is based on unquoted diary entries. In addition, the BBC archives at Caversham have been consulted over a number of years.

Further information and quotations have been taken from:

BRIGGS, A. (1965). *The History of Broadcasting in the UK*, vols 1 and 2. Oxford University Press.

BROME, V. (1988). *J. B. Priestley*. Hamish Hamilton.

BRIDSON, D. G. (1971). *Prospero and Ariel. The rise and fall of radio.* Gollancz.

CARPENTER, H. (1996). *The Envy of the World. Fifty years of the BBC Third Programme and Radio 3, 1946–1996.* Weidenfeld & Nicolson.

DE-LA-NOY, M. (1988). *Eddy. The life of Edward Sackville-West.* Arcadia.

DRUMMOND, J. (2000). *Tainted by Experience. A life in the Arts.* Faber and Faber.

GIELGUD, V. (1947). *Years of the Locust*. Nicholson & Watson.

GIELGUD, V. (1957). *British Radio Drama*. Harrap.

GILLIAM, L. (1950). *Introduction to BBC Features*. Evans Bros.

GRENFELL, J. (1976). *Joyce Grenfell Requests the Pleasure*. Macmillan.

HEPPENSTALL, R. (1969). *Portrait of the Artist as a Professional Man.* Peter Owen.

HOGGART, R. (1993). *An Imagined Life.* Oxford University Press.

JENKINS, A. (1980). *Stephen Potter – Inventor of Gamesmanship.* Weidenfeld & Nicolson.

MACLAREN-ROSS, J. (1965). *Memoire of the Forties.* Alan Ross Ltd. Unfinished and published posthumously.

MACKENZIE, C. *Octave 8.* Chatto & Windus.

MACLEOD, J. (1947). *A Job at the BBC.* William Maclellan.

NEWBY, P. H. (1981). *Feelings have changed,* Faber and Faber.

PRIESTLEY, J. B. (1962). *Margin Released.* William Heinemann.

PRIESTLEY, J. B. (1967). *All England Listened.* Chilmark Ltd.

PURVES, L. (2002). *Radio: a true love story,* Hodder & Stoughton.

RODGER, I. (1982). *Radio Drama.* Macmillan.

SIEVEKING, L. DE G. (1934). *The Stuff of Radio.* Cassell & Co.

STALLWORTHY, J. (1995) *Louis MacNeice.* Faber and Faber.

WHITEHEAD, K. (1989). *The Third Programme: a literary history.* Clarendon Press.

Back numbers of *The Listener* and the *Radio Times.*

BBC Year Books.

Index

Index of those alive in the forties with more than a passing reference in the text.